Psychotherapy for Depression in Older Adults

Wiley Series in Clinical Geropsychology
Series Editor, Sara H. Qualls

Psychotherapy for Depression in Older Adults
Sara H. Qualls and Bob G. Knight, Eds.

Forthcoming: *Change in Decision-Making Capacity in Older Adults*
Sara H. Qualls and Michael A. Smyer, Eds.

Forthcoming: *Aging Families and Caregiving*
Sara H. Qualls and Steven H. Zarit, Eds.

Psychotherapy for Depression in Older Adults

Edited by

Sara H. Qualls and Bob G. Knight

WILEY

John Wiley & Sons, Inc.

This book is printed on acid-free paper. ∞

Copyright © 2006 by John Wiley & Sons, Inc. All rights reserved.

Published by John Wiley & Sons, Inc., Hoboken, New Jersey.
Published simultaneously in Canada.

Library of Congress Cataloging-in-Publication Data:

Qualls, Sara Honn.
    Psychotherapy for depression in older adults / by Sara H. Qualls and Bob G. Knight.
        p.   cm. — (Wiley series in clinical geropsychology)
    Includes bibliographical references.
    ISBN-13: 978-0-470-03797-3 (cloth)
    ISBN-10: 0-470-03797-0 (cloth)
    1. Depression in old age—Treatment.   2. Psychotherapy for older people.   I.
Knight, Bob.   II. Title.   III. Series.
    RC537.5.Q34 2007
    618.97'68527-—dc22
                                                                    2006005812

Printed in the United States of America.

10   9   8   7   6   5   4   3   2   1

Contents

Preface   *ix*

Contributors   *xiii*

PART I: Depression and Aging   1
Sara H. Qualls

1 **Unique Aspects of Psychotherapy with Older Adults**   3
   Bob G. Knight
   Background: The Contextual, Cohort-Based Maturity/
      Specific Challenge Model   3
   Adapting Psychotherapy for Work with Older Clients   13
   Conclusion   23
   References   25

2 **The Nature of Depression in Later Life**   29
   Amy Fiske
   Definition   29
   Etiology   31
   Risk and Protective Factors   33
   Course   37
   Presentation   38
   Conclusion   39
   References   40

3 **Assessing Depression in Older Adults**   45
   Melissa Snarski and Forrest Scogin
   The Purpose of Geriatric Depression Assessment   46
   Instruments Commonly Used to Assess
      Geriatric Depression   52
   Assessment Methods   58

Interdisciplinary Nature of Depression Assessment in
Older Adults   69
References   70

PART II: Therapy Systems   **79**
Bob G. Knight

4   **Cognitive Behavior Therapy with Older Adults**   **83**
Ken Laidlaw
Appropriateness with Older Adults   84
The Application of Cognitive Behavior Therapy with
Older Adults   87
Suitability for Cognitive Behavior Therapy   90
Modifying Cognitive Behavior Therapy with Older Adults   91
A New Conceptualization Framework for Cognitive
Behavior Therapy with Older Adults   92
Transitions in Role Investments   93
Summary of Conceptualization Framework for Cognitive
Behavior with Older Adults   97
Conclusion   105
References   106

5   **Interpersonal Psychotherapy with Older Adults**   **111**
Gregory A. Hinrichsen
The Structure and Ethos of Interpersonal Psychotherapy   112
Interpersonal Psychotherapy in the Treatment of Late
Life Depression   115
Issues in the Application of Interpersonal Psychotherapy
to Depressed Older Adults   118
Comments on the Case of Helen   125
Conclusion   127
References   127

6   **Problem-Solving Therapy with Older Adults**   **133**
Patricia A. Areán and Terri Huh
Support for Problem-Solving Therapy in Older Adults   135
Modifying Problem-Solving Therapy for Older Adults   136
Conclusion   147
References   149

Afterword   **152**

7   **Evidence-Based Psychological Treatment with Older Adults**   157
    Forrest Scogin and Adriana Yon
        The Evidence-Based Practice Movement   158
        Meta-Analyses with Older Adults   159
        Categorical Reviews with Older Adults   161
        Identifying Evidence-Based Treatments   169
        Exemplary Studies of Geriatric Depression   169
        Conclusion   171
        References   172

        Part III: The Contexts of Geropsychology Practice   177
        Sara H. Qualls

8   **The Social and Cultural Context of Psychotherapy with Older Adults**   179
    Martha R. Crowther, Gia Robinson Shurgot,
    Martinique Perkins, and Rachel Rodriguez
        Defining Race, Ethnicity, Culture, and Minority Status   180
        The Role of Culture   182
        Adapting Psychotherapy to Work with Older
           Ethnic Minorities   189
        Conclusion   193
        Recommended Reading   194
        References   195

9   **Psychotherapy in the Context of Long-Term Care**   201
    Deborah W. Frazer
        General Principles across All Residential Settings   201
        Characteristics of Residents in Residential Settings   203
        Ethical Issues in Residential Settings   222
        Conclusion   226
        Recommended Reading   226
        References   227

10 **The Basics of Building and Managing a Geropsychology Practice**   229
    Paula E. Hartman-Stein
        Know Thy Business   230
        Know Thy Market and Thy Customer   241

Conclusion   246
Appendix A: Sample Form for Case Progress
    Notes for Psychotherapy and Health and
    Behavior Interventions   247
References   247

Author Index   251

Subject Index   263

Preface

Media attention to the mushrooming Baby Boomer population has raised public awareness of the discrepancy between predicted demand for health services and the network of providers available to meet it. Mental health disciplines face what has been described as a crisis (Halpain, Harris, McClure, & Jeste, 1999) due to the very limited pipeline of training programs that are preparing future professionals in geriatric service specialization. No discipline has successfully addressed this problem, nor has the federal government responded in a substantial way to address the need for expansion of training programs in geriatric health care.

An alternative mechanism for expansion of mental health services for older adults is to train existing practitioners in the knowledge and skills that are distinctive to geriatric practice (Qualls, 1998). A survey in the late 1990s documented the growing interest in aging populations among practicing psychologists (Qualls, Segal, Norman, Niederehe, & Gallagher-Thompson, 2002). The same survey documented the relatively low rate of formal graduate school and internship training preparation in aging that was accessed by persons who now are interested in aging.

A major challenge to any effort to expand capacity through continuing education is the absence of a coherent curriculum that covers the full array of skills and knowledge needed to practice proficiently. Thankfully, consensus about the knowledge and skill base that is needed for geriatric mental health practice is growing. For example, the field of psychology has adopted a set of guidelines that specifies *what* needs to be known (American Psychological Association, 2004). Unfortunately, mechanisms for obtaining advanced training in the full array of topics needed by general practitioners have not previously been developed.

In June 2005, a National Clinical Geropsychology Conference series was launched in Colorado Springs, Colorado, with mental health professionals attending from across the United States. The goal of the conference series is to provide an intensive training opportunity for seasoned mental health providers wishing to expand their practice to include services for older adults. With primary sponsorship of the Gerontology Center at the University of Colorado at Colorado Springs, continuing education credits were granted in collaboration with the Adult Development and Aging Division of the American Psychological Association and the National Association of Social Workers.

Wiley recognized the value of this type of systematic training opportunity for practitioners and contracted for a book series designed specifically for mental health professionals who have a growing interest in providing services to older adults. Based on the topic of the first conference, this book is the first in the series. The next two topics are *Aging and Decision-Making Capacity: Clinical, Legal, and Family Issues* and *Aging Families and Caregiving*.

The contributors to this book are all active in clinical practice and seasoned writers. The chapters were written specifically to benefit experienced professionals who have a strong basis for practice but little expertise in serving aging populations. Case examples and practical advice are interwoven with research findings from the scientific literature. We hope you find this useful and that you will look for opportunities to expand your knowledge of geriatric mental health needs and services through the conference series, this book series, and the other training opportunities that are becoming available in practitioner-friendly venues.

SARA H. QUALLS, PhD
BOB G. KNIGHT, PhD

REFERENCES

American Psychological Association. (2004). APA guidelines for psychological practice with older adults. *American Psychologist, 59*(4), 236–260.

Halpain, M. C., Harris, M. J., McClure, F. S., & Jeste, D. V. (1999). Training in geriatric mental health: Needs and strategies. *Psychiatric Services, 50*, 1205–1208.

Qualls, S. H. (1998). Training in geropsychology: Preparing to meet the demand. *Professional Psychology: Research and Practice, 29,* 23–28.

Qualls, S. H., Segal, D. L., Norman, S., Niederehe, G., & Gallagher-Thompson, D. (2002). Psychologists in practice with older adults: Current patterns, sources of training, and need for continuing education. *Professional Psychology: Research and Practice, 33,* 435–442.

Contributors

Patricia A. Areán, PhD
Department of Psychiatry
University of California
San Francisco, California

**Martha R. Crowther,
PhD, MPH**
Department of Health Behavior
University of Alabama
Birmingham, Alabama

Amy Fiske, PhD
Department of Psychology
West Virginia University
Morgantown, West Virginia

Deborah W. Frazer, PhD
Genesis Healthcare
Philadelphia, Pennsylvania

Paula E. Hartman-Stein, PhD
Center for Healthy Aging
Kent, Ohio

Gregory A. Hinrichsen, PhD
Psychological Services
Zucker Hillside Hospital
Glen Oaks, New York

Terri Huh, PhD
Department of Psychiatry
University of California
San Francisco, California

Bob G. Knight, PhD
School of Gerontology
University of Southern California
Los Angeles, California

Ken Laidlaw, MA, MPhil
School of Health in Social Science
University of Edinburgh
Edinburgh, Scotland

Martinique Perkins, MA
Department of Psychology
University of Alabama
Birmingham, Alabama

Sara H. Qualls, PhD
Department of Psychology
University of Colorado
Colorado Springs, Colorado

Rachel Rodriguez, MA
Department of Psychology
University of Alabama
Birmingham, Alabama

Forrest Scogin, PhD
Department of Psychology
University of Alabama
Tuscaloosa, Alabama

Gia Robinson Shurgot, PhD
Andrus Gerontology Center
University of Southern California
Los Angeles, California

Melissa Snarski, MA
Department of Psychology
University of Alabama
Birmingham, Alabama

Adriana Yon, MA
Department of Psychology
University of Alabama
Tuscaloosa, Alabama

PART

I

⟫⟩◆⟨⟪

Depression and Aging

SARA H. QUALLS

Americans like beginnings better than endings, so aging is often associated with depression, based on the intuitive notion that "I would be depressed if . . ." Even seasoned mental health professonals presume that greater knowledge of depression and grief is what they need before working with older adults for the first time (Qualls, Segal, Norman, Niederehe, & Gallagher-Thompson, 2002). Hence, we started with that topic for the first book in a series devoted to providing learning opportunities for mental health professionals interested in expanding their practice to include older adults. Readers may, however, be surprised by what they learn in the chapters in this first section.

By building rich frameworks for the distinctive aspects of psychotherapy with older adults, the first three chapters challenge simplistic notions of later life as a period of inevitable loss that creates depression. In the opening chapter, Knight invites the reader to step back to view the cohort, cultural, developmental, and clinical contexts of his work. Knight's contextual, cohort-based maturity/specific challenge (CCMSC) model organizes findings from multiple disciplines, including sociology and life span developmental psychology, to focus attention on what therapists will experience in their work with older clients as compared with work with younger adults. Readers may want to mark the pages to highlight aspects of this model that surprise them and reflect on the implications of those markings for countertransference and the need for further training.

In Chapter 2, Fiske reviews the literature on depression in older adults, providing readers with opportunities to challenge their previous assumptions about prevalence, symptom presentation, etiology, risk and protective factors, and course. Practitioners learn how naive reliance on the *Diagnostic and Statistical Manual* (DSM) system may lead to underidentification of late life depression, under what conditions commonly stressful occurrences such as bereavement and caregiving are linked to depression, and how the etiology of depression is (and is not) distinctive in later life. A very large literature is summarized quite succinctly here for practitioners who need to figure out how the distinctive nature of depression in later life matters to their professional work.

The complexities of depression in later life require thoughtful approaches to assessment to protect the client and the therapist from launching an inappropriate intervention. Snarski and Scogin offer a practical approach in Chapter 3 of conducting assessment in the context of the initial sessions of psychotherapy. Once again, the focus is on what is different in the initial interview with older adults compared with other populations. The authors review and analyze self-report assessment tools for their strengths and weaknesses and offer practical, useful strategies and principles for conducting initial diagnostic interviews with older adults.

A *warning:* Readers are strongly discouraged from skipping this section of the book under the presumption that they know this material based simply on their general professional education. Mental health professionals have many mistaken notions about aging that may lead them astray in designing and implementing interventions for depressed elderly persons. We invite you to start at the beginning. Enjoy!

REFERENCES

Qualls, S. H., Segal, D. L., Norman, S., Niederehe, G., & Gallagher-Thompson, D. (2002). Psychologists in practice with older adults: Current patterns, sources of training, and need for continuing education. *Professional Psychology: Research and Practice, 33,* 435–442.

CHAPTER

1

Unique Aspects of Psychotherapy with Older Adults

BOB G. KNIGHT

In the past, older clients were often subjected to negative stereotyping and inaccurate generalizations that hindered their access to and success in psychotherapy. A loss-deficit model of aging took a negative approach to life span development and portrayed the normative course of later life as a series of losses and the typical response as depression (Berezin, 1963; Gitelson, 1948). More recently, writing about therapy with older adults has drawn on scientific gerontology rather than stereotypes and has portrayed the process of aging in a more positive light (Knight, Nordhus, & Satre, 2003; Knight & Satre, 1999). This has led to the proposal of a contextual, cohort-based maturity/specific challenge model (CCMSC; Knight, 2004).

BACKGROUND: THE CONTEXTUAL, COHORT-BASED MATURITY/SPECIFIC CHALLENGE MODEL

The CCMSC model is informed by research on aging in such diverse fields as developmental and cognitive psychology, medicine, and sociology. According to this model, the special social context of older adults and the fact that they are members of earlier-born cohorts raised in different sociocultural circumstances may require adaptations to psychotherapy that are not dictated by the developmental processes of aging. Older adults are more mature than younger ones in certain respects but also are facing some of the hardest challenges that life presents, such as chronic illness, disability, and grieving for others. Each of these areas—contextual factors, cohort differences, and maturation—has significant relevance to working with older adults in therapy.

Social Context Factors

Therapists working with older adults should have general familiarity with their distinctive social contexts. These include specific environments (e.g., age-segregated housing, social and recreational centers, the aging services network) and laws affecting older adults (e.g., Medicare regulations, Older Americans' Act regulations, and conservatorship law). This information is not difficult to acquire, and the lack of it among psychotherapists at large may contribute to misunderstanding the world in which older adults live. Informal visiting at locations where the elderly receive services can help create an experiential framework for understanding the environments of the elderly.

Cohort Differences

Cohort differences are explained by membership in a group defined by birth year. Each generation is socialized into beliefs, attitudes, personality dimensions, and even academic abilities that remain relatively stable and that distinguish a cohort from generations born earlier and later. In understanding the effects of aging, therefore, it is important to separate the effects of maturation from the effects of cohort membership. This separation is accomplished in studies using sequential designs that can compare individuals of the same age from different cohorts. In some areas of social gerontology, it has been discovered that many of the differences between the old and the young previously attributed to the aging process are actually due to cohort effects. For example, in the United States, later-born cohorts have more years of formal schooling than cohorts born earlier in the twentieth century, up to the 1970s.

Cohort differences in intellectual skills have also been identified. Later-born cohorts tend to be superior in reasoning ability and spatial orientation (Schaie, 1996). However, some earlier-born cohorts (people who are now older) are superior in arithmetic ability and verbal fluency (Schaie, 1996), showing that some differences between cohorts favor the older group. The absence of developmental change does not imply that older people today are not different from today's younger people because differences can be explained by cohort effects rather than aging. Personality is also affected by birth cohort. For example, Schaie (1995) found that from 1900 until World War II, successive cohorts declined in extroversion, but in the cohorts that followed, extroversion increased. Likewise, threat reactivity has increased with each cohort since the beginning of the twentieth century (Schaie, 1995). These findings suggest that the personality differences observed between younger and older adults are often cohort differences rather than developmental aspects of aging.

Even though cohort differences are not developmental, they are nevertheless real effects that distinguish older adults from younger ones. To conduct psychotherapy effectively with older adults, it is useful to learn about historical forces and social norms that shaped earlier-born cohorts. Developing a working knowledge of psychologically significant cohort effects is just as essential as learning about cultural differences before working with clients from another country.

Maturity-Related Differences

The most pervasive cognitive change with developmental aging is the slowing that occurs in all cognitive tasks where speed of response is a factor (Salthouse, 1996). Although slowing reaction time can be partially reversed in older adults through practice, exercise, and other interventions, age differences are seldom completely eliminated.

Memory is a complex topic in the study of cognitive changes in late life. Recent longitudinal investigations of memory change in older adults over time have generally confirmed decline with age on some memory functions, such as word recall (e.g., Small, Dixon, & Hultsch, 1999; Zelinski & Burnight, 1997). In the same studies, other functions seem to be relatively preserved, such as recognition memory. Older adults do better with structured material, more time to study the material, and greater environmental support (e.g., when able to use notes; recognition and cued recall are better than free recall; see Smith, 1996, for a review).

In general, what is known about memory now suggests that even differences between current younger and older adults in memory performance are not large when the material is meaningful and relevant to the older adult and the older adult is motivated to learn (Hultsch & Dixon, 1990; Smith, 1996). Of special interest for psychotherapy, there is evidence that older adults retain emotional material better than neutral material (Carstensen & Turk-Charles, 1994). Older adults benefit from memory training (Verhagen, Marcoen, & Goossens, 1992), and so the lower memory functioning compared to younger adults is at least partially reversible.

A two-factor model distinguishing fluid from crystallized intelligence was proposed by Cattell and expanded by Horn (see Dixon, 2003, for a review). Fluid intelligence, and its components of speed of processing, encoding newly learned material, and inferential reasoning, show clear evidence of aging-related change. Crystallized intelligence, and its general fund of information and vocabulary, show little age-related change until age 70 or later (Schaie, 1996). These changes in average level of intellectual abilities are observed but are not universal and may be caused by early dementia or illness-related deficits (Schaie, 1996). Baltes and Staudinger (2000) made a similar distinction between the mechanics of intelligence (how we acquire knowledge) and the pragmatics of intelligence (the content of what we know) with parallel age trajectories.

Drawing on the information-processing "mind as computer" metaphor, Rybash, Hoyer, and Roodin (1986) argued that increased experience can be seen as operating like an "expert system" program. Accumulation of experience provides older adults with a considerable store of knowledge that is informed by their work and family experiences. Older adults may outperform younger adults in these expert domains. Conversely, greater processing speed may help younger adults successfully process new information without the advantage of an expert system.

Similarly, Paul Baltes and colleagues with the Berlin Aging Study have proposed a model of the development of wisdom in later life. Wisdom is composed of rich factual and procedural knowledge, life span contextualism, relativism of values and priorities, and recognition and management of uncertainty (e.g., Baltes & Staudinger, 2000). In general, wisdom in this sense should be an asset for the work of therapy and make older clients easier to work with. Working with clients who have more wisdom than you do can be inspiring or somewhat daunting and anxiety arousing, depending on the therapist.

Emotional changes over the adult life span are a topic of considerable importance for psychotherapists working with older adults. Carstensen (1992) proposed a theory of emotion across the life span called socioemotional selectivity theory. This theory began with the observations that our social support network gets smaller as we age (much of the change occurs in the 30s), but life satisfaction stays stable. Carstensen suggested that younger adults have a motivational focus on information seeking and finding a mate and so need a large network of contacts. Later in adulthood, the motivational focus shifts to maintaining emotional balance. This motivational focus underlies a shift toward positive affect as adults age (e.g., Carstensen, Fung, & Charles, 2003).

The Specificity of Challenges in Late Life

Practitioners working with older adults may well be thinking that this view of aging is overly optimistic. The outline of evidence for increasing maturation has intentionally focused on normal development through the life span. Yet many elderly clients seeking help in therapy are struggling with problems that threaten psychological homeostasis at any point in the life span: chronic illness, disability, the loss of loved ones to death, and prolonged caregiving for family members with severe cognitive or physical frailty. These problems are not unique to late life but are more likely in the last third of life. In addition, late life is not immune to vicissitudes common throughout the life span: disappointment in love, arguments with family members, and failing at the tasks we set ourselves. Finally, many people who have struggled with depression, anxiety, substance abuse, or psychosis all of their lives eventually become older adults who continue to struggle with these problems.

In brief, clients come into psychotherapy because they have problems that produce emotional distress. Older people in hospitals or nursing homes are there because they are physically ill, and often chronically ill. Stated clearly, these facts are entirely obvious; however, it is not uncommon to implicitly assume that these problems are due to advanced age rather than to the underlying illness, psychological disorder, or severe life stress. The tendency to identify young-old and old-old periods within the older years and to equate young-old with a healthy, leisure-oriented postretirement lifestyle and the old-old years with illness, frailty, and disability is common. Such problems are stochastically more common in the old-old years, and this fact is likely due to underlying biological changes in the "wear and repair" systems of the body. However, the actual shift from the healthy, active years of aging to physical or mental frailty is due to specific disease processes that differ across individuals and that differ in age of onset. These individual variations, which are common, lead to our observations that an 80-year-old does not seem old (i.e., she is still healthy and mentally alert), whereas a 60-year-old seems very old (she has severe arthritis and moderately severe dementia). In some instances, these individual variations can result in an old-old parent caring for a disabled young-old child. Common everyday notions of what old age is like are wound up in notions about illness and disability. The reality involves some association between aging and frailty, but the association is far from a one-to-one correspondence, and the belief that they are identical causes many problems for older adults.

The *specific* nature of these problems is important to the practice of psychotherapy with individual older persons. Just as the deficit side of the loss-deficit model ignored evidence for maturation, the perception that *generic* losses are normative in late life fails to do justice to the *specific* nature of the losses incurred. Clinical experience suggests that it matters whether what is lost is one's spouse, one's vision, or the use of one's legs. Recognizing the specificity of loss and reconceptualizing losses as challenges implies that some losses can be overcome through rehabilitation counseling as well as adjusted to through grief counseling. Turning from a loss-deficit model to a maturity/specific challenge model also helps us to recognize when depression is not normative for a given life experience. For example, depression following retirement may be seen in this model as atypical (because most older adults enjoy freedom from the demands of work) and therefore in need of careful therapeutic assessment.

Chronic Illness and Disability

Clinical experience with older adults has made it clear to me that working with emotionally distressed older adults very often means working with older adults who are chronically ill and/or physically disabled and who are struggling to adjust to these problems. In setting out to do psychological work with older adults, I have had to learn about chronic illnesses and their psychological impact, pain control, adherence to medical treatment, rehabilitation strategies, and how to assess behavioral signs of medication reactions. This work has taken me into hospitals, nursing homes, cardiac rehabilitation programs, emergency rooms, and to the bedside of many severely disabled older adults.

In doing this work, I have become acquainted with physicians and nurses and have learned how to talk to and with them. I have learned much about the limitations of medicine and about the demands that patients place on doctors. I have learned to think about hospitals and other medical settings as organizational systems inhabited by human beings but operating according to distinctive social rules. I have come to better appreciate my own expertise by observing that many people with medical training are as uncomfortable with emotionality, psychosis, and suicidal threats as I am with blood, physical symptoms, and medical emergencies. Learning to work with other disciplines in this way is an essential aspect of doing psychotherapy with older adults (cf. Zeiss & Steffen, 1996).

This aspect of working with older adults involves specialized knowledge and specialized skills, as compared to other areas of psychotherapeutic practice where physical problems and the physical dimension of the person can be more safely ignored. The increased proportion of chronic illness and disability with each decade of life and the increased correlation of the physical and the psychological in later life require therapists to discuss physical problems and to understand when a problem may have physical causes. This principle does not mean that every psychotherapist working with the elderly must be a physician. It does mean that we must be able to talk intelligently and cooperatively with physicians and with older clients who need to discuss the very real physical problems they face.

The specific-challenges part of the CCMSC model differs from the loss-deficit model in that the loss-deficit model argues that the work of therapy with the elderly is adjustment to the natural losses of late life and grieving for them. This model is wrong on two counts. First, there is nothing especially *natural* about blindness or heart disease or cancer. The fact that they happen more frequently to older adults does not make these diseases and disabilities part of normal development. It certainly does not make the individual older person experience these problems as normal or as less of a crisis than they would be for a younger adult.

Second, the loss-deficit model fails to suggest the next step of optimizing functioning. Rehabilitation may start by accepting the deficit in functioning, but it does not end there. The next step is to consider how life may be improved. The goal is often not the return to premorbid levels of functioning and mood, but there is always room for improvement over the level of mood and functioning present when the client enters therapy. It should be noted that the presence of these issues in work with older clients makes assessment more complex and challenging, that many psychotherapists are uncomfortable discussing physical problems or even being with clients who are ill and disabled, and that seeking improvement (but not total return to pre-illness mood levels) in the lives of clients with serious and chronic health problems is different from seeking the complete remission of acute depression.

These issues may be even more troubling when the illness is a dementia that produces cognitive impairment. The progressive nature of most of the dementias makes the long-term outlook negative, and the diminishing cognitive ability will eventually directly interfere with verbally oriented therapy. Nonetheless, there can be considerable value in working with older adults in the early to middle phases of a progressive dementia, in a way that parallels the value of work with persons with a terminal illness. The therapist must continually monitor the level of cognitive impairment and the client's ability to benefit from the therapy. (See Knight, 2004, for a more extended discussion of this complex topic.)

Grief

In a similar manner, working with older adults in outpatient therapy often involves grief work. Although loved ones die throughout our lives, the experience is more common in later life. Older adults seeking help for depression frequently have experienced the deaths of several loved ones in the preceding months or years. Much of psychotherapy with older adults will involve some grief work.

As was true for chronic illness and disability, older adults do not seem to experience grief as a normal and expectable part of later life. Losing a loved one, even a loved one who has been ill for some time, is often experienced as surprising and tragic. The loss may be experienced more deeply because of the length of the relationship.

Unlike the loss-deficit model, the maturity/specific challenges model goes beyond emotional grief work and the acceptance of loss to explore the question of what the remainder of the grieving client's life will be like. Grief work is not only about accepting loss, but about finding a new way of living without the deceased in one's life.

Caregiving

Given the relatively high levels of illness and disability in later life, many older adults who are not themselves ill or disabled will be caring for a family member who is. The nature of the caregiving will depend in part on the nature of the underlying illness of the care receiver, in the sense that this will determine the nature of the tasks of caregiving, the length of the caregiving period, and the degree of strain likely to be experienced. In broad terms, it is known that caring for a person with dementia is more stressful than caring for a physically frail family member (Ory, Hoffman, Yee, Tennstedt, & Schulz, 1999), although individual reactions will vary.

Compared to noncaregivers, caregivers experience higher levels of symptoms of emotional distress (Schulz, O'Brien, Bookwala, & Fleissner, 1995) and have been found to have higher levels of clinical depression and clinical anxiety disorders (Dura, Stukenberg, & Kiecolt Glaser, 1991). There is some evidence for effects of caregiving on physical health as well, although this evidence is less consistent across studies (Schulz et al., 1995). My own involvement with services for caregivers initially grew out of noticing that a substantial proportion of therapy clients in the caseload of the senior services program that I managed in a community mental health center were caregivers. The emotional distress of caregivers is typically considered within a stress and coping framework (Aranda & Knight, 1997; Knight, Silverstein, McCallum, & Fox, 2000; Lazarus & Folkman, 1984) in which the perception of caregiving as burdensome, the caregiver's coping style, and the available social support are key influences on mental health outcomes.

Caregiving always occurs in the context of a family relationship and is typically a relationship with a long history. At least implicitly, and often explicitly, working with a caregiver will require some conceptualization of the family system in which the caregiving takes place and may well require family sessions or ongoing family therapy (see Knight & McCallum, 1998; Qualls, 1996).

In brief, the specific-challenges part of the CCMSC model recognizes the gravity of the problems faced by older adults. It emphasizes the specificity of the problems and assumes that problems in later life can be overcome. In fact, one implication of the model is that work with older adults facing a specific problem should draw on the available knowledge about helping all adults with similar problems. Therapy with older adults should not become so specialized that techniques and concepts developed for other clients are not readily generalized to older adults and that techniques and concepts developed in gerontological counseling are not tried with younger adults as appropriate.

Summary

The CCMSC model portrays older adults in a complex light that draws on scientific gerontology. The normal developmental process of maturation is seen as making older adults more mature in some ways and as producing mild deficits in other cognitive processes. In general, the normal developmental processes of adulthood and later life are characterized by small, slow changes and an overall picture of continuity rather than marked change. However, cohort differences shape many distinctions between young and old adults, and these differences affect psychotherapy with older adults, both in terms of building rapport and often in communication and understanding between client and therapist when they come from different cohorts. The social contexts in which many older adults live invite us to understand older adults in a specific context and to consider the context as a source of their problems and as a target of change to benefit them. Finally, some of the problems faced by older adults are encountered more frequently in later life and have come to be identified with old age. Although these problems require specific expertise, they should not be overidentified with the age of the client: Younger adults have chronic illness, disabilities, grief, and caregiving responsibilities as well, if less frequently than older persons.

ADAPTING PSYCHOTHERAPY FOR WORK WITH OLDER CLIENTS

Drawing on the previous discussion of general findings in gerontology, the following discussion explores the possible changes to be made in therapy to maximize success with older clients. Adaptation might be required by the social circumstances of older adults, cohort effects, or developmental changes that take place during adulthood. Each of these three sources of change has different implications for the nature and scope of adaptation in therapy with older adults. The specific challenges of later life form a fourth basis for adaptation of therapy, one that is problem specific rather than client specific.

Therapy with older adults may need to adapt to specific social circumstances: retirement, widowhood, segregated housing, nursing homes, and so on. As noted before, working in nursing homes requires expertise in the social setting of the nursing home as much as it requires knowledge of the process of aging. These adaptations need to respond to change in the social definition and context of the elderly. For example, the past decade or so has seen the rise and proliferation of assisted-care homes as a new level of long-term care for older adults.

Changes due to cohort effects will differ with each cohort and will require that adaptations in therapy be constantly revised as each cohort becomes old. Adaptations based on cohort differences imply that knowledge and skills specific to a given cohort will remain useful with that cohort as it ages. For example, if we have norms for a psychological test for people in their 60s and those norms are now 20 years old, we would use those norms with today's 60-year-olds if developmental influences are primary and with today's 80-year-olds if cohort differences are the operative influence. Developmental changes affect all older adults and are relatively consistent over time. If most adaptations were due to development, then therapy with older adults might be different from therapy with younger adults, as is therapy with children.

Adaptations Based on the Social Context of Older Adults

To the extent that older clients inhabit the specific social world of older adults in American society (and not all older people do), the older client must be understood in relation to his or her external social environment. This concept, and especially interventions derived from it, has its roots in social learning theory, which emphasizes the interrelatedness of person and environment and the need to understand both to plan appropriate interventions (Bandura, 1977; Rotter, 1954). In this sense, the "older American" is created by social policy and by stereotypical thinking of others in our society.

Older people are usually retired and therefore living on a fixed income. Their health care decisions are influenced by Medicare regulations. They often (although not as often as is thought) live in age-segregated areas. The men are usually married, and the women are usually alone; the discrepancy creates pressures on both men and women in later life. Stereotypical thinking about aging means that many older people find their relationships with others, including other older people, conditioned by certain misconceptions, such as "All older people get Alzheimer's disease," "All elderly people are isolated and lonely," "Older people are (or ought to be) asexual," or "Older people are greedy geezers."

Therapists have three interests in the subculture of the elderly. One is to understand the various ways our society makes life difficult for the elderly and so creates some of the emotional problems that the therapist is trying to ameliorate. With regard to this interest, without some exploration of the subculture and our formal and informal social policies, the therapist will often be perplexed as to when the client is being realistic about being insulted or discriminated against as opposed to when there is some psychologically important level of suspiciousness indicating anxiety or paranoia.

The second interest is that the therapist needs to understand the social context in which the client lives to be able to understand the client and work effectively with him or her. The social ecology of the organizations in which older adults live, seek health care, spend leisure time, and so on affect the individual's self-concept and shape options for behavior. The way that this plays out in residential settings is described by Frazer in Chapter 9.

Residential settings are only one of many special characteristics of the older adult lifestyle. Programs funded by the Older Americans Act and other social programs for senior citizens have created a variety of social settings with special characteristics, including congregate meal sites, senior recreation centers, senior volunteer programs, and various advisory and advocacy councils. For many seniors, doctors' waiting rooms, hospital emergency rooms, and other health care settings also function as major social outlets. Those readers who have tried to make social chitchat with a busy physician can understand the likelihood of frustration for both doctor and patient. For the therapist to function effectively and to understand what clients are talking about, some exposure to each of these settings is very useful. Preferably, visits should take place when the therapist (or therapist in training) can be somewhat removed from the professional role and more of a participant observer in the anthropological sense.

The third interest of the therapist in the social context of older clients relates to the need to understand the social context well enough to be of active assistance to the older client when this is needed. Most discussions of psychotherapy with the elderly emphasize—and correctly so—the complex nature of the problems faced by elderly persons and the need for intervention in nonpsychological areas of their lives (e.g., Smyer & Qualls, 1999; Zarit & Zarit, 1998). Various authors have suggested the need to do casework for older clients, the need to work within a biopsychosocial model, and the need to take a more interdisciplinary focus. Casework services, which can include a wide variety of activities, are used here to refer to two types of activities on the part of the therapist working with older clients. One is providing accurate information on available services for problems the client has that do not fall within the scope of the problems that therapy is likely to resolve; the other is actually providing or setting up services for the client.

Each community will have a somewhat different network of services. Important services to look for in any local context are the following:

- Physicians who are knowledgeable about and comfortable with the elderly
- Various types of residences available to older adults, including independent living, assisted living, residential care, and skilled nursing facilities
- Geriatric case management services
- Specialized services for older persons with dementia
- Services for caregivers of frail older adults
- Congregate meal sites and home-delivered meal programs
- Senior recreation centers
- Day care centers for the elderly
- Income assistance programs
- Transportation services
- Hospital-based programs
- Legal services, including regulations and agencies that cover guardianship of dependent adults or elderly
- Home health services
- Emergency services that provide monetary loans or food or pay utility bills in bad weather
- Elder abuse laws and hotlines

To locate supportive services, good initial sources are the local Area Agency on Aging, Alzheimer's Association chapters, geriatric case managers, the aging service section of public social services, ombudsman programs, adult protective services, self-help groups, and hospital discharge planners. Remember that both public and private resources must be considered.

At times, the decision to refer is quite clear-cut. The client needs a given service that is available, and providing the information is the easiest way to resolve the issue. In other cases, there is a judgment to be made about whether clients would do better to resolve the problem on their own. In one instance, a client who was quite delusional and disorganized in her thinking was facing eviction from an apartment where the rent had been raised beyond her fixed retirement income. While proceeding with therapy, the therapist actively attempted to secure a placement in public housing. This was not an easy task as the supply was far smaller than the demand. While the housing bureaucracy was being dealt with, the client recovered sufficiently to implement her own plan: the recruitment of three roommates to share expenses. The arrangement lasted for 2 years.

The outcome of the preceding example points to a potential conflict between the values of psychotherapy and those of case management. Therapy is generally oriented toward increasing client independence and working to have clients do things for themselves and solve problems for themselves. Casework is often about solving problems for people by providing concrete service solutions. As the preceding example indicated, it is not always easy to know when an impaired client can still solve a problem independently. The other end of this conflict is illustrated by considering whether it makes more sense to pursue therapy with clients who are so depressed that they have not eaten well in weeks or to immediately refer them to home-delivered meals services and start therapy after a few days of good meals.

Cohort-Based Adaptations

As noted, there are many sources of differences between younger and older adults that are due to cohort dissimilarities rather than to developmental changes. These differences include variations across cohorts in cognitive abilities, educational levels, word usage preferences, normative life trajectories, and the sociohistorical context within which the individual's life story unfolds. These differences hold implications for the adaptation of therapy with older clients who, in this context, are better described as earlier-born clients. This phrasing emphasizes that it is the era into which one is born, rather than the current position in the life cycle, that is the basis of the adaptation.

The lower levels of education in earlier cohorts suggest that therapists should rely less on abstraction and complex terminology and not assume that the client will share the therapist's psychological worldview. Older adults may require simpler language to describe therapeutic processes and a lengthier explanation of the nature of therapy. These changes are similar to those used when doing therapy with clients of lower socioeconomic status (Goldstein, 1973; Lorion, 1978). The focus on cohort differences and education as the causes of these changes reminds us that more highly educated cohorts will be getting older in the near future and that not all older clients require this adaptation, but only the ones who do have less education.

Life patterns change across cohorts, and then (sometimes) change back. Knowing what is normative for a client depends a great deal on understanding these cohort differences. The psychological significance of a woman not marrying but pursuing a career may be very different for a woman who came of age in the 1940s or 1950s as compared to one who came of age in the 1970s or later. The social stigma and psychological distress of growing up as the child of divorced parents was different for children in the 1930s and 1940s than for children of the late-twentieth century. The later-born therapist can miss such cues by interpreting a 1940s (or 1950s) young adult life by early twenty-first-century standards.

To understand the client's life history, it is helpful to be able to place him or her in the flow of historical time. That is, to some extent, working with earlier-born clients implies a need to understand in outline the history of the twentieth century and especially the events that often have great personal or familial significance: World War I, World War II, the Great Depression, the waves of immigration from Europe in the 1920s, the Jazz Age, the ebb and flow of progressive and conservative politics and moral thinking, and so on. In trying to understand clients, I find myself constantly doing mental arithmetic to construct a sense of the client's life cycle and how it fits into historical time. It is generally helpful to keep in mind when a client reached adulthood and to think about the history and values of that period. To keep the math simple, I add 20 years to the birth year to get an approximate sense of the cohort that the client reached young adulthood with. Then I transform statements about "I changed jobs 12 years after I married" into "That means he was 34 then, and so it was 1944. Why wasn't he in military service during WWII?" The life course paradigm in sociological conceptions of aging describes this process as using "multiple time clocks" to track where the individual is in the life cycle and to place him or her in the flow of historical time (as well as in the changing roles of the family context over time; see Bengtson & Allen, 1993).

Cohort-based changes may be some of the more significant changes confronting therapists working with clients who are earlier born and whose lives are shaped by events that the therapist does not recall from personal experience. It implies some need to have an understanding of history, not always common among psychotherapists. Much of what one needs to know can be learned from the client, especially as the real issue in all cases is what the client understood the impact of these historical events to be. The questions must be asked, however, and I often find that younger therapists do not want to ask such questions for fear of displaying ignorance or of calling attention to the age difference between them and the older client. On the whole, I find that clients appreciate being asked such questions and feel more clearly understood when they explain events of which the therapist is ignorant.

Cohort differences provide one basis for thinking of older adults as a special population. In a sense, older adults present problems similar to those of clients who are fluent in English but raised in a different culture: Words are the same but may be used in different ways, and the client's experiences are rooted in a social context with which we are not familiar and may be influenced by values different from our own. Earlier-born cohorts are from a different time rather than a different place, but the same responses apply: sensitivity to cues that words are used in different ways, awareness of not sharing a similar background, and being willing to use one's ignorance constructively to learn from the client about the client's experience.

Adaptations Due to Development and Maturation

The earlier overview of gerontology suggested that consistent developmental changes occurring with aging are seen in the slowing of cognitive processing, changes in cognitive abilities and in memory performance, changes in emotional complexity, and the opportunity to have developed expertise in relationships. Much of maturation in adulthood is characterized by stability or by positive change, with negative changes often being small, not important for socially significant functioning, and compensated for by use of other intact abilities. In addition, it was emphasized that adult developmental change is far from consistent either across individuals or among any one individual's various characteristics. The potential impact of each of the consistently observed factors on the practice of psychotherapy is considered in this section.

Slowing

The slowing of cognitive processes that occurs with normal aging, which is increased with many chronic diseases, can become a noticeable influence on communication between older and younger adults. The smaller capacity of working memory in later life is likely to have a similar impact on processing conversation and written materials. It is especially noticeable if the younger professional is feeling rushed or talks quickly as a matter of habit, or when the older person has the additional slowing that comes with depression, hypertension, dementia, or other disorders with psychomotor slowing as a symptom. In any case, the recommendation is clear: If there appears to be some uncertainty in communication, the younger therapist should relax and slow down the pace of the conversation.

The impact of slowing in therapy is that the conversational flow of each session is usually slower than with younger adults in both the pacing of sentences and the latency between client speech and therapist speech. Speaking quickly often leads to communication inaccuracy and the need to repeat. The therapist working with older clients will need to be more aware of pacing in sessions and may need to resist actively any personal tendency to speak quickly in response to time pressure, anxiety, or excitement.

If these changes were not compensated in other ways, one would expect that therapeutic progress as a whole would be slower with older adults in terms of number of sessions required to reach therapeutic goals. In a meta-analysis of therapy outcome studies with older adults, Pinquart and Sörensen (2001) reported that studies using more than nine sessions achieved better outcomes than shorter interventions. One study of therapist-rated change suggested that the old-old need more sessions to achieve gains comparable to the young-old (Knight, 1988).

Memory

Changes in the capacity of working memory in later life (Light, 1990; Salthouse, 1991) may also require some modification of communication style in the therapy setting. Working memory is the active processing capacity of memory—the number of things that can be actively held in memory and worked on at one time. This limited capacity store may be slightly smaller in later life. If so, it may account for changes in comprehension of speech and in problem-solving abilities. Both of these changes can be compensated for by slowing the pace of speech, simplifying sentence structure, and presenting problems in smaller pieces.

Fluid versus Crystallized Intelligence

To the extent that therapy mostly draws on well-learned information about oneself and the world, there is not likely to be any major effect of developmental aging on the therapeutic process. The tasks associated with fluid intelligence often have a timed component or involve visually mediated processing. Reasoning is usually associated with fluid intelligence. If reasoning declines with aging, it may have some impact on therapy. The required changes are likely to be similar to those that one might make working with less educated adults; that is, one may have to use more concrete examples and do more of the inferential work oneself rather than relying on the client to think through the implications of abstract interpretations.

Expertise and Greater Cognitive Complexity

The development of expertise through life experience will, in general, be an asset when working with older adults. Older clients often have expertise that is relevant to the problem they brought to therapy. Their accumulated knowledge of people and relationships can be brought to bear on current relationship problems. Tapping into this expertise can be an adaptation for the therapist in a couple of ways. First, therapists working with younger adults may be more used to encouraging people to explore themselves to discover untapped strengths. Switching to helping people recall and use already existing strengths is not more difficult, but it is different. Second, working with clients who have more experience and expertise than you do is a change of perspective for the therapist. It can be quite exciting for therapists who are open to learning from clients; it may be anxiety arousing for therapists who are uncertain of their own abilities.

When older adults do exhibit greater cognitive complexity, these attributes are likely to be helpful in therapy. An ability to appreciate the ebb and flow of change in life, to take the other person's viewpoint, to appreciate differences in perspective based on cultural, religious, or family differences are all beneficial to the work of therapy. As with expertise, it can be unsettling to work with clients who may have more of these abilities than you do. Older adults may explain to you how they resolved a problem or may explain their understanding of an interpersonal event because it is outside of your comprehension. For example, my own understanding of how parents negotiate adult-to-adult relationships with grown children while still retaining vivid memories of this individual as a child and a deeply felt sense of needing to protect him or her comes from clients who explained it to me.

Emotional Changes in Later Life

Emotionality is thought to be more complex and probably less intense in later life. In general, my experience has been that sessions with older clients involve less expression of emotion than sessions with younger adults. Older people are less inclined to cry (especially to sob), less inclined to shout in anger, and less inclined to bounce up and down for joy. They often describe complex mixes of emotional reactions to the events of their lives. An argument between an older client and her middle-aged daughter may arouse a mixture of anger, sadness, guilt, and pride; the same incident in a younger client may well be associated with only one of these emotions.

CONCLUSION

We have considered and rejected the presumed pessimism about therapeutic work with older adults. The discussion of possible adaptations of therapy with the elderly has considered the following three perspectives on why modification might be needed:

1. The contextual view points to differences due to socially created and modifiable differences in lifestyle between the young and the old. These differences are specific to those elderly who are in that social contexts: retired, live in segregated environments, become senior advocates, and so forth.

2. Cohort differences are differences between groups born at different times. There is a need to comprehend the historical background and the values of the generational groups that are now older and to be aware that these differences are specific to persons of a given era. Future generations of elders will, of course, be different from the current ones. There is some evidence (e.g., Schaie, 1996) that differences between cohorts born in the early to midtwentieth century are larger than cohort differences between those born in midcentury and later, at least with regard to differences in intellectual functioning. Whether this will be true for values, life experiences, and so forth remains to be seen.

3. The developmental perspective suggests that modification may be needed because of developmental changes in the adult as he or she ages. The conclusion so far is that such changes primarily mean a possible need to slow down the therapeutic conversation and rely less on the client's inferential reasoning abilities and also to recognize the client's greater maturity, expertise based on adult life experiences, greater cognitive and emotional complexity, and more mature coping strategies.

The discussion of these sources of change has laid a groundwork for arguing that the major adaptations to therapy with the elderly will arise from cohort effects and social context effects rather than from developmental changes. This perspective makes the therapist's task in approaching work with the older client easier in that comprehending persons of different backgrounds is easier than comprehending stages of life that one has not yet experienced. It also brings the work of understanding the elderly within the range of familiar skills: Most therapists have had exposure to different cohorts and to persons of different social backgrounds. In addition, reflection on therapeutic experience suggests positive characteristics of older clients that may make them very well suited to the work of therapy.

Before leaving the topic of adaptations to therapy, there are other observations based on clinical experience that lead to an optimistic attitude toward therapy with older people. Older people bring to therapy a broad range of experience, richer psychological histories, and opportunities to experiment that are characteristic of the postretirement lifestyle.

Perhaps the most obvious thing that can be said about the potential for change in older adults is that they have lived longer than younger adults. This implies a broader range of experience and more time to have learned about themselves and others. The more traditional, largely pessimistic, view has been that adult development and increased experience make people rigid and set in their ways. Yet some clinicians working with the elderly have felt that the effect is quite the reverse: that growth and experience teach adults to be more flexible, less dogmatic, and more aware that there are different ways of looking at life.

A closely related reason for optimism about therapeutic change with the elderly is that older adults have a much richer psychological history with which to work. Although there is seldom time to work through all of it, exploration of any given theme in life can produce multiple examples that provide the therapist with much richer data to build a conceptualization of the person's approach to that special aspect of his or her life. If, for example, the client is concerned about some quality of the relationships in his or her life, the older client can relate the rich experience of a lifetime of diverse relationships with friends, lovers, spouse(s), children, coworkers in various job settings, grandchildren, and others. If the issue has been of concern for some time, there likely are examples of many different ways that the client has approached the problem in the past with various patterns of success and failure. The therapeutic challenge is to be able to absorb as much information as possible and to interpret and reinterpret the data of the client's life in new and helpful ways that are relevant to current issues.

Therapy involves more than simply understanding oneself and learning new ways of looking at things. Once the understanding is reached there is usually a need to do some things differently. For making these changes, some of the very factors that are traditionally considered losses in old age remove significant barriers to change. When a younger adult reaches a new understanding in therapy and wants to follow up with changes in life outside the therapy room, there is often considerable pressure to remain the same from coworkers, spouse, and family. In addition to actual pressure from others, the energy drain of working and raising a family may seriously reduce the ability to devote time and energy to making the change. The postretirement older adult with more leisure time and relatively little involvement in stable and stabilizing social environments such as work and family is in an excellent position to explore various alternative ways of acting and being. Virtually any change that clients desire to make can be experimented with in the context of the options provided by enhanced leisure time and decreased social pressure.

This spirit of optimism about the possibility for change in late life runs counter to common folk wisdom about aging and clinical lore about older adults. It is, however, based on an understanding of aging gathered from gerontological knowledge and clinical experience with a large number of older adults in various community settings. In the absence of ill health, not only is there no block to normal therapeutic work with the elderly, but these positive factors can make working with the elderly a very rewarding experience for the therapist.

REFERENCES

Aranda, M. P., & Knight, B. G. (1997). The influence of ethnicity and culture on the caregiver stress and coping process: A sociocultural review and analysis. *Gerontologist, 37,* 342–354.

Baltes, P. B., & Staudinger, U. M. (2000). A metaheuristic (pragmatic) to orchestrate mind and virtue toward excellence. *American Psychologist, 55,* 122–136.

Bandura, A. (1977). *Social learning theory.* Englewood Cliffs, NJ: Prentice-Hall.

Bengtson, V. L., & Allen, K. R. (1993). The life course perspective applied to families over time. In P. G. Boss, W. J. Doherty, R. LaRossa, W. R. Schumm, & S. K. Steinmetz (Eds.), *Sourcebook of family theories and methods: A contextual approach* (pp. 469–498). New York: Plenum Press.

Berezin, M. (1963). Some intrapsychic aspects of aging. In N. E. Zinberg & I. Kaufman (Eds.), *Normal psychology of the aging process*. New York: International Universities Press.

Carstensen, L. L. (1992). Social and emotional patterns in adulthood: Support for socioemotional selectivity theory. *Psychology and Aging, 7,* 331–338.

Carstensen, L. L., Fung, H. H., & Charles, S. T. (2003). Socioemotional selectivity theory and the regulation of emotion in the second half of life. *Motivation and Emotion, 27,* 103–123.

Carstensen, L. L., & Turk-Charles, S. (1994). The salience of emotion across the adult life span. *Psychology and Aging, 9,* 259–264.

Dixon, R. A. (2003). Themes in the aging of intelligence: Robust decline with intriguing possibilities. In R. J. Sternberg & J. Lautrey (Eds.), *Models of intelligence: International perspectives* (pp. 151–167). Washington, DC: American Psychological Association.

Dura, J. R., Stukenberg, K. W., & Kiecolt-Glaser, J. (1991). Anxiety and depressive disorders in adult children caring for demented parents. *Psychology and Aging, 6,* 467–473.

Gitelson, M. (1948). The emotional problems of elderly people. *Geriatrics, 3,* 135–150.

Goldstein, A. P. (1973). *Structural learning therapy: Toward a therapy for the poor.* New York: Academic Press.

Hultsch, D. F., & Dixon, R. A. (1990). Learning and memory in aging. In J. E. Birren & K. W. Schaie (Eds.), *Handbook of the psychology of aging* (3rd ed., pp. 259–274). New York: Academic Press.

Knight, B. G. (1988). Factors influencing therapist-rated change in older adults. *Journal of Gerontology, 43,* 111–112.

Knight, B. G. (2004). *Psychotherapy with older adults* (3rd ed.). Thousand Oaks, CA: Sage.

Knight, B. G., & McCallum, T. J. (1998). Family therapy with older clients: The contextual, cohort-based, maturity/specific challenge model. In I. H. Nordhus, G. VandenBos, S. Berg, & P. Fromholt (Eds.), *Clinical geropsychology* (pp. 313–328). Washington, DC: American Psychological Association.

Knight, B. G., Nordhus, I. H., & Satre, D. D. (2003). Psychotherapy with the older client: An integrative approach. In I. B. Weiner (Series Ed.) & G.

Stricker & T. A. Widiger (Vol. Eds.), *Comprehensive handbook of psychology: Vol. 8. Clinical psychology* (pp. 453–468). New York: Wiley.

Knight, B. G., & Satre, D. D. (1999). Cognitive behavioral psychotherapy with older adults. *Clinical Psychology: Science and Practice, 6,* 188–203.

Knight, B. G., Silverstein, M., McCallum, T. J., & Fox, L. S. (2000). A socio-cultural stress and coping model for mental health outcomes among African-American caregivers in southern California. *Journal of Gerontology: Psychological Sciences, 55B,* P142–P150.

Lazarus, R. S., & Folkman, S. (1984). *Stress, appraisal, and coping.* New York: Springer.

Light, L. L. (2000). Memory changes in adulthood. In S. H. Qualls & N. Abeles (Eds.), *Psychology and the aging revolution: How we adapt to longer life* (pp. 73–97). Washington, DC: American Psychological Association.

Lorion, R. P. (1978). Research on psychotherapy and behavior change with the disadvantaged. In S. L. Garfield & A. E. Bergin (Eds.), *Handbook of psychotherapy and behavior change* (pp. 903–938). New York: Wiley.

Ory, M., Hoffman, R. R., Yee, J. L., Tennstedt, S., & Schulz, R. (1999). Prevalence and impact of caregiving: A detailed comparison between dementia and nondementia caregivers. *Gerontologist, 39,* 177–185.

Pinquart, M., & Sörensen, S. (2001). How effective are psychotherapeutic and other psychosocial interventions with older adults? A meta-analysis. *Journal of Mental Health and Aging, 7,* 207–243.

Qualls, S. (1996). Family therapy with aging families. In S. H. Zarit & B. G. Knight (Eds.), *A guide to psychotherapy and aging: Effective interventions in a life-stage context* (pp. 121–138). Washington, DC: American Psychological Association.

Rotter, J. B. (1954). *Social learning and clinical psychology.* Englewood Cliffs, NJ: Prentice-Hall.

Rybash, J. M., Hoyer, W. J., & Roodin, P. A. (1986). *Adult cognition and aging.* New York: Pergamon Press.

Salthouse, T. A. (1991). *Theoretical perspectives on cognitive aging.* Hillsdale, NJ: Erlbaum.

Salthouse, T. A. (1996). The processing-speed theory of adult age differences in cognition. *Psychological Review, 103,* 403–428.

Schaie, K. W. (1995). *Intellectual development in adulthood: The Seattle Longitudinal Study.* New York: Cambridge University Press.

Schaie, K. W. (1996). Intellectual development in adulthood. In J. E. Birren & K. W. Schaie (Eds.), *Handbook of the psychology of aging* (4th ed., pp. 266–286). San Diego, CA: Academic Press.

Schulz, R., O'Brien, A. T., Bookwala, J., & Fleissner, K. (1995). Psychiatric and physical morbidity effects of dementia caregiving: Prevalence, correlates, and causes. *Gerontologist, 35,* 771–791.

Small, B. J., Dixon, R. A., & Hultsch, D. F. (1999). Longitudinal changes in quantitative and qualitative indicators of word and story recall in young-old and old-old adults. *Journal of Gerontology: Psychological Sciences, 54B,* P107–P115.

Smith, A. D. (1996). Memory. In J. E. Birren & K. W. Schaie (Eds.), *Handbook of the psychology of aging* (4th ed., pp. 236–250). San Diego, CA: Academic Press.

Smyer, M. A., & Qualls, S. H. (1999). *Aging and mental health.* Malden, MA: Blackwell.

Verhagen, P., Marcoen, A., & Goossens, L. (1992). Improving memory performance in the aged through mnemonic training: A meta-analytic study. *Psychology and Aging, 7,* 242–251.

Zarit, S. H., & Zarit, J. M. (1998). *Mental disorders in older adults: Fundamentals of assessment and treatment.* New York: Guilford Press.

Zeiss, A. M., & Steffen, A. M. (1996). Interdisciplinary health care teams: The basic unit of geriatric care. In L. L. Carstensen, B. A. Edelstein, & L. Dornbrand (Eds.), *The practical handbook of clinical gerontology* (pp. 423–450). Thousand Oaks, CA: Sage.

Zelinski, E. M., & Burnight, K. P. (1997). Sixteen year longitudinal changes in memory and cognition in older adults. *Psychology and Aging, 12,* 503–513.

2

——⟫◆⟪——

The Nature of Depression in Later Life

Amy Fiske

Depression occurs in late life, but is not a normal part of aging. Depression in late life is both similar to and different from depression in other age groups. Age differences in etiological influences, clinical presentation, course, and outcomes have been noted. Among older adults, depressive experiences are remarkably heterogeneous, suggesting that there are multiple pathways to depression in late life. This chapter examines the nature of depression in late life, including etiology, risk factors, course, and clinical presentation.

DEFINITION

The fourth edition of the *Diagnostic and Statistical Manual of Mental Disorders* (*DSM-IV*; American Psychiatric Association, 1994) contains several categories of mood disorders, including Major Depressive Disorder and Dysthymic Disorder.* Major Depressive Disorder is defined by the presence of five of nine symptoms, one of which must be pervasive dysphoria or anhedonia. Other possible symptoms are fatigue, sleep disturbance, appetite disturbance, psychomotor retardation or agitation, feelings of guilt, difficulty

---

* Bipolar Disorder and cyclothymia are rare in late life and appear to be etiologically distinct from the unipolar disorders. For that reason, they are not covered in this chapter.

concentrating, and thoughts of death or suicide. The diagnosis of dysthymia requires fewer symptoms but symptoms must be present for at least 2 years with no symptom-free periods of 2 months or more. Other commonly used diagnostic categories include Mood Disorder Due to a General Medical Condition, and Adjustment Disorder with Depressed Mood.

Late life depression is not well captured by this system, however. Whereas 1% to 3% of adults age 65 and older meet diagnostic criteria for Major Depressive Disorder (Hasin, Goodwin, Stinson, & Grant, 2005; Weissman, Bruce, Leaf, Florio, & Holzer, 1991), as many as 15% to 25% of all older adults report depressive symptoms at a level considered clinically significant (Jeste et al., 1999). Numerous new categories have emerged, some formally proposed and others used informally, in an effort to reflect the range of depressive experiences that do not fulfill diagnostic criteria for any disorder. For example, minor depression was included in *DSM-IV* with a set of criteria proposed for further study. These criteria specify either dysphoria or anhedonia, like the criteria for Major Depressive Disorder, but require additional symptoms to reach a total of only two to four symptoms (unlike major depression, which requires a total of five). Symptoms must be pervasive and last 2 weeks and must cause distress or impairment. The term *minor depression* is also in common use among investigators to refer to depression not meeting diagnostic criteria for Major Depressive Disorder. A category that has been used in research but is not yet represented in the *DSM* is "subsyndromal depressive symptoms" (Judd, 1997). This category has been defined as two or more symptoms that are pervasive, lasting at least 2 weeks, and must cause distress or impairment, but without meeting criteria for minor depression. An even broader set of criteria, labeled "clinically significant nonmajor depression," has recently been proposed (Kumar, Lavretsky, & Elderkin-Thompson, 2004).

The etiological distinctiveness of these additional diagnostic categories remains to be demonstrated. Kumar and colleagues (2004) argue, based on their own work as well as that of other investigators, that Major Depressive Disorder resembles minor (or subsyndromal) depression in many ways, including neuroimaging findings, family history, risk factors, phenomenology, and sequelae, suggesting that distinctions between them are somewhat arbitrary. An alternative to the categorical (i.e., diagnostic) perspective is the dimensional approach, which describes the experience of depression in late life in terms of frequency and/or severity of depressive symptoms. This chapter addresses the etiology and outcomes of late life depression from both diagnostic and dimensional perspectives.

When considering depressive disorders, a distinction can be made based on age of onset. Among older adults with depression, it appears that half experienced the first episode in late life, whereas the other half entered old age with a history of depression (e.g., Brodaty et al., 1997). Late-onset depression has been associated with poorer cognitive performance, abnormalities on neuroimaging, and decreased likelihood of family history of depression compared to early-onset disorder, suggesting etiological differences (Alexopoulos, Meyers, Young, Campbell, et al., 1997). However, age of onset does not necessarily define etiologically homogeneous groups. Older adults who entered late life with a history of depressive disorder may also develop depression due to age-related factors, and conversely, survival to old age without a history of depression does not necessarily imply the absence of genetic risk or other early life vulnerabilities. Thus, in the sections that follow, early- and late-onset depression are considered together, noting specifically where evidence suggests differences in etiology, clinical presentation, and course.

ETIOLOGY

One way to conceptualize the etiology of depression in late life is to consider the ways the psychological, biological, and environmental influences on depression wax and wane—and interact—across the life span and into old age. Gatz and colleagues (Gatz, Kasl-Godley, & Karel, 1996; Karel, 1997) proposed a developmental diathesis-stress model that takes each of these dimensions into account. Psychological vulnerability to depression is thought to decrease in late life as older adults become more adept at coping with stressors. Genetic risk for depression also appears to be less prominent in late life. Other types of biological vulnerability, however, become more frequent, including age-associated neurobiological changes that may predispose to depression. Although stressors are present at all stages of life, certain stressors increase in frequency in late life, including bereavement, caregiving responsibilities, and illness-related disability. Taken together, the model would explain the increased levels of depressive symptoms found in late life relative to midlife (Mirowsky & Ross, 1992). According to this model, different etiological factors would be expected to play a role in late life depression compared to earlier in the life span. Biological vulnerability and certain age-related stressors are likely to be more important in explaining late life depression, whereas psychological vulnerability is less likely to play a role. In the discussion that follows, psychological and biological dimensions are reviewed. Following that, specific stressors shown to be risk factors for depression in this age group are discussed.

Several lines of research support the proposition that the psychological diathesis for depression may decrease in late life. When known risk factors for depression are statistically controlled, older adults actually have lower levels of depressive symptoms than do middle-aged adults (Mirowsky & Ross, 1992), suggesting a role for maturity in protecting against depression. Further, negative affectivity decreases across the adult life span (Charles, Reynolds, & Gatz, 2001). Thus, growing older may convey psychological protection against depression.

Another etiological factor that may diminish with age is genetic susceptibility to depression. Family history of depression is less common among older adults with either major depression or dysthymia than among younger adults with these disorders, suggesting that genetic influences on depression may be less prominent in late life (Devanand et al., 2004). In mixed-age samples, the heritability of Major Depressive Disorder is between 33% and 42% (for a meta-analysis, see Sullivan, Neale, & Kendler, 2000). Examining depressive symptoms without regard to syndromal criteria yields somewhat lower heritability estimates (Gatz, Pedersen, Plomin, Nesselroade, & McClearn, 1992).

In contrast, other biological factors appear to play a larger role in depression with age. Age-related biological changes that have been linked to depression generally involve disease processes rather than normal aging. Several diseases and medical conditions have well-established relationships with depression, including Parkinson's disease, Alzheimer's disease, stroke, and heart disease. Even in the absence of disease, however, cerebrovascular risk factors such as hypertension and diabetes are associated with depressive disorders in older adults (Alexopoulos, Meyers, Young, Campbell, et al., 1997). Depression associated with vascular risk factors, referred to as "vascular depression," is characterized by late onset and a distinctive symptom profile that includes psychomotor retardation, executive functioning deficits, and impaired insight and is less likely to include agitation and guilt (Alexopoulos, Meyers, Young, Kakuma, et al., 1997). Findings from neuroimaging studies are consistent with the possibility of a vascular subtype of depression, indicating that depressed patients with white matter abnormalities, which have been shown to be ischemic in origin, are more likely to have late-onset depression and to report psychomotor retardation (Simpson, Baldwin, Jackson, Burns, & Thomas, 2000) than depressed patients without such abnormalities. In studies measuring symptoms rather than depressive disorders, similar relationships have been reported between vascular risk and depressive symptoms (Mast, Azar, & Murrell, 2005). Although some investigations do not find the expected relationship between vascular risk factors and depression (see Cervilla, Prince, & Rabe-Hesketh, 2004), the lack of an effect may simply indicate that not enough is currently known about vascular depression. For example, Mast and colleagues have recently demonstrated that the association between vascular burden and depression is present primarily among the oldest old (85 and older; Mast et al., 2005) and among those with poor executive functioning (Mast, Yochim, MacNeill, & Lichtenberg, 2004). Taken together, research on vascular depression clearly demonstrates the importance of considering vascular burden when evaluating depression in older adults.

RISK AND PROTECTIVE FACTORS

Older women are at greater risk than older men for depressive disorders and significant depressive symptoms, but some evidence indicates that the gender gap seen in midlife may be narrowed or even reversed in late life (Bebbington et al., 1998). Other sociodemographic risk factors in midlife, including socioeconomic disadvantage and low levels of educational attainment, are also related to depression in late life (Mojtabai & Olfson,

2004). Other stressors discussed in this section are stressful life events, physical disability, bereavement, and caregiving for a frail family member. Social support is also discussed in terms of moderating the effects of these stressors.

Negative Life Events

Aggregate measures of stressful life events have been associated with both depressive disorders and increases in depressive symptom levels among older adults, although the effect is moderate (for a meta-analysis, see Kraaij, Arensman, & Spinhoven, 2002). Effects may also be time limited, lasting less than 6 months (Norris & Murrell, 1987). Notably, depressive symptoms in older adults have also been shown to predict later negative life events (Fiske, Gatz, & Pedersen, 2003), suggesting that a recursive effect may lead to a downward spiral if not interrupted.

Existing diatheses appear to moderate the effects of stressful life events. Ormel, Oldenhinkel, and Brilman (2001) reported that negative events were associated with depressive symptoms only in individuals with neurotic personality traits. Recent work in younger adult samples has demonstrated that the effect of negative life events on both depressive disorders and depressive symptoms is moderated by variation in the promoter region of the serotonin transporter (5-HTT) gene (Caspi et al., 2003). The same genotype moderated the effects of hip fracture on depression in a small sample of older adults (Lenze, Munin, & Ferrell, 2005).

Physical Illness and Disability

Physical health status has been one of the most commonly cited correlates of depressive symptoms and depressive disorders in late life. The association between illness burden and depressive symptoms is of a similar magnitude in late life as in middle age (Fiske et al., 2003), but the high prevalence of physical illness among older adults makes it an important risk factor. There are several, possibly overlapping, explanations for the correlation. Depression onset may be a psychological reaction to the physical illness, as will be discussed presently. In addition, poor health may have been precipitated by the depression, as accumulating evidence shows that depression increases risk for cardiovascular and other disease (Frasure-

Smith, Lesperance, & Talajic, 1993). In addition, a pathological process may be associated with both physical disease and depressive symptoms, as in vascular depression. With respect to the psychological reaction to illness, evidence indicates that disability plays a prominent role in mediating the effects of physical illness on depressive symptoms and disorders (for a review, see Zeiss, Lewinsohn, & Rohde, 1996). Severity of disability appears to be of importance, as Yang and George (2005) reported that in basic activities of daily living either onset or maintenance of impairment was associated with depressive symptom level, but for lesser forms of impairment only onset led to increases in depressive symptoms. These findings suggest that over time, older adults adapt to all but the most severe limitations.

Bereavement

Bereavement is another stressor that increases in frequency in late life and is associated with symptoms of depression. Although symptoms usually resolve over time without treatment, this is not always the case. According to *DSM-IV* criteria, a diagnosis of Major Depressive Disorder is given in the context of bereavement if the symptoms last more than 2 months or include marked functional impairment, morbid preoccupation with worthlessness, suicidal ideation, psychotic symptoms, or psychomotor retardation. Vulnerability factors influence the likelihood of depression following bereavement. Zisook and Shuchter (1993) reported that risk for depression following death of the spouse was highest in individuals with interpersonal difficulties and poor health, and risk for depression that endured for 2 years after the loss was highest in those with a family history of depression. Using prospective data, Bonanno and colleagues (2002) were able to distinguish between bereaved spouses with chronic depression that was present before the loss and those in whom enduring depressive symptoms developed only after bereavement. Excessive levels of dependency (both trait dependency and dependency on the spouse), low levels of instrumental support, and having a healthy spouse best predicted the development of enduring depressive symptoms after the loss.

Some investigators have distinguished complicated grief from bereavement-related depression, based in part on differential symptom presentation. Prigerson and colleagues (Latham & Prigerson, 2004) define complicated grief as a reaction to the death of a loved one that continues for at least 6 months, involves long-term functional impairment, and includes symptoms of separation distress (e.g., intrusive thoughts about the deceased, yearning, searching, or excessive loneliness) and traumatic distress (e.g., feelings of purposelessness, numbness, and disbelief). Similarly, Bonanno, Wortman, and Nesse (2004) reported that among bereaved spouses with enduring depressive symptoms, those without preloss depression were more likely to report searching for meaning, yearning, emotional pangs, and thinking and talking about the deceased, in contrast to spouses with prebereavement depression, who were more likely to perceive difficulties associated with widowhood (e.g., cleaning, paying bills). Complicated grief may have a worse prognosis than bereavement-related depression. It has been associated with increased morbidity, suicidal thoughts, and suicidal behaviors (Latham & Prigerson, 2004).

Caregiving

Both rates of depressive disorders (Cuijpers, 2005) and levels of depressive symptoms (Schulz & Williamson, 1991) are elevated in caregivers. Caregiving differs from many of the other stressors of late life in that it is more likely to be ongoing, resulting in chronic rather than acute stress. Perception of role captivity predicts chronicity of depressive symptoms (Liming Alspaugh, Parris Stephens, Townsend, Zarit, & Greene, 1999). Severity of problem behaviors in the care recipient has been linked to depressive symptoms that are time limited (Liming Alspaugh et al., 1999), but if a severe problem of this nature occurs early in the caregiving career, the effects on depression can be more profound and long-lasting (Gaugler, Kane, & Kane, 2005). Other factors associated with depressive symptoms include feelings of role overload and interpersonal or financial stressors (Liming Alspaugh et al., 1999; Schulz & Williamson, 1991). Women are more likely than men to fill the caregiving role, and women caregivers are more likely to be depressed than men caregivers, a finding that can be explained in part by underrecognition or underreporting of distress by male caregivers, and in part by socialization of women to use the less effective escape-avoidance coping style (Lutzky & Knight, 1994). Ethnic differences have also been reported. European American caregivers appraise caregiving as more burdensome than do African American caregivers, although levels of depressive symptoms are equivalent, in part because African American caregivers are younger, are in poorer health, and use emotion-focused coping, all of which are associated with greater levels of distress (Knight, Silverstein, McCallum, & Fox, 2000).

Social Factors

Among older adults, social factors can provide protection against depression or, alternatively, contribute to risk (for a review, see Hinrichsen & Emery, 2005). Social support has been examined as a possible buffer against the effects of various stressors. Findings consistently indicate that perceived support mitigates the effects of stressors, whereas objective measures of the structure or adequacy of the social support network do not. There is a limit, however, beyond which additional support may have a detrimental effect. Further, certain relationships may be depressogenic. Hinrichsen and Emery found higher levels of "expressed emotion" (expressions of criticism and/or emotional overinvolvement) in families of depressed older adults than in families of nondepressed older adults. Thus, an older adult's social context may be either helpful or harmful, depending in part on the nature of the relationship and the older adult's appraisal of it as supportive.

Several conclusions can be drawn regarding these risk factors for depressive disorders and depressive symptoms in late life. First, most of the stressors discussed here, including bereavement, onset of disability, and negative life events generally, appear to have time-limited effects. Second, these stressors appear to have the greatest effect on individuals with existing vulnerabilities, as predicted by diathesis-stress models, although more research is needed to examine these interactions. Further, perception of social support is instrumental in mitigating the effects of stressors on depressive outcomes.

COURSE

Depression appears to follow a more chronic course in late life than earlier in the life span, although heterogeneity exists. As a group, older adults treated for depression recover as rapidly as do individuals in other age groups, but they relapse more quickly (Mueller et al., 2004). Residual symptoms of depression after an episode has remitted increase the likelihood of relapse (Chopra, Zubritsky, & Knott, 2005). These findings suggest that depression treatment should be continued even after an episode has resolved until residual symptoms are also ameliorated. It is also possible, however, that for some older adults residual symptoms are a marker of neurobiological changes associated with increased vulnerability to depression, as in vascular depression. Executive dysfunction, which is characteristic of vascular depression, has been associated with chronicity as well as relapse and recurrence of depressive episodes (Alexopoulos et al., 2000). Indeed, longitudinal research shows that, at least in some cases, older adults with chronic depression go on to develop dementia (Tuma, 2000), suggesting that the depression was a prodromal symptom. Depression in older adults also leads to increased mortality, due to suicide (reviewed by Conwell, 2004) or all causes (Gallo et al., 2005).

A similar picture of the course and outcome of depression emerges when depressive symptoms rather than depressive disorders are considered. Depressive symptom levels are remarkably stable in older samples (Fiske et al., 2003). Like depressive disorders, elevated levels of depressive symptoms are associated with increased risk of mortality, including suicide (Ross, Bernstein, Trent, Henderson, & Paganini-Hill, 1990). The extent to which treatment for depression can prevent suicide or other premature mortality needs further investigation.

PRESENTATION

Depression in later life is characterized by a somewhat different symptom profile than depression in younger and middle-aged adults. The general pattern that emerges is that older adults are less likely to endorse dysphoria (Gallo, Rabins, & Anthony, 1999), ideational symptoms of guilt (Gallo, Anthony, & Muthén, 1994), or suicidal ideation (Blazer, Bachar, & Hughes, 1987). Symptoms that are more likely to be endorsed by older adults include somatic symptoms, such as fatigue (Gallo et al., 1994), insomnia (Christensen et al., 1999; Gallo et al., 1994), psychomotor retardation (Christensen et al., 1999; Gallo et al., 1994) or agitation (Brodaty et al., 1991), and diminished appetite or weight loss (Blazer et al., 1987; Brodaty et al., 1991, 1997). In addition, cognitive deficits are more common in late life depression, and particularly in depression with first onset in late life (Rapp et al., 2005). Other symptoms that have been reported to be more common in older adults are hopelessness and helplessness (Christensen et al., 1999), anhedonia (Christensen et al., 1999), and thoughts or wishes of death that are distinct from suicidal ideation (Gallo et al., 1994).

Few studies have evaluated sex differences in depressive symptom presentation in this age group. Findings to date indicate that at the same overall level of depression, men are more likely to report agitation (Christensen et al., 1999; Kockler & Heun, 2002), whereas women are more likely to report appetite disturbance (Kockler & Heun, 2002), worry, panic, pain, neck or back tension, feeling miserable, and feeling depressed (Christensen et al., 1999).

In summary, there are notable differences in clinical presentation of depression among older adults compared to middle-aged or younger adults. Older adults overall are less likely to endorse sadness or ideational symptoms of depression but more likely to endorse somatic symptoms and display cognitive deficits. Further, older adults are at greater risk of death by suicide but are less likely to endorse suicidal ideation.

CONCLUSION

The nature of depression among older adults is similar to depression in midlife adults in many respects, but differences are notable. Diagnostic rubrics appear less likely to capture the most common forms of depressive experience in this age group; for that reason, a dimensional perspective that considers the frequency and severity of a range of depressive symptoms may be particularly useful. Further, the increased heterogeneity of depression in this age group makes it important to consider multiple etiologies, which may include biological, psychological, and social factors. The effects of stressors on depression in this age group are similar to the effects in middle-aged adults, but because stressors such as disability, bereavement, and caregiving are particularly characteristic of late life, they should be considered routinely. Although the picture is mixed with regard to course of depression among older adults, there is also reason for optimism, both with regard to treatment and prevention. Older adults improve as rapidly with treatment as nonelderly. Furthermore, it is becoming increasingly clear that depression is not a normal part of aging, but rather the result of a varied set of causes, each of which could be a target for prevention.

REFERENCES

Alexopoulos, G. S., Meyers, B. S., Young, R. C., Campbell, S., Silbersweig, D., & Charlson, M. (1997). The "vascular depression" hypothesis. *Archives of General Psychiatry, 54*, 915–922.

Alexopoulos, G. S., Meyers, B. S., Young, R. C., Kakuma, T., Silbersweig, D., & Charlson, M. (1997). Clinically defined vascular depression. *American Journal of Psychiatry, 154*, 562–565.

Alexopoulos, G. S., Meyers, B. S., Young, R. C., Kalayam, B., Kakuma, T., Gabrielle, M., et al. (2000). Executive dysfunction and long-term outcomes of geriatric depression. *Archives of General Psychiatry, 57*, 285–290.

American Psychiatric Association. (1994). *Diagnostic and statistical manual of mental disorders* (4th ed.). Washington, DC: Author.

Bebbington, P. E., Dunn, G., Jenkins, R., Lewis, G., Brugha, T., Farrell, M., et al. (1998). The influence of age and sex on the prevalence of depressive conditions: Report from the National Survey of Psychiatric Morbidity. *Psychological Medicine, 28*, 9–19.

Blazer, D., Bachar, J. R., & Hughes, D. C. (1987). Major depression with melancholia: A comparison of middle-aged and elderly adults. *Journal of the American Geriatrics Society, 35*, 927–932.

Bonanno, G. A., Wortman, C. B., Lehman, D. R., Tweed, R. G., Haring, M., Sonnega, J., et al. (2002). Resilience to loss and chronic grief: A prospective study from preloss to 18-months postloss. *Journal of Personality and Social Psychology, 83*, 1150–1164.

Bonanno, G. A., Wortman, C. B., & Nesse, R. M. (2004). Prospective patterns of resilience and maladjustment during widowhood. *Psychology and Aging, 19*, 260–271.

Brodaty, H., Luscombe, G., Parker, G., Wilhelm, K., Hickie, I., Austin, M.-P., et al. (1997). Increased rate of psychosis and psychomotor change in depression with age. *Psychological Medicine, 27*, 1205–1213.

Brodaty, H., Peters, K., Boyce, P., Hickie, I., Parker, G., Mitchell, P., et al. (1991). Age and depression. *Journal of Affective Disorders, 23*, 137–149.

Caspi, A., Sugden, K., Moffitt, T. E., Taylor, A., Craig, I. W., Harrington, H., et al. (2003). Influence of life stress on depression: Moderation by a polymorphism in the 5-HTT gene. *Science, 301*, 386–389.

Cervilla, J., Prince, M., & Rabe-Hesketh, S. (2004). Vascular disease risk factors as determinants of incident depressive symptoms: A prospective community-based study. *Psychological Medicine, 34*, 635–641.

Charles, S. T., Reynolds, C. A., & Gatz, M. (2001). Age-related differences and change in positive and negative affect over 23 years. *Journal of Personality and Social Psychology, 80*, 136–151.

Chopra, H. P., Zubritsky, C., & Knott, K. (2005). Importance of subsyndromal symptoms of depression in elderly patients. *American Journal of Geriatric Psychiatry, 13*, 597–606.

Christensen, H., Jorm, A. F., MacKinnon, A. J., Korten, A. E., Jacomb, P. A., Henderson, A. S., et al. (1999). Age differences in depression and anxiety symptoms: A structural equation modelling analysis of data from a general population sample. *Psychological Medicine, 29*, 325–339.

Conwell, Y. (2004). Suicide. In S. P. Roose & H. A. Sackeim (Eds.), *Late-life depression* (pp. 95–106). New York: Oxford University Press.

Cuijpers, P. (2005). Depressive disorders in caregivers of dementia patients: A systematic review. *Aging and Mental Health, 9*, 325–330.

Devanand, D. P., Adorno, E., Cheng, J., Burt, T., Pelton, G. H., Roose, S. P., et al. (2004). Late onset dysthymic disorder and major depression differ from early onset dysthymic disorder and major depression in elderly outpatients. *Journal of Affective Disorders, 78*, 259–267.

Fiske, A., Gatz, M., & Pedersen, N. L. (2003). Depressive symptoms and aging: The effects of illness and non-health related events. *Journal of Gerontology: Psychological Sciences, 58*, P320–P328.

Frasure-Smith, N., Lesperance, F., & Talajic, M. (1993). Depression following myocardial infarction: Impact on six-month survival. *Journal of the American Medical Association, 270*, 1819–1825.

Gallo, J. J., Anthony, J. C., & Muthén, B. O. (1994). Age differences in the symptoms of depression: A latent trait analysis. *Journal of Gerontology: Psychological Sciences, 49*, P251–P264.

Gallo, J. J., Bogner, H. R., Morales, K. H., Post, E. P., Ten Have, T., & Bruce, M. L. (2005). Depression, cardiovascular disease, diabetes, and two-year mortality among older, primary-care patients. *American Journal of Geriatric Psychiatry, 13,* 748–755.

Gallo, J. J., Rabins, P. V., & Anthony, J. C. (1999). Sadness in older persons: 13-year follow-up of a community sample in Baltimore, Maryland. *Psychological Medicine, 29,* 341–350.

Gatz, M., Kasl-Godley, J. E., & Karel, M. J. (1996). Aging and mental disorders. In J. E. Birren & K. W. Schaie (Eds.), *Handbook of the psychology of aging* (4th ed., pp. 365–382). San Diego, CA: Academic Press.

Gatz, M., Pedersen, N. L., Plomin, R., Nesselroade, J. R., & McClearn, G. E. (1992). Importance of shared genes and shared environments for symptoms of depression in older adults. *Journal of Abnormal Psychology, 101,* 701–708.

Gaugler, J. E., Kane, R. L., & Kane, R. A. (2005). The longitudinal effects of early behavior problems in the dementia caregiving career. *Psychology and Aging, 20,* 100–116.

Hasin, D. S., Goodwin, R. D., Stinson, F. S., & Grant, B. F. (2005). Epidemiology of major depressive disorder: Results from the National Epidemiologic Survey on Alcoholism and Related Conditions. *Archives of General Psychiatry, 62,* 1097–1106.

Hinrichsen, G. A., & Emery, E. E. (2005). Interpersonal factors and late-life depression. *Clinical Psychology: Science and Practice, 12,* 264–275.

Jeste, D. V., Alexopoulos, G. S., Bartels, S. J., Cummings, J. L., Gallo, J. J., Gottlieb, G. L., et al. (1999). Consensus statement on the upcoming crisis in geriatric mental health: Research agenda for the next two decades. *Archives of General Psychiatry, 56,* 848–853.

Judd, L. L. (1997). The clinical course of unipolar major depressive disorders. *Archives of General Psychiatry, 54,* 989–991.

Karel, M. J. (1997). Aging and depression: Vulnerability and stress across adulthood. *Clinical Psychology Review, 17,* 847–879.

Knight, B. G., Silverstein, M., McCallum, T. J., & Fox, L. S. (2000). A sociocultural stress and coping model for mental health outcomes among African American caregivers in southern California. *Journals of Gerontology: Psychological Science, 55,* P142–P150.

Kockler, M., & Heun, R. (2002). Gender differences of depressive symptoms in depressed and nondepressed elderly persons. *International Journal of Geriatric Psychiatry, 17,* 65–72.

Kraaij, V., Arensman, E., & Spinhoven, P. (2002). Negative life events and depression in elderly persons: A meta-analysis. *Journal of Gerontology: Psychological Sciences, 57B,* P87–P94.

Kumar, A., Lavretsky, H., & Elderkin-Thompson, V. (2004). Nonmajor clinically significant depression in the elderly. In S. P. Roose & H. A. Sackeim (Eds.), *Late-life depression* (pp. 64–80). New York: Oxford University Press.

Latham, A. E., & Prigerson, H. G. (2004). Suicidality and bereavement: Complicated grief as a psychiatric disorder presenting greatest risk for suicidality. *Suicide and Life-Threatening Behavior, 34,* 350–362.

Lenze, E. J., Munin, M. C., & Ferrell, R. E. (2005). Association of the serotonin transporter gene-linked polymorphic region (5-HTTLPR) genotype with depression in elderly persons after hip fracture. *American Journal of Geriatric Psychiatry, 13,* 428–432.

Liming Alspaugh, M. E., Parris Stephens, M. A., Townsend, A. L., Zarit, S. H., & Greene, R. (1999). Longitudinal patterns of risk for depression in dementia caregivers: Objective and subjective primary stress as predictors. *Psychology and Aging, 14,* 34–43.

Lutzky, S. M., & Knight, B. G. (1994). Explaining gender differences in caregiver distress: The roles of emotional attentiveness and coping styles. *Psychology and Aging, 9,* 513–519.

Mast, B. T., Azar, A. R., & Murrell, S. A. (2005). The vascular depression hypothesis: The influence of age on the relationship between cerebrovascular risk factors and depressive symptoms in community dwelling elders. *Aging and Mental Health, 9,* 146–152.

Mast, B. T., Yochim, B., MacNeill, S. E., & Lichtenberg, P. A. (2004). Risk factors for geriatric depression: The importance of executive functioning within the vascular depression hypothesis. *Journals of Gerontology: Biological Sciences and Medical Sciences, 59A,* 1290–1294.

Mirowsky, J., & Ross, C. E. (1992). Age and depression. *Journal of Health and Social Behavior, 33,* 187–205.

Mojtabai, R., & Olfson, M. (2004). Major depression in community-dwelling middle-aged and older adults: Prevalence and two-year and four-year follow-up symptoms. *Psychological Medicine, 34,* 623–634.

Mueller, T. I., Kohn, R., Leventhal, N., Leon, A. C., Solomon, D., Coryell, W., et al. (2004). The course of depression in elderly patients. *American Journal of Geriatric Psychiatry, 12,* 22–29.

Norris, F. H., & Murrell, S. A. (1987). Transitory impact of life-event stress on psychological symptoms in older adults. *Journal of Health and Social Behavior, 28,* 197–211.

Ormel, J., Oldenhinkel, A. J., & Brilman, E. I. (2001). The interplay and etiological continuity of neuroticism, difficulties, and life events in the etiology of major and subsyndromal, first and recurrent depressive episodes in later life. *American Journal of Psychiatry, 158,* 885–891.

Rapp, M. A., Dahlman, K., Sano, M., Grossman, H. T., Haroutunian, V., & Gorman, J. M. (2005). Neuropsychological differences between late-onset and recurrent geriatric major depression. *American Journal of Psychiatry, 162,* 691–698.

Ross, R. K., Bernstein, L., Trent, L., Henderson, B. E., & Paganini-Hill, A. (1990). A prospective study of risk factors for traumatic death in the retirement community. *Preventive Medicine, 19,* 323–334.

Schulz, R., & Williamson, G. M. (1991). A two-year longitudinal study of depression among Alzheimer's caregivers. *Psychology and Aging, 6,* 569–578.

Simpson, S., Baldwin, R. C., Jackson, A., Burns, A., & Thomas, P. (2000). Is the clinical expression of late-life depression influenced by brain changes? MRI subcortical neuroanatomical correlates of depressive symptoms. *International Psychogeriatrics, 12,* 425–434.

Sullivan, P. F., Neale, M. C., & Kendler, K. S. (2000). Genetic epidemiology of major depression: Review and meta-analysis. *American Journal of Psychiatry, 157,* 1552–1562.

Tuma, T. A. (2000). Outcome of hospital-treated depression at four and a half years: An elderly and a younger adult cohort compared. *British Journal of Psychiatry, 176,* 224–228.

Weissman, M. M., Bruce, M. L., Leaf, P. J., Florio, L. P., & Holzer, C., III. (1991). Affective disorders. In L. N. Robins & D. A. Regier (Eds.), *Psychiatric disorders in America* (pp. 53–80). New York: Free Press.

Yang, Y., & George, L. K. (2005). Functional disability, disability transitions, and depressive symptoms in late life. *Journal of Aging and Health, 17,* 263–292.

Zeiss, A. M., Lewinsohn, P. M., & Rohde, P. (1996). Functional impairment, physical disease, and depression in older adults. In P. M. Kato & T. Mann (Eds.), *Handbook of diversity issues in health psychology* (pp. 161–184). New York: Plenum Press.

Zisook, S., & Shuchter, S. R. (1993). Major depression associated with widowhood. *American Journal of Geriatric Psychiatry, 1,* 316–326.

3

Assessing Depression in Older Adults

MELISSA SNARSKI AND FORREST SCOGIN

Assessment of depression is a routine aspect of mental health practice with older adults. In fact, we believe that depression screening should be a routine aspect of general health care for older adults. This is not to suggest that all older adults are depressed, or that all older adults seen for behavioral health care are depressed. However, depression is a relatively prevalent and highly comorbid disorder among older adults seen across health care settings. Thus, assessment of depression symptoms is integral to proper diagnosis and treatment planning for elders. In this chapter, we discuss the purpose of geriatric depression assessment, the methods used, and the issues that arise and adaptations to be considered in assessment of depressed elders. Our focus is on depression assessment as part of the treatment implementation process rather than as used in research or screening activities. We also focus on some of the difficulties that can be encountered in geriatric depression assessment. This focus should not be interpreted as meaning that all cases are difficult; in fact, most cases are relatively uncomplicated. Our intention is to write this chapter in a rather informal voice and make practical suggestions where possible.

THE PURPOSE OF GERIATRIC
DEPRESSION ASSESSMENT

Geriatric depression should be routinely assessed due to the frequent co-morbidities of physical and mental health conditions seen in older patients. Older adults face health conditions and psychological stressors such as loss of relatives and independence. For example, some evidence suggests that cerebrovascular disease may play a key role in determining which older adults develop depression in late life (Alexopoulos et al., 1997). These conditions may predispose older adults to developing depression. There is an 8% to 25% prevalence rate of clinically significant depression in older adults (Blazer, 1993).

Although depressive symptoms are quite prevalent in older adults, they are often difficult to diagnose. Some reasons for this difficulty are the many somatic symptom confounds present in older adults. For example, an older adult may suffer from several painful physical conditions that increase fatigability and make sleep difficult. The same symptoms in another older adult may be clearly attributable to a depressive episode. More commonly, the causes and correlates of symptoms are inextricably bound in a holistic fashion. Major depression and depressive symptoms have been correlated with increased medical morbidity (Bush et al., 2001; Hansen et al., 2001). However, for diagnostic and treatment reasons it is important to tease apart the differences. Some of these overlapping problems may include sleep problems, weight loss, fatigue, and irritability (Jamison & Scogin, 1992).

Another potential confound is cognitive ability. Often, depressed individuals have complaints such as memory problems, confusion, and concentration problems. These types of symptoms make it difficult to differentiate between depression and age-related changes in cognition or dementia. The relation of dementia and depression is quite complex. Depression has been reported as a risk factor for developing dementia (Jorm, 2000). Overlapping symptoms that occur in both depression and dementia make it difficult to differentiate between the two (Purandare, Burns, Craig, Faragher, & Scott, 2001). In addition, there are many cases in which depression and dementia coexist. Studies examining depression in demented patients typically report prevalence rates of 20% to 30% (Wragg & Jeste, 1989).

A study conducted by Muller-Thomsen and colleagues (Muller-Thomsen, Arlt, Mann, Mab, & Ganzer, 2005) examined the difference in prevalence of depressive symptoms dependent on severity of dementia. To do this, four different scales were used: the Geriatric Depression Scale—Short Form (GDS-SF), the Montgomery and Asperg Depression Scale, the Cornell Scale for Depression in Dementia (CSDD), and the Nurses' Observation Scale for Geriatric Patients. Participants were divided into two groups: mild Alzheimer's disease (score on the Mini Mental State Exam [MMSE] > 18) and moderate to severe Alzheimer's disease (MMSE < 18). Results indicated higher prevalence rates of depression in the moderate to severe Alzheimer's disease group (36.3% to 68.4%) than in the mild Alzheimer's disease group (27.5% to 53.4%). These results are contrary to previous findings that depression and dementia had the greatest rates of comorbidity in the earliest stages.

The difficulty in diagnosing depression in older adults may result in either unrecognized symptoms or overdiagnosis of symptoms. There are low recognition rates of geriatric depression in settings such as primary care, where older adults are most likely present (D'Ath, Katona, Mullan, Evans, & Katona, 1994). One reason for this underrecognition is the high frequency of somatic symptoms compared to cognitive-affective symptoms of depression reported by older adults in comparison to younger cohorts (Fiske, Kasl-Godley, & Gatz, 1998; Goldberg, Breckenridge, & Sheikh, 2003; Kasl-Godley, Gatz, & Fiske, 1998). In the absence of reports of symptoms such as sadness and guilt, depression can go unnoticed (Gatz & Hurwicz, 1990). Because the psychological symptoms of depression often go undetected in older adults, there is a low utilization rate of antidepressant medication in this population (Weatherall, 2000).

Another reason depression is underrecognized is that often individuals do not have symptoms that qualify for a diagnosis of major depression. Instead, a large percentage of depressed older adults suffer from a less severe condition, known as minor depression. Although common opinion holds that older adults are more depressed than other age groups, cross-sectional studies have shown that older adults report lower rates of depression than younger adults (Goldberg et al., 2003). More specifically, studies have typically found that although there are lower rates of major depression, there are higher rates of depressive symptoms in older adults versus younger adults (Fiske et al., 1998; Kasl-Godley et al., 1998). Minor depression could be diagnosed for these individuals reporting subclinical levels of depression. However, due to the limited symptomatology, minor depression often can pass under the diagnostic radar.

In contrast, sometimes depression is overdiagnosed. Some studies noted that somatic complaints due to physical conditions may be mistakenly attributed to depression (Goldberg et al., 2003; Lewinsohn, Seeley, Roberts, & Allen, 1997). Both circumstances demonstrate the difficulty of teasing apart somatic symptoms, which have the potential to be psychological; physiological; or, more complicated still, simultaneous in etiology and presentation.

In addition to minor and major depression, the older patient's depressive symptoms may be indicative of other disorders. Disorders such as dysthymia and vascular depression are two such conditions. Dysthymia consists of milder symptoms than Major Depressive Disorder and may last for several years, with intermittent periods of up to 2 months without any of the depressive symptoms; another criterion is depressed mood for most of the day, for more days than not, for at least 2 years. Vascular depression may be diagnosed in individuals whose mood is likely influenced by cerebrovascular disease. The key component of vascular depression is evidence of ischemic small-vessel pathology via a magnetic resonance image (MRI). One study of vascular depression found that increased levels of white matter hypertensities (WMH) may be evidence for the vascular origin of late-life depressions. In this study, 1 participant out of the 13 had higher levels of WMH at baseline, which increased over time and may have led to his diagnosis of major depression 3 years later (Nebes et al., 2002). Typically, these individuals experience their first episode of major depression late in life and also exhibit cognitive impairments, especially in executive functioning (Nebes et al., 2002).

Findings indicate that striatofrontal dysfunctions may cause these deficits in executive functioning (Tranel, Anderson, & Benton, 1994). These dysfunctions may contribute to the development of depression (Alexopoulos et al., 1997). In addition, older adults suffering from depression due to executive dysfunction have a slower response to antidepressants and show an earlier relapse rate (Alexopoulos et al., 2000; Kalayam & Alexopoulos, 1999). There are some clinical implications of these findings. One implication involves incorporating evaluations of psychomotor activity and executive functioning as a key element of the assessment of depressed elders (Kiosses, Alexopoulos, & Murphy, 2000). Clinicians can assess the origin of depressive symptoms to determine if the symptoms stem from executive dysfunction. Several instruments measure executive dysfunction, which is often recognized in tasks involving following set (Trails B), verbal fluency (Controlled Oral Word Association Test), response inhibition (Stroop Color-Word Interference Test), and sorting (Wisconsin Card Sorting Task; La Rue, 1999).

A primary purpose of a depression assessment and diagnosis is to promote communication. Diagnoses are useful in professional communication across health care disciplines. A diagnosis of depression or anxiety provides meaningful information to another health care provider. Therefore, diagnosis serves an important function by simplifying communication among the disciplines, which is important given the interdisciplinary nature of optimal geriatric health care.

An accurate diagnosis is important to both older clients and their caregivers. A diagnosis of depression can help individuals understand their behaviors and feelings. In addition, a precise description of the patient's problems may help both the patient and caregiver by lessening confusion and distress resulting from the patient's behavioral changes (Kaszniak, 1996). Having an accurate diagnosis or label may provide relief for older adults who have been concerned about their symptoms for many years. The following is a composite case example.

Case Example: Rita, Depression

Rita is a 60-year-old European American woman who was has been suffering from an undiagnosed illness for the past 10 years. Rita feels weak and unmotivated with a great deal of pain. She described her problem in this way:

> I get nervous and sad when I am alone at home. I am especially upset about going out and getting my chores done. I do not have any desire to go to the grocery store and see people. When I go to the grocery store, I usually go at a time when it is less crowded and make it quick.

Her depression was especially bothersome when it prohibited her from getting important daily tasks done:

> I do not sleep very well. It takes me hours to actually get to sleep. When I wake up in the morning, I have no energy. I have lots to do around the house and errands to run, but I feel like I can't move. I am not motivated to do simple things like cook and clean. I do not even make meals sometimes because I don't feel hungry. I do not have any interest in being with my friends or family who call me all the time with invitations. I used to be a social butterfly, but since the loss of my husband 10 years ago, I just stay home and feel sick.

After listening to this description, her clinician told her, "It sounds like you're describing a mood disorder. The experiences you're mentioning sound like major depression." Following the diagnosis, the clinician discussed the criteria of major depression and the client was very eager to point out that they matched her experiences. It relieved her to have a diagnosis or name for her problem. Moreover, it comforted her to find the potential cause of her disorder and to know that there were effective treatment options available.

Previous to sessions with her clinician, this client felt that her complaints were not taken seriously. Family members and friends did not understand her and told her that she just needed to get out. Her physicians told her that there was nothing physically wrong with her. She was extremely relieved to have someone validate her concerns and free her of this confusion.

Many older adults' experiences are similar to Rita's. Their depressive symptoms may include somatic symptoms and are often undetected. Therefore, the use of screening measures for depression in primary care settings could greatly improve the detection rates of geriatric depression (Callahan et al., 1994). However, having instruments that are valid with older adults as well as conducting carefully structured and unstructured interviews for accurate detection are necessary.

Depression assessment and accurate detection also allow the clinician to plan and monitor the client's treatment progress and outcome. The results of depression screening tools, such as the GDS, have the potential to guide the course of treatment. The GDS provides a good quick overview of the client's current mood status. If a client scores above the cutoff score on the GDS, a clinical interview is recommended and may be able to make further determinations of the client's particular disorder (e.g., Major Depressive Disorder, dysthymia). However, depression scores on the GDS do indeed determine the level of severity of the person's symptoms.

Assessing the severity level of the patient's depression helps in the treatment planning process. For example, a client with a score of 28 out of 30 on the GDS requires more intensive treatment than an individual with a score of 12. Therefore, a client's score on the GDS may determine which treatment is appropriate. Some research findings suggest that for mildly and moderately depressed older adults (scores of 5 to 20) psychotherapy is the treatment of choice and that severely depressed clients (scores over 20) should seek pharmacotherapy for more rapid relief of their symptoms (Hanson, Scogin, Welsh, & Karpe, 2004). In addition, an approach combining psychotherapy and antidepressant medication may be especially beneficial to those with scores of 15 to 30 on the GDS suffering from moderate to severe depression.

Once a treatment plan has been initiated, the depression screener can continue to be used as a means of monitoring treatment progress and outcome. Weekly depression assessments can help determine if that particular treatment is in fact decreasing depressive symptoms. If assessments indicate that a particular treatment is not working (i.e., depression scores are not declining), an alternative treatment may be implemented. However, if weekly depression scores do show a decline, it is important to continue to monitor the client's progress to prevent a relapse (Hanson et al., 2004). Usually, the GDS is administered at the beginning of the weekly session and discussed with the patient when it is used for treatment monitoring. Specifically, if the client continually endorses specific symptoms or suicidal thoughts, a follow-up session is conducted. Over time,

GDS scores can be graphed to show a patient's progress. If the GDS administration is too time-consuming, the GDS-SF can be used.

After a client has completed the course of therapy, depression assessment tools such as the GDS can be used to measure the outcome of therapy. This can be implemented in several ways. First, the GDS can be used to measure depressive symptoms in a time of remission. Second, the GDS can be used at the end of therapy to determine if there has been a change from the baseline score. Third, the GDS can be used as an indicator of when therapy should end. To fulfill this purpose, a certain score on the GDS would determine that the client was now in a healthy range. Overall, the GDS is useful as an outcome assessment tool and allows clients to map their progress.

Accurate detection of the disorder and its progress helps identify appropriate treatments. There exist several evidence-based interventions, both pharmacological and psychological, that can reduce the burden of depression. Chapter 4 in this book discusses the status of empirical support for psychological interventions for geriatric depression, and Chapters 5 through 7 examine in detail several of these interventions. The existence of these interventions make assessment more meaningful as it can lead directly to the implementation of beneficial treatment.

INSTRUMENTS COMMONLY USED TO ASSESS GERIATRIC DEPRESSION

The *Diagnostic and Statistical Manual of Mental Disorders, fourth edition, text revision* (*DSM-IV-TR*; American Psychiatric Association, 2000), provides the most frequently used diagnostic criteria for depressive disorders. The diagnosis of major depression requires that five of the nine listed symptoms of depression are present for a period of 2 weeks. Minor depression, a diagnosis under consideration for inclusion in the next edition of the *DSM*, is the presence of at least two but fewer than five of the symptoms. The nine symptoms are depressed mood, significant weight loss or gain, insomnia or hypersomnia, decreased interest in activities, fatigue or decreased energy, psychomotor agitation or retardation, diminished thinking or concentration, feelings of guilt and worthlessness, and suicidal ideation.

Various instruments that are widely used to detect depression throughout the life span have been used in geriatric populations. The Center for Epidemiologic Studies Depression Scale (CES-D; Radloff, 1977), the Beck Depression Inventory II (BDI-II; Beck, Steer, & Brown, 1996), and the Hamilton Rating Scale for Depression (HRSD; Hamilton, 1960) have been among the most popular. Although sound psychometrically, none was developed with older adults in mind and each has characteristics that complicate its use with older adults. In contrast, the GDS (Yesavage, Brink, Rose, Lum, et al., 1983) alleviates some of these problems by taking into account issues specific to older adults. In addition, the CSDD (Alexopoulos, Abrams, Young, & Shamoian, 1988) is often used in older adults to measure depression and differentiate between major and minor depression.

The Center for Epidemiologic Studies Depression Scale

The CES-D is a commonly used depression scale that has the added advantage of being in the public domain and thus free of charge. The CES-D is used to measure depression severity and yields a four-factor structure model of depressed affect, positive affect, somatic activity, and interpersonal issues (Radloff, 1977). The CES-D has been found to be psychometrically sound and to represent these four factors in nonmedical geriatric samples (Hertzog, Van Alstine, Usala, & Hultsch, 1990), in primary care older adult patients (Lyness, King, Cox, Yoediono, & Caine, 1999), and in ethnically diverse older adults (Liang, Tran, Krause, & Markides, 1989). However, there are some possible disadvantages to using the CES-D with an older population. First, it relies on somatic items to indicate depression, which, as mentioned before, can be difficult to disentangle. In addition, one study has shown that the CES-D needs to be modified for Black and Hispanic elders (Callahan & Wolinsky, 1994). The CES-D overall has good internal consistency in older adults (Areán & Miranda, 1997) and is said to be robust in its utility with community-residing older adults (Lewinsohn et al., 1997).

The Beck Depression Inventory II

The BDI-II is a widely used and well-known inventory that measures depression via a multiple-choice format. The original BDI (Beck, Ward, Mendelson, Mock, & Erbaugh, 1961) has good psychometric properties with an older adult sample. Both internal consistency and test-retest reliability have been demonstrated in both nondepressed and depressed outpatient older adults (Gallagher, Breckenridge, Steinmetz, & Thompson, 1983; Gallagher, Nies, & Thompson, 1982). The BDI has also shown clinical sensitivity and specificity in elderly inpatient and outpatient populations, with a cutoff score of 10 out of 21 items (Norris, Gallagher, Wilson, & Winograd, 1987; Rapp, Parisi, Walsh, & Wallace, 1988). Similar results have been found in the short version of the BDI, which contains 13 items with a cutoff score of 5 (Scogin, Hamblin, Beutler, & Corbishley, 1988).

The 23-item BDI-II is a revised version of the BDI with the omission of four previously used items, the addition of new items, and two altered items. In addition, many items were restated for clarity. The BDI-II has good psychometric properties with an older adult sample and has been shown to be highly correlated with the GDS ($\alpha = .707$) as well as having good internal consistency ($\alpha = .85$; Jefferson, Powers, & Pope, 2000). Thus, the changes made in the BDI-II do not seem to have changed its utility with older adults. Some changes, such as the inclusion of both increases and decreases in sleep and eating, may have actually allowed the BDI-II to be more comparable to the GDS in terms of multiple endorsement rate (Jefferson et al., 2000). However, Jefferson et al. note in closing that some professionals may choose to use the GDS because it was developed specifically for the geriatric population. This suggestion was implied by a difference in the nonresponse rate found. Participants left significantly more items blank on the BDI-II than on the GDS. Some of the older women in the study reported that some of the BDI-II questions did not apply to them, such as the "sexual interest" question.

The Hamilton Rating Scale for Depression

The HRSD is a commonly used structured interview to screen for depression and rate depression severity. One of the advantages of using this measure with older adults is its brevity. The HRSD takes approximately 30 minutes and is sensitive to changes in depression severity (Rabkin & Klein, 1987). The HRSD has several versions, including 17- and 21-item rating scales with items ranked on scales from 0 to 4, 0 to 2, and 0 to 3. A score of 18 to 20 on the Full-Scale Hamilton Depression Inventory is used as the cutoff for a clinical level of depressive symptomology. One of the disadvantages of the HRSD is its reliance on somatic items. This may make it especially ineffective when screening older adults who have many somatic complaints due to physical conditions. Although the HRSD is a valid measurement for detecting depression, it was not developed with older adults in mind and must be used with caution by the assessor.

The Geriatric Depression Scale

The most commonly used depression screening instrument for older adults is the GDS (Yesavage, Brink, Rose, Lum, et al., 1983). The omission of somatic items and the simple yes/no format make it an attractive measure for use with older adults. The GDS consists of 30 items with simple phrasing. A score of 11 is considered the cutoff score for mild depression. The GDS has high internal consistency (Yesavage, Brink, Rose, Lum, et al., 1983) and is valid for depression screening in older outpatients and inpatients (Scogin, 1987; Yesavage, Brink, Rose, & Adey, 1983).

Several studies have attempted to find distinct subdimensions of the GDS by conducting factor analyses. One of the earliest GDS factor analysis in the literature was conducted by Parmalee and colleagues (Parmalee, Lawton, & Katz, 1989). Parmalee's principal components analysis (PCA) included the following six factors: dysphoria, worry, withdrawal-apathy, vigor, decreased concentration, and anxiety (Adams, Matto, & Sanders, 2004). Adams (2001) followed up on the work of Parmalee and others and examined a six-factor solution of the GDS. The findings implied a similar factor structure to Parmalee's, with slight differences in categorization. For example, the dysphoria factor was separated into two factors, one representing negative affect and the other representing hopelessness and helplessness. In addition, other factors were combined or added. Interestingly, Adams also found some correlations of the factors to demographic and health variables. For example, the withdrawal-apathy and lack of vigor factors correlated with increasing age and functional impairment. To better understand the value of the subdimensions of the GDS, Adams et al. conducted a confirmatory factor analysis (CFA) on the GDS based on previous results from several PCAs (Adams, 2001; Parmalee et al., 1989). The resulting CFA included 26 of the 30 items on the GDS with five factors.

These five factors suggest possible subscales of the GDS and allow these differences in subscales to be seen (Mitchell, Mathews, & Yesavage, 1993). These differences in subscales may be instrumental in determining the type of depression an individual is suffering from, as geriatric depression has many subtypes (Blazer, 2003). Therefore, the various subscales may have clinical implications in the future. For example, it may be that a certain subscale would discriminate between subtypes of depression, such as vascular and nonvascular major depression.

The GDS also has a short form, the GDS-SF (Sheikh & Yesavage, 1986), which contains 15 items. Research found a strong correlation ($r = .84$) between the short form and the long form when comparing individuals who took both. A score of 3 to 5 is a typical cutoff score for depression on the short form (Watson & Pignone, 2003). An even briefer five-item version has been developed for use in depression screening (Hoyl et al., 1999).

Although the GDS is considered by many to be the best depression screening measure for older adults, it is not free of problems. The GDS may not be the instrument of choice in demented patients and may vary in its usefulness by culture. The CSDD may be more appropriate in demented populations. An additional problem may be the client's understanding of the questions. Flacker and Spiro (2003) examined the effect of question comprehension on the utility of the GDS in older African Americans. In this study, 50 African American patients were given the GDS-SF as a part of their routine care. Any item about which the patient asked for clarification or looked confused and was still unable to answer after repetition was marked "not understood." On average, each patient did not understand one question, and there were four particular questions that more than 10% of the patients did not understand (Flacker & Spiro, 2003). Results of linear regression analyses showed that the number of questions not understood was associated with age and MMSE score, but not with educational attainment. Findings of this study indicate that lack of understanding of some questions on the GDS-SF may be a limitation of this instrument. This is particularly important because such misunderstandings could lead a professional to inaccurately detect depression. The authors of this study state two possible reasons for these misunderstandings. One potential explanation is cognitive impairment. The other possibility is the effect of culture and religion on understanding items on the

GDS-SF. Flacker and Spiro urge professionals to use the GDS-SF simply as a screening instrument and not as a diagnostic tool. Instead, the final diagnosis of depression lies in clinical judgment. Although the GDS is a reliable and valid screening instrument, it is suggested that a clinical or structured interview should follow the GDS to confirm the presence of a disorder (Segal, Coolidge, & Hersen, 1998).

The Cornell Scale for Depression in Dementia

The CSDD (Alexopoulos et al., 1988) is a 19-item, clinician-administered depression scale. This scale can be used in older adults with and without dementia, but it is especially useful in dementia patients because it incorporates the cooperation of collateral sources. The CSDD relies on information from interviews with both the patient and the caregiver, as well as direct observation of the patient (Alexopoulos et al., 1988). The clinician administers the same items to both the patient and the caregiver. Discrepancies between the two sources are clarified by the caregiver and then left to the clinician's judgment to evaluate. The CSDD is widely used in demented populations, and research shows that it is a consistent measure for detecting depression independent of the severity of dementia (Muller-Thomsen et al., 2005).

Although the CSDD is usually used as a unidimensional measure, some studies examined possible subscales of the measure by exploring factor analyses. In particular, Kurlowicz and colleagues (Kurlowicz, Evans, Strumpf, & Maislin, 2002) fit a four-factor model consisting of 16 items from the original 19-item CSDD. The four factors were depression, anxiety, somatic/vegetative, and disturbed sleep (Kurlowicz et al., 2002). These findings are similar to an earlier factor analysis study finding four factors of depression, rhythm disturbances, agitation, and physical symptoms (Harwood, Ownby, Barker, & Duara, 1998).

Summary

Professionals should be careful when selecting from these screening tools to include both symptom frequency (CES-D) and symptom discomfort (Hopkins Symptom Checklist) measures, as well as interviews. Chodosh, Buckwalter, Blazer, and Seeman (2004) conducted a study in which they examined whether older adults respond differently to depression instruments measuring frequency versus severity of symptoms. They found that older adults did differ in their responses between the two types of depression instruments. Furthermore, there were differences by socioeconomic status (SES), with higher SES groups endorsing more bother/severity of symptoms than symptom frequency. Therefore, Chodosh et al. suggest that professionals use both measures of frequency and severity when assessing depression in older adults.

In summary, several depression measurements not specifically designed for older adults have demonstrated utility with this population. For self-report, we prefer the GDS for the reasons mentioned. However, clinicians working with clients across the life span may prefer to use the BDI-II or CES-D to foster practice consistency and avoid switching instruments based on client age. In addition, due to the heterogeneous population of older adults, findings suggest that professionals should assess both symptom discomfort and symptom frequency to obtain accurate assessment (Chodosh et al., 2004).

ASSESSMENT METHODS

Assessing depression in older adults is usually accomplished through a blend of unstructured and structured interviews, self-report measurement, interdisciplinary input when available, and report by significant others. The contribution of these sources of information varies by site (e.g., outpatient mental health setting versus nursing home) and older adult functional ability (e.g., moderately demented versus no functional limitations).

Structured and Unstructured Interviews

Both structured and unstructured interviews are used to assess depression in older adults. Each has advantages and disadvantages. At its extreme, in a structured interview each question is scripted, with a primary goal to gather only factual information. One example of a comprehensive structured interview that has been used reliably with older adults is the Structured Clinical Interview for *DSM-III-R* (SCID; Spitzer, Williams, Gibbon, & First, 1990).

A structured interview has many advantages. It provides more objective coverage of disorders and is not as likely to fall prey to problems such as clinician bias. Structured interviews thus have improved reliability and validity over unstructured interviews (Segal, 1997). Generally, if rapport is built early on and the interview procedures are clearly spelled out, a structured interview is the older adult's preference due to its comprehensive nature and extra time with the interviewer (Segal et al., 1998).

One drawback is the amount of time that some structured interviews take due to their comprehensive nature. Because a goal with older adults is to keep sessions as short and simple as possible, an interview such as the SCID may not be preferable or practical when considering the client's needs. Another concern with using the SCID in older adults is that many of the behavioral and somatic complaints included in the criteria of disorders may actually reflect a normal part of aging. In addition, training is often required to administer structured interviews reliably.

Unstructured interviews, when conducted with skill, are very useful. Compared to more structured interviewing, open-ended, nonscripted questioning may lead to richer information and aid in establishing rapport. However, extreme examples of unstructured interviewing, such as the therapist silently waiting for the client to set the direction for the session, may be disconcerting to a depressed client. Such an unstructured stance can catalyze and lead to stream-of-consciousness responding, especially in cognitively compromised older adults.

Most clinical interviews are unstructured unless they are a part of a research protocol. So, although we have several structured interviews that have been used with older adults, they are not commonly used. However, experience with assessing depression via interviews such as the SCID and the HRSD results in more effective unstructured interview-based assessments of depression.

Taking these issues into consideration, we recommend that a more structured interview be used with depressed older adults. However, a particular structured interview, such as the SCID, may be modified or shortened to eliminate fatigue effects common in depressed older adults. We also suggest having an agenda and using less complex questions. This style may help things go more smoothly in addition to being the preferred process for older adults who are used to a more formal relationship between doctor and patient.

Initial Interview

In many clinical environments, the initial session with the client is the most pivotal in terms of assessment and treatment engagement. Use of the depression-specific instruments may be a part of the initial assessment, but for many clinicians, especially those in outpatient settings, the initial interview may be conducted with less formal assessment. In this section, we discuss the initial interview and depression assessment in that session.

The initial clinical interview and history of the client has been cited as being the "most important assessment approach" and a true "cornerstone" of the assessment process (National Institutes of Health, 1991). The first interview is the foundation on which treatment rests and a key to its success. Although many other measurements are used to assess depression in clients, such as self-report measures, the clinical interview helps to establish a depression diagnosis for the client.

An important issue to be mindful of is the pace of the interview and questioning. A clever idea that we paraphrase was coined by clinical geropsychologist Bob Knight, coeditor of this book: Slow down the pace to speed up the process. Because many older adults show some decline in working memory capacity, the speed at which information is presented and how much information is presented must be modified. Talking at a normal pace with an average level of content may be less than optimal with older adults, especially with depressed older adults whose concentration and memory may be impaired. The therapist may have to repeat or clarify ideas, which may be quite time-consuming. In addition, the assessment and beginning therapeutic process may be damaged by the constant repetition and clarification. Depressed older adults may be particularly sensitive to such actions and become self-critical about their difficulties. Thus, it may be more valuable to speak somewhat slower and use simpler sentence structure when working with older adults. Clearly, such determinations are made on a case-by-case basis.

The pattern of complex, rapid speech that may actually be the adaptive way to communicate on a daily basis in interactions with colleagues requires greater attentional resources and working memory capacity. By slowing down to help the depressed older adult better understand you, more may actually get done. A simple example of this is to make sure you are asking only one question at a time. It is easy to fall into a pattern in which we ask several questions in one breath. Although slowing down and simplifying may take conscious effort, the benefits may be more time spent productively exploring the older client's concerns.

Thorough History

One of the most important goals of the initial interview is to gather relevant information about the client's history. The clinical interview is a good opportunity to ask specific questions about the client's recent or past illnesses and injuries, as well as family history of psychological and neurological disease. It is also important to ask clients questions about their medication use and substance abuse, both of which may affect their mental status. Other important information includes education, employment past and present, financial status, marital status, and current living situation. In addition, cultural variables should be examined, such as marriage and family relations, ethnicity, religion, hobbies, social activity, and entertainment (Kaszniak, 1996). Each of these social variables may have an impact on the client's mood, and many of them impact the way individuals respond to questions regarding depressive symptoms. Some research has found that different cultures and religions associate different meanings with certain words (Flacker & Spiro, 2003). Socioeconomic status also has an influence on how older adults report depression (Chodosh et al., 2004). Chodosh and colleagues found that older adults with higher SES responded more to questions regarding severity and bother, whereas lower SES individuals typically responded more to symptom frequency items.

Functional Abilities and Daily Activities

Depression assessment with older adults should go beyond the scope of traditional psychological diagnosis. Functional ability level is an important consideration in work with older adults and an important correlate of depression. It can be measured by examining the individual's daily activities. Functional ability is the maintenance of independent self-care and function in various environments and is generally broken down into two categories: Bathing, feeding, and toileting are examples of basic activities of daily living; using the telephone and cooking meals are examples of instrumental and advanced activities of daily living. Often, asking clients a simple question, such as "Do you have any trouble doing things around the house?" leads to much of the information necessary to assess their activity abilities. Functional ability screening is a natural complement to cognitive and mood screening. When assessing functional abilities, it is sometimes discovered that cognitive or mood impairments are responsible for the functional difficulties.

Two popular scales, the Activities of Daily Living Scale (ADLS; Katz, Ford, Moskowitz, Jackson, & Jaffe, 1963) and the Instrumental Activities of Daily Living Scale (IADLS; Lawton & Brody, 1969) are commonly used to measure functioning. The ADLS examines activities such as feeding and toileting, whereas the IADLS examines activities such as managing money and using transportation. With some clients, it is appropriate to give both of these measures because a client in early stages of dementia may not have obvious difficulties. A collateral source is another important tool to use when measuring functional abilities. A spouse, caregiver, or family member may be able to provide additional information regarding functional strengths and weaknesses.

Depression can sometimes exaggerate an individual's functional ability deficits. The anhedonia and lack of initiation sometimes seen with depression may create the appearance of greater disability than warranted relative to an older adult's optimal functioning. Treatment of depression may reduce some of these limitations.

Assessing functional abilities is an important part of diagnosis; often, these measurements help to predict outcome. In addition, testing functional ability levels aids family members in their understanding of the client's condition. Therefore, assessing patient ability level makes it easier to educate the family about the client's condition and develop a treatment plan.

Consulting Others

Although treating the depressed older adult as an autonomous individual and with a great deal of respect is important, it is also important to get information from others close to the client, which may allow you to treat the patient with beneficence. Often interviews with family members, friends, and caregivers are included to supplement the information given by the client, especially clients with moderate to severe dementia. This additional information often includes important aspects about the client's condition that were not reported by the clients themselves. With demented clients, who may not be able to accurately answer self-report questions, it is most important to get information by proxy from a caregiver or close relative (Kaszniak & Scogin, 1995). One way to collect information by proxy is with the collateral source version of the GDS. In the GDS-CS, the 30-item scale changes the word "you" to the word "they." Some findings indicate that more depressive symptoms are endorsed by the collateral sources than by the older adult patients (Nitcher, Burke, Roccaforte, & Wengel, 1993). In this case, the authors of the study suggest that a higher cutoff score be used when scoring items from a collateral source. Additionally, it may be important to assess the caregiver and his or her level of distress.

Family assessment is useful with most depressed older clients and not simply confined to work with demented older adults. In a first session with a depressed senior, it may be important to include family members in the meeting. However, it is important to get the client's permission before doing so. As treatment progresses, it will probably be more appropriate to meet only with the older client and periodically update the family (Scogin, 2000). When assessing a family, you should get a sense of the client's current and historical role in the family (Knight & McCallum, 1998). For example, an older adult's depression may be influenced by his or her change in role from caregiver to recipient of care. It is important to appreciate the client's perspective and any major changes that have taken place. In addition, knowing the perspective and conditions of the family members is helpful. Family members themselves may be impaired. In some families, depression, psychological assessment, and treatment may carry stigmas (Knight & McCallum, 1998). This information would be useful in determining a diagnosis, as well as preparing the individual for the potential consequences of a diagnostic label.

Assessing Mental Status

Certain types of cognitive functioning become less efficient with aging (Salthouse, 1998). Therefore, it is important to determine if there is impairment in this area so that the necessary assessment and treatment decisions will be made. Such impairment may interfere with accurate depression assessment or may be a resulting symptom of depression. In some cases, the need for a formal cognitive evaluation is evident. The following is a case example of a patient referred by her family for memory complaints.

Case Example: Dorothy, Alzheimer's Family Caregiver

Dorothy, 45 years old, was concerned about the possibility that her mother had Alzheimer's disease. She wanted to know if her mother really had dementia and if so, how far along in the disease process she was. She expressed concern about her mother, such as "We are afraid Mama is going to do something to hurt herself if she is left alone." Although Dorothy was warned that her mother may be resistant to being tested, she agreed that an evaluation would help the family. To the surprise and relief of the daughter, the mother was very cooperative with the assessment. Significant care and attention was paid to rapport building before formal testing began. This may have lessened the expected resistance.

Generally, when the patient is referred by family members you first have contact with the individual making the referral. However, at the first interview, it is a good idea to talk first to the patient alone so that the patient can express his or her own concerns and thoughts before beginning a formal cognitive assessment (Scogin, 2000). When an older adult has cognitive impairments, such as difficulties with memory, ruling out other causes such as depression or head injury is important. Additionally, if an older adult has a preexisting diagnosis of dementia it may be best to order more formal neuropsychological testing rather than completing a brief cognitive screener such as the MMSE. A challenge when assessing cognitive functioning is that a lot of individuals fall in the "in between" category on a screener, which makes diagnosis difficult.

When examining older adults for memory impairment, it is important to ask them what their specific memory deficits are and their subjective appraisal of their memory. Because all people experience some degree of memory change, determining whether the changes are significant and how much distress the changes are causing them becomes important. For example, you might ask "How often does remembering names present a memory problem for you?" and "How much does forgetting things bother you?" The following are indications that an older adult has a memory problem:

- Taking a long time to respond to questions (response latency)
- Frequently losing one's train of thought
- Having difficulty with relatively undemanding memory tasks

Examples of questions that tap recent memory include:

- Who is the president of the United States?
- When did you last eat?
- When was your last doctor's appointment?

The most commonly used instrument for cognitive screening is the MMSE (Folstein, Folstein, & McHugh, 1975). This brief instrument is broadly used for both research and clinical purposes. Because this is a widely used instrument, it is easy for professionals across disciplines to discuss a case. For example, if a geropsychologist tells a geriatrician that the client has a 20 on the MMSE, the geriatrician would have a rough idea of the client's overall cognitive functioning. The MMSE assesses cognitive functions such as orientation, attention, recall, and receptive and expressive language. Most important, the MMSE is very easy to administer and score. It also contains cutoff scores for various levels of impairment.

Generally, anyone scoring over 23 (maximum of 30) is considered unlikely to have dementia-level impairment. Scores of 23 or lower indicate that the patient has significant cognitive impairment. The MMSE is often used to classify the severity level of cognitive impairment in a patient. The following cutoff scores are recommended by the authors: normal cognitive function = 24 to 30, mild cognitive impairment = 21 to 23, moderate cognitive impairment = 10 to 20, and severe cognitive impairment = 0 to 9. Because the MMSE was developed for the purpose of screening for cognitive impairment, it should not be used to make a diagnosis of dementia or to discriminate among various types of dementia. However, patients scoring 23 or below likely have some impairment and should seek further evaluation. This criterion drops to a score of below 18 in cases where literacy or lack of formal education is a factor. Overall, the MMSE is a reliable and efficient screening instrument. It requires no equipment and can be done rather easily as part of an overall evaluation.

Additionally, the Telephone Interview for Cognitive Status (TICS; Brandt, Spencer, & Folstein, 1988) is a good alternative measure to use with older adults who are unable to complete the MMSE face to face. Conducting a telephone screening for cognitive impairment also has some efficiency advantages in terms of time and travel. However, it does require plans for handling situations in which significant cognitive impairment is discovered in a potential participant. The TICS is a brief measure that may take a maximum of 10 minutes to complete and assesses domains such as orientation, short-term memory, and concentration (Barber & Stott, 2004). Findings indicate that the TICS has a 90% rate of agreement with the MMSE when screening for dementia (Ferrucci et al., 1998). The TICS is accurate in its measurement of cognitive impairment in both Alzheimer's and poststroke patients. There is also a 13-item modified version of the TICS (TICS-m) that has many of the original items in addition to some questions that assess delayed recall (Barber & Stott, 2004).

Medical Status, Medication, and Substance Use

The medical status of a depressed older adult may affect diagnosis and treatment. Many older adults have chronic medical conditions and are prescribed several different medications. Some common medical conditions are Parkinson's disease, cardiovascular disease, arthritis, respiratory disorders, stroke, pain, incontinence, and digestive disorders. Many of these age-related medical complications require modifications to the assessment and treatment. In addition, some of these conditions may be the source of the client's depression.

Awareness of medical status is necessary as you begin the depression assessment with older adults. It is best to ask the client direct questions, such as "Are you experiencing any medical problems?" and "What medications are you taking now?" Medication use is a salient issue with older adults. Older adults consume a disproportionate amount of medications relative to other age groups and metabolize drugs at a slower rate than younger adults do. Both of these factors put them at risk for possible drug interactions (Segal et al., 1998).

Another medical issue that should be addressed when working with older adults is alcohol consumption. Alcohol consumption may affect mental status and medication use. Good opening questions are "What types of alcoholic beverages do you like?" and "How much do you usually drink at one time?"

Because medical status is an important part of assessment when working with an older adult, it is important to include other health care professionals from various disciplines. For example, an older client's primary physician can provide a thorough history of that individual's health and medical conditions, and a pharmacist can provide information about medications and possible interactions. This information may be especially important when a client's psychological complaint stems from another medical illness. One personal example of this was a client of the first author who was diagnosed with Parkinson's disease. She did not accept her diagnosis and was resistant to medication. I worked together with her physician and pharmacist to put together an educational component to our therapy sessions. This interdisciplinary collaboration allowed me to educate my client about her disorder and discuss the benefits of her medications and how they would improve her physical and mental health. Such collaboration was successful in informing the client about her options and helping her cope with her diagnosis.

Sensory Issues

Clinicians should be aware of sensory changes experienced by the depressed older adult. These sensory changes influence the clinician's selection of assessment tools, the structure of the assessment environment, and the interpretation of results. There are multiple sensory changes that individuals may experience as they age. Older adults often show loss of visual acuity and hearing precision and overall response slowing. These changes may contribute to the onset and maintenance of depressive symptoms in older adults.

Visual acuity usually begins to decline around age 40. By age 65, about half of all individuals have a visual acuity of 20/70 or less (Owsley & Sloane, 1990; Schieber, 1992). It is important to consider visual difficulties before selecting assessment instruments. Certain procedures and instruments may not be feasible given the older adult's visual capabilities. Severe vision problems have psychological consequences in older adults, such as decreased self-esteem and depression (Hersen, Kabacoff, et al., 1995; Hersen, Van Hasselt, & Segal, 1995).

Hearing precision is another ability that declines with age (Schieber, 1992). Research has shown that rates of serious impairments are higher in hearing than in vision. Nearly 50% of older adults experience a severe hearing impairment (Cavanaugh, 1997). Hearing difficulties that lead to difficulty in word comprehension can create invalid assessment results (Peters, Potter, & Scholer, 1988). In addition, hearing loss can sometimes be confused with dementia (Becker, 1981). Psychological consequences such as depression are associated with impairments in hearing (Segal et al., 1998).

Some simple modifications may help with sensory difficulties and make assessment less challenging. With hearing impaired older adults, a good idea is to talk somewhat louder, though not shouting. Slowing down the rate of speech and enunciating clearly will also help. It is important for clients to clearly see your face, particularly your mouth, when you are talking to them. In addition, good lighting and sitting close enough so that clients can see you without violating their personal space is important. These tips may help an older adult with hearing impairment to understand you through the motoric and nonverbal means of communication. Another helpful measure is minimizing background noise such as conversations from nearby rooms or other noises coming from the outside.

For visually impaired respondents, reading items to them from the GDS or similar instruments may expedite the assessment process. The use of response cards that demonstrate answer options is also useful for some older clients. Clients may give subtle hints about sensory problems they are experiencing, but the clinician must be attuned to the process and aware of the issues their clients are facing. Accommodating depressed clients with such impairments may lessen their sensitivity to their difficulties.

In some instances, these accommodations are not enough to create an acceptable assessment environment. Other impediments may stand in the way of successful depression assessment. For example, the measures being used may be inappropriate or unrealistic for the client's ability level. One example of this is when clients do not understand the questions (Flacker & Spiro, 2003). In these instances, it may be necessary to modify or individualize the measurement tools used. As another example, a typical 1- to 1.5-hour interview session may be too lengthy for a frail older client. Depressed clients may become fatigued and unable to answer the interviewer's questions.

INTERDISCIPLINARY NATURE OF DEPRESSION ASSESSMENT IN OLDER ADULTS

A desirable, arguably necessary, component of working with older adults is interdisciplinary care (Speer & Schneider, 2003; Zeiss & Gallagher-Thompson, 2003). Interdisciplinary teams of physicians, caregivers, and other health care professionals collaborate to plan, implement, and evaluate the outcomes of health care (Zeiss & Gallagher-Thompson, 2003). One study examining the relationship between depression and dementia is a perfect example of how interdisciplinary involvement can benefit the assessment process. Muller-Thomsen and colleagues (2005) examined the relationship between depression and severity of dementia by using four different scales. All four depression scales were performed by independent raters. A physician, neuropsychologist, and caregiver assessed the depression of the patient, and the demented patient was given the GDS self-rating scale. By incorporating all four assessments, the researchers gained a more complete insight into the patient's condition. In addition, each independent rater could supplement his or her scale with information on the patient's physical condition, neurological condition, or functioning at home.

The interdisciplinary team model is integral to understanding and serving the complex interaction of the physical and mental health needs of older adults (Zeiss & Steffen, 1998). In regard to assessment, the psychological problems of older adults require attention to complex biopsychosocial factors. Therefore, the American Psychological Association recommends that referrals be made to other health professionals as necessary (APA Working Group on the Older Adult, 1998) and when such referrals are within the means of the clients.

The obvious benefit to having an interdisciplinary team of professionals is that each individual may add a different perspective about the client's needs. For example, a client may have an impairment, such as hearing difficulty, that requires a certain accommodation. This sensory impairment may be identified by only one member of the team but may be an important accommodation to consider.

REFERENCES

Adams, K. B. (2001). Depressive symptoms, depletion, or developmental change? Withdrawal, apathy, and lack of vigor in the Geriatric Depression Scale. *Gerontologist, 41*, 768–777.

Adams, K. B., Matto, H. C., & Sanders, S. (2004). Confirmatory factor analysis of the Geriatric Depression Scale. *Gerontologist, 44*(6), 818–826.

Alexopoulos, G. S., Abrams, R. C., Young, R. C., & Shamoian, C. A. (1988). Cornell Scale for Depression in Dementia. *Biological Psychiatry, 23*(3), 271–284.

Alexopoulos, G. S., Meyers, B. S., Young, R. C., Campbell, S., Silbersweig, D., & Charlson, M. (1997). "Vascular depression" hypothesis. *Archives of General Psychiatry, 54*, 915–922.

Alexopoulos, G. S., Meyers, B. S., Young, R. C., Kakuma, T., Gabrielle, M., Sirey, J., et al. (2000). Executive dysfunction and long-term outcomes of geriatric function and long-term outcomes of geriatric depression. *Archives of General Psychiatry, 57*, 285–290.

American Psychiatric Association. (2000). *Diagnostic and statistical manual of mental disorders* (4th ed., text rev.). Washington, DC: Author.

APA Working Group on the Older Adult. (1998). What practitioners should know about working with older adults. *Professional Psychology: Research and Practice, 29(5)*, 413–427.

Areán, P. A., & Miranda, J. (1997). The utility of the Center for Epidemiological Studies Depression Scale in older primary care patients. *Aging and Mental Health, 1(1)*, 47–56.

Barber, M., & Stott, D. J. (2004). Validity of the Telephone Interview for Cognitive Status (TICS) in post-stroke patients. *International Journal of Geriatric Psychiatry, 19*, 75–79.

Beck, A. T., Steer, R. A., & Brown, G. K. (1996). *Beck Depression Inventory-II*. San Antonio, TX: Psychological Corporation.

Beck, A. T., Ward, C. H., Mendelson, M., Mock, J., & Erbaugh, J. (1961). An inventory for measuring depression. *Archives of General Psychiatry, 4*, 53–63.

Becker, G. (1981). *The disability experience: Educating health professionals about disabling conditions*. Berkeley: University of California Press.

Blazer, D. G. (1993). *Depression in late life* (2nd ed.). St. Louis, MO: Mosby.

Blazer, D. G. (2003). Depression in late life: Review and commentary. *Journal of Gerontology: Medical Sciences, 58A*, M249–M265.

Brandt, J., Spencer, M., & Folstein, M. (1988). The Telephone Interview for Cognitive Status. *Neuropsychiatry, Neuropsychology, and Behavioral Neurology, 1*, 111–117.

Bush, D. E., Ziegelstein, R. C., Tayback, M., Richter, D., Stevens, S., Zahalsky, H., et al. (2001). Even minimal symptoms of depression increase mortality risk after acute myocardial infarction. *American Journal of Cardiology, 88(4)*, 337–341.

Callahan, C., Hendrie, H. C., Hihus, R. S., Brater, D. C., Hui, S. I., & Teirny, W. M. (1994). Improving the treatment of late-life depression in primary care. *Journal of the American Geriatrics Society, 8*, 839–846.

Callahan, C. M., & Wolinsky, F. D. (1994). The effect of gender and race on measurement properties of the CES-D in older adults. *Medical Care, 32*, 341–356.

Cavanaugh, J. C. (1997). *Adult development and aging* (3rd ed.). Pacific Grove, CA: Brooks/Cole.

Chodosh, J., Buckwalter, J. G., Blazer, D. G., & Seeman, T. E. (2004). How the question is asked makes a difference in the assessment of depressive symptoms in older persons. *American Journal of Geriatric Psychiatry, 12*, 75–83.

D'Ath, P., Katona, P., Mullan, E., Evans, S., & Katona, C. (1994). Screening, detection, and management of depression in elderly primary care attenders: The acceptability and performance of the 15 item Geriatric Depression Scale (GDS15) and the development of short versions. *Family Practice—An International Journal, 11*, 260–266.

Ferrucci, L., Del Lungo, I., Guralnik, J. M., Bandinelli, S., Benvenuti, E., Salani, B., et al. (1998). Is the Telephone Interview for Cognitive Status a valid alternative in persons who cannot be evaluated by the Mini-Mental Status Examination? *Aging, 10*, 332–338.

Fiske, A., Kasl-Godley, J. E., & Gatz, M. (1998). Mood disorders in late life. In A. S. Bellack & M. Hersen (Eds.), *Comprehensive clinical psychology* (Vol. 7, pp. 193–229). Oxford: Elsevier Science.

Flacker, J. M., & Spiro, L. (2003). Does question comprehension limit the utility of the Geriatric Depression Scale in older African Americans? *Journal of the American Geriatrics Society, 51*(10), 1511–1512.

Folstein, M. F., Folstein, S. E., & McHugh, P. R. (1975). Mini-mental state: A practical method for grading the cognitive state of patients for the clinician. *Journal of Psychiatric Research, 12*, 189–198.

Gallagher, D., Breckenridge, J., Steinmetz, J., & Thompson, L. (1983). The Beck Depression Inventory and research diagnostic criteria: Congruence in an older population. *Journal of Consulting and Clinical Psychology, 51*, 945–946.

Gallagher, D., Nies, G., & Thompson, L. W. (1982). Reliability of the Beck Depression Inventory with older adults. *Journal of Consulting and Clinical Psychology, 50*, 152–153.

Gatz, M., & Hurwicz, E. A. (1990). Are old people more depressed? Cross sectional data on CES-D factors. *Psychology and Aging, 5*, 284–290.

Goldberg, J. H., Breckenridge, J. N., & Sheikh, J. I. (2003). Age differences in symptoms of depression and anxiety: Examining behavioral medicine outpatients. *Journal of Behavioral Medicine, 26*(2), 119–132.

Hamilton, M. (1960). A rating scale for depression. *Journal of Neurology and Neurosurgical Psychiatry, 23*, 56–62.

Hansen, M. S., Fink, P., Frydenberg, M., Oxhoj, M., Sondergaard, L., & Munk-Jorgensen, P. (2001). Mental disorders among internal medical inpatients: Prevalence, detection, and treatment status. *Journal of Psychosomatic Research, 50*(4), 199–204.

Hanson, A. E., Scogin, F. R., Welsh, D. L., & Karpe, J. M. (2004). Geriatric Depression Scale. In M. E. Maruish (Ed.), *The use of psychological testing for treatment planning and outcomes assessment* (pp. 379–397). Mahwah, NJ: Erlbaum.

Harwood, D. G., Ownby, R. L., Barker, W. W., & Duara, R. (1998). The factor structure of the Cornell Scale for Depression in Dementia among probable Alzheimer's disease patients. *American Journal of Geriatric Psychiatry, 6,* 212–220.

Hersen, M., Kabacoff, R. I., Van Hasselt, V. B., Null, J. A., Ryan, C. F., Melton, M. A., et al. (1995). Assertiveness, depression, and social support in older visually impaired adults. *Journal of Visual Impairment and Blindness, 7,* 524–530.

Hersen, M., Van Hasselt, V. B., & Segal, D. L. (1995). Social adaptation in older visually impaired adults: Some comments. *International Journal of Rehabilitation and Health, 1,* 49–60.

Hertzog, C., Van Alstine, J., Usala, P. D., & Hultsch, D. F. (1990). Measurement properties of the CES-D in older populations. *Psychological Assessment, 24,* 64–72.

Hoyl, M. T., Alessi, C. A., Harker, J. O., Josephson, K. R., Pietruszka, F. M., Koelfgen, M., et al. (1999). Development and testing of a five-item version of the Geriatric Depression Scale. *Journal of the American Geriatric Society, 47*(7), 873–878.

Jamison, C., & Scogin, F. (1992). Development of an interview-based Geriatric Depression Scale. *International Journal of Aging and Human Development, 35*(3), 193–204.

Jefferson, A. L., Powers, D. V., & Pope, M. (2000). Beck Depression Inventory-II (BDI-II) and the Geriatric Depression Scale (GDS) in older women. *Clinical Gerontologist, 22*(3/4), 3–12.

Jorm, A. F. (2000). Is depression a risk factor for dementia or cognitive decline? A review. *Gerontology, 46,* 219–227.

Kalayam, B., & Alexopoulos, G. S. (1999). Prefrontal dysfunction and treatment response in geriatric depression. *Archives of General Psychiatry, 56,* 713–718.

Kasl-Godley, J. E., Gatz, M., & Fiske, A. (1998). Depression and depressive symptoms in old age. In I. H. Nordhus, G. R. VandenBos, S. M. Bergstrom, & P. Fromholt (Eds.), *Clinical geropsychology* (pp. 211–217). Washington, DC: American Psychological Association.

Kaszniak, A. W. (1996). Techniques and instruments for assessment of the elderly. In S. H. Zarit & B. G. Knight (Eds.), *A guide to psychotherapy and aging: Effective clinical interventions in a life-stage context* (pp. 163–219). Washington, DC: American Psychological Association.

Kaszniak, A. W., & Scogin, F. R. (1995). Assessing for dementia and depression in older adults. *Clinical Psychologist, 48*(2), 17–24.

Katz, S., Ford, A. B., Moskowitz, R. W., Jackson, B. A., & Jaffe, M. W. (1963). Studies of illness in the aged: The index of ADL—A standardized measure of biological and psychosocial function. *Journal of the American Medical Association, 185*, 914–919.

Kiosses, D. N., Alexopoulos, G. S., & Murphy, C. (2000). Symptoms of striatofrontal dysfunction contribute to disability in geriatric depression. *International Journal of Geriatric Psychiatry, 15*, 992–999.

Knight, B. G., & McCallum, T. J. (1998). Psychotherapy with older adult families: The contextual, cohort-based maturity/specific challenge model. In I. H. Nordhus, G. R. VandenBos, S. Berg, & P. Fromholt (Eds.), *Clinical geropsychology* (pp. 313–328). Washington, DC: American Psychological Association.

Kurlowicz, L. H., Evans, L. K., Strumpf, N. E., & Maislin, G. (2002). A psychometric evaluation of the Cornell Scale for Depression in Dementia in a frail, nursing home population. *American Journal of Geriatric Psychiatry, 10*, 600–608.

La Rue, A. (1999). Geriatric neuropsychology: Principles of assessment. In P. A. Lichtenberg (Ed.), *Handbook of assessment in clinical gerontology* (pp. 381–416). New York: Wiley.

Lawton, M. P., & Brody, E. (1969). Assessment of older people: Self-maintaining and instrumental activities of daily living. *Gerontologist, 9*, 179–185.

Lewinsohn, P. M., Seeley, J. R., Roberts, R. E., & Allen, N. B. (1997). Center for Epidemiological Studies Depression Scale (CES-D) as a screening instrument for depression among community-residing older adults. *Psychology and Aging, 12*(2), 277–287.

Liang, J., Tran, T. V., Krause, N., & Markides, K. S. (1989). Generational differences in the structure of the CES-D in Mexican-Americans. *Journal of Gerontology, 44*, S110–S120.

Lyness, J. M., King, D. A., Cox, C., Yoediono, Z., & Caine, E. D. (1999). The importance of subsyndromal depression in older primary care patients: Prevalence and associated functional disability. *Journal of the American Geriatric Society, 47*, 647–652.

Mitchell, J., Mathews, H. F., & Yesavage, J. A. (1993). A multidimensional examination of depression among the elderly. *Research on Aging, 15*, 198–219.

Muller-Thomsen, T., Arlt, S., Mann, U., Mab, R., & Ganzer, S. (2005). Detecting depression in Alzheimer's disease: Evaluation of four different scales. *Archives of Clinical Neuropsychology, 20*, 271–276.

National Institutes of Health. (1991). *Consensus development conference statement: Diagnosis and treatment of depression in late life.* Washington, DC: Author.

Nebes, R. D., Reynolds, C. F., III, Boada, F., Meltzer, C. C., Fukui, M. B., Saxton, J., et al. (2002). Longitudinal increase in the volume of white matter hypertensities in late-onset depression. *International Journal of Geriatric Psychiatry, 17,* 526–530.

Nitcher, R. L., Burke, W. J., Roccaforte, W. H., & Wengel, S. P. (1993). A collateral source version of the Geriatric Depression Rating Scale. *American Journal of Geriatric Psychiatry, 1,* 143–152.

Norris, J. T., Gallagher, D., Wilson, A., & Winograd, C. H. (1987). Assessment of depression in geriatric medical outpatients: The validity of two screening measures. *Journal of the American Geriatrics Society, 35,* 989–995.

Owsley, C., & Sloane, M. E. (1990). Vision and aging. In F. Boller & J. Grafman (Eds.), *Handbook of neuropsychology* (Vol. 4, pp. 229–249). Amsterdam: Elsevier.

Parmalee, P. A., Lawton, M. P., & Katz, I. R. (1989). Psychometric properties of the Geriatric Depression Scale among the institutionalized aged. *Psychometric Assessment: A Journal of Consulting and Clinical Psychology, 1,* 331–338.

Peters, C. A., Potter, J. F., & Scholer, S. G. (1988). Hearing impairment as a predictor of cognitive decline in dementia. *Journal of the American Geriatrics Society, 36,* 981–986.

Purandare, N., Burns, A., Craig, S., Faragher, B., & Scott, K. (2001). Depressive symptoms in patients with Alzheimer's disease. *International Journal of Geriatric Psychiatry, 16,* 960–964.

Rabkin, J. G., & Klein, D. F. (1987). The clinical measurement of depressive disorders. In A. J. Marsella, R. M. A. Hirschfeld, & M. M. Katz (Eds.), *The measurement of depression* (pp. 30–83). New York: Guilford Press.

Radloff, L. S. (1977). The CES-D scale: A self-report depression scale for research in the general population. *Applied Psychological Measurement, 1,* 385–401.

Rapp, S. R., Parisi, S. A., Walsh, D. A., & Wallace, C. E. (1988). Detecting depression in elderly medical inpatients. *Journal of Consulting and Clinical Psychology, 56,* 509–513.

Salthouse, T. A. (1998). Cognitive and information-processing perspectives on aging. In I. H. Nordhus, G. R. VandenBos, S. Berg, & P. Fromholt (Eds.), *Clinical geropsychology* (pp. 49–59). Washington, DC: American Psychological Association.

Schieber, F. (1992). Aging and the senses. In J. E. Birren, R. B. Sloane, & G. D. Cohen (Eds.), *Handbook of mental health and aging* (pp. 251–306). San Diego, CA: Academic Press.

Scogin, F. R. (1987). The concurrent validity of the Geriatric Depression Scale with depressed older adults. *Clinical Gerontologist, 7*, 23–31.

Scogin, F. R. (2000). *The first session with seniors: A step-by-step guide*. San Francisco: Jossey Bass.

Scogin, F. R., Hamblin, D., Beutler, L., & Corbishley, A. (1988). Reliability and validity of the short-form Beck Depression Inventory with older adults. *Journal of Clinical Psychology, 44*, 853–857.

Segal, D. T. (1997). Structured interviewing and *DSM* classification. In S. M. Turner & M. Hersen (Eds.), *Adult psychopathology and diagnosis* (3rd ed., pp. 25–57). New York: Wiley.

Segal, D. T., Coolidge, F. L., & Hersen, M. (1998). Psychological testing of older people. In I. H. Nordhus, G. R. VandenBos, S. Berg, & P. Fromholt (Eds.), *Clinical geropsychology* (pp. 231–257). Washington, DC: American Psychological Association.

Sheikh, J. I., & Yesavage, J. A. (1986). Geriatric Depression Scale (GDS): Recent Evidence and development of a shorter version. *Clinical Gerontologist, 5*(1/2), 165–173.

Speer, D. C., & Schneider, M. G. (2003). Mental health needs of older adults and primary care: Opportunity for interdisciplinary geriatric team practice. *Clinical Psychology: Science and Practice, 10*(1), 85–101.

Spitzer, R. L., Williams, J. B. W., Gibbon, M., & First, M. B. (1990). *Structured Clinical Interview for DSM-III-R (SCID)*. Washington, DC: American Psychiatric Press.

Tranel, D., Anderson, S. W., & Benton, A. (1994). Development of the concept of "executive function" and its relationship to frontal lobes. In F. Boller, H. Spinnler, & J. A. Hendler (Eds.), *Handbook of neuropsychology* (Vol. 9, pp. 125–148). Amsterdam: Elsevier.

Watson, L. C., & Pignone, M. P. (2003). Screening accuracy for late-life depression in primary care: A systematic review. *Journal of Family Practice, 52*, 956–964.

Weatherall, M. (2000). A randomized controlled trial of the Geriatric Depression Scale in an inpatient ward for older adults. *Clinical Rehabilitation, 14*, 186–191.

Wragg, R. E., & Jeste, D. V. (1989). Overview of depression and psychosis in Alzheimer's disease. *American Journal of Psychiatry, 146*, 577–587.

Yesavage, J. A., Brink, T. L., Rose, T. L., & Adey, M. (1983). The Geriatric Depression Scale: Comparison with other self-report and psychiatric rating scales. In T. Crook, S. Ferris, & R. Bartus (Eds.), *Assessment in geriatric psychopharmacology* (pp. 153–167). New Canaan, CT: Mark Powley Associates.

Yesavage, J. A., Brink, T. L., Rose, T. L., Lum, O., Huang, V., Adey, M. B., et al. (1983). Development and validation of a geriatric depression screening scale: A preliminary report. *Journal of Psychiatric Research, 17*, 37–49.

Zeiss, A. M., & Gallagher-Thompson, D. (2003). Providing interdisciplinary geriatric team care: What does it really take? *Clinical Psychology: Science and Practice, 10*, 115–119.

Zeiss, A. M., & Steffen, A. (1998). Interdisciplinary health care teams in geriatrics: An international model. In A. S. Bellack & M. Hersen (Series Eds.) & B. Edelstein (Vol. Ed.), *Comprehensive clinical psychology: Vol. 7. Clinical geropsychology* (pp. 551–570). London: Pergamon Press.

II

Therapy Systems

Bob G. Knight

In this section of the book, we have asked three expert proponents of psychotherapy with older adults to discuss their system of therapy and then to apply that system to a specific case example. This section closes with a chapter that summarizes the current evidence base for psychological treatment of depression in older adults. The systems were chosen because they represent the most common approaches to working with older adults in the current literature and because each system has a strong empirical basis with younger adults and a supporting empirical literature with older adults. The authors of these chapters are each important contributors to that literature and to training new therapists to work with older adults.

The case example they were asked to respond to follows.

Case Example: Helen

When she first started therapy, Helen was in her mid-60s, unemployed, and living with her parents. Her father had been taking care of her mother, who was reported to have been moderately to severely demented for a number of years. Her mother also had arthritis and osteoporosis. Her father was described as a small man with severe curvature of the spine and a bad heart condition. He was also subject to periodic bouts of severe depression.

Helen described herself as assisting her father in his care of her mother. However, as she talked in more detail, it emerged that she could more accurately be described as taking care of both of them. Her parents argued and yelled at one another quite often, a continuation of a lifelong pattern but one that she had not been regularly exposed to since her teenage years. Her mother at this time was suspicious of both of them, accusing them of taking her money and of plotting to kill her. Helen also found her father's depressions overwhelming and contagious, especially as she had a prior history of treatment for depression herself. She saw her mother's situation as hopeless and overwhelming to her father. A home visit by other members of an outreach team confirmed this picture as well as her description of her father as intensely depressed. Her father refused therapy and also refused to see his doctor in response to Helen's concerns about his physical health. He was also adamant about keeping his wife at home until the end.

Helen's situation was further complicated by relative isolation from friends, as she had lived much of her adult life in a nearby city and most of her friends were there rather than in her parents' hometown. After moving, she had worked for a while for a juvenile corrections center, but her job had been eliminated in government cutbacks. Her father had encouraged her to live with and help them. Though financially convenient, this left her dependent on her parents and without outside structured activity or support for her self-esteem.

When she first came in, she was severely depressed at times and moderately depressed chronically. She felt fatigued and described her situation as being hopeless and felt helpless to change it. She worried about her own mental abilities and feared that she would follow her mother into dementia. The only reported cognitive changes were better understood as problems in concentration and decision making, which are common to depression. For example, she often was unable to finish a book or a magazine article and would become quite confused trying to decide what she could do with her life now. She expressed considerable guilt about not doing more for her parents, not working, and having negative feelings toward her parents, who were both quite ill and disabled.

She thought often about death, usually in an abstract way, but more recently had incidents in which she started planning to kill herself. Further exploration of this revealed relatively indefinite plans: She had no target date and thought that the means would either be an ancient gun that she thought her father owned or some pills, though she had none and did not know what kind she would use. She had had suicidal impulses in the past in conjunction with other depressions and could recall having been taken to the emergency room and admitted to a psychiatric hospital on one occasion, but felt that she had not, in fact, been close to dying from the attempt. She had trouble sleeping at night and then would often be lethargic and sit in one chair most of the day. She tended to overeat when depressed and had been gaining weight.

The outreach team referred her to the team psychiatrist for antidepressant medication. Her objections centered on a prior bad experience with lithium. Careful questioning failed to reveal any clear history of manic episodes, although this interview did reveal an admission to a psychiatric day treatment program several years previously. On reassurance that we would not duplicate her experience with lithium toxicity (which had resulted in acute confusion and a residual hand tremor that lasted several months after the lithium was discontinued), she saw the psychiatrist. She was started on relatively low doses of an antidepressant and carefully monitored for possible manic changes. The psychiatrist felt that some of her history was suggestive of hypomanic episodes, although no clear manic episode was described by Helen or in the records of her previous psychiatrist.

Earlier history with parents. In talking about her father and her relationship with him, it came out that as a child she had felt responsible to protect her mother from him. Her father had been distant from her but often hostile toward her mother, including both verbal abuse and physical fights. As a young adult, Helen had once hit him with a frying pan to keep him from attacking her mother. After that, she had distanced herself from both of them. They had later divorced, married other people, divorced those people, and remarried. She described her shock and disbelief when they called to tell her they were back together again. She had remained distant from them until her mother's illness aroused her sense of responsibility to care for them. She felt that age and disability had mellowed her father and that they had forgiven one another for past events, although he had remained a distant, cold man.

Helen made an early attempt to escape by marrying a young man in the military; they had one son. But her mother forced her to leave the military base and return to her parents' house. Her mother also interfered in Helen's raising her son. It was only after a divorce and leaving the area that Helen achieved some independence. Finding herself back with her mother again, now as her caregiver, gave her the feeling that her mother had won a lifelong struggle between them.

4

Cognitive Behavior Therapy with Older Adults

KEN LAIDLAW

Cognitive behavior therapy (CBT) is recognized as a well-established, empirically validated treatment for depression and anxiety (Chambless et al., 1996), with recent research suggesting that it may be more effective at preventing relapse in depression than antidepressant medication (Hollon et al., 2005). Cognitive behavior therapy is probably best known in the form developed by Aaron T. Beck (see Beck, 1987; Beck, Rush, Shaw, & Emery, 1979). In this model, depression is characterized by the activation of underlying dysfunctional beliefs or schemata consequent to confrontation with idiosyncratically stressful events (the stress-diathesis model) that lead to errors in the processing of information that are important for understanding the onset and maintenance of depressive symptoms (Clark, Beck, & Alford, 1999).

The primary mode of effectiveness in CBT is driven by the identification and modification of dysfunctional thoughts, beliefs, and actions, where symptom amelioration occurs through cognitive restructuring and behavioral change (Persons, 1989). Cognitive behavior therapy can be differentiated from other forms of psychotherapy by its emphasis on the empirical investigation of the patient's thoughts, appraisals, inferences, and assumptions. In CBT, the meanings patients ascribe to their experiences are the data with which therapists work.

Since the early 1980s, CBT researchers have provided evidence for the utility of this approach as a treatment for late life depression (for reviews, see Koder, Brodaty, & Anstey, 1996; Laidlaw, 2001; Scogin & McElreath, 1994). Although the literature base is still rather small with regard to the empirical evaluation of psychotherapy with depressed elders, CBT for late life depression is an efficacious treatment (Gatz et al., 1998) and a much needed addition and alternative to physical treatments for depressed elders (Gerson, Belin, Kaufman, Mintz, & Jarvik, 1999).

APPROPRIATENESS WITH OLDER ADULTS

Cognitive behavior therapy is particularly appropriate as an intervention for older adults because it is skills enhancing, present oriented, and problem focused and takes into account normal age-related changes in the formulation of an individualized treatment plan (Glantz, 1989; Steuer & Hammen, 1983; Thompson, 1996; Zeiss & Steffen, 1996).

Morris and Morris (1991) provide a number of reasons why cognitive-behavioral interventions are particularly effective with older people:

- CBT focuses on the *"here and now,"* meaning the individual's current needs are identified and interventions are developed to target specific stressors.
- CBT develops *practical problem-solving skills*, where individuals are taught specific ways to manage their individual stressors.
- CBT sessions are *structured*, with the organized nature of therapy meaning that the person remains oriented to tasks within and across sessions even in the presence of cognitive impairment.
- CBT employs *self-monitoring*, where the individual is taught to recognize mood fluctuations and emotional vulnerabilities and to develop coping strategies that reduce depressive symptomatology.
- CBT utilizes a *psycho-educative approach*, to emphasize the connection between thoughts, mood, and behavior in understanding how problems may have developed and for understanding what interventions may be necessary.

- CBT is *goal oriented*, and challenges negative age stereotypical beliefs, such as, "You can't teach an old dog new tricks" or "it is depressing to be old."

It used to be thought that older people would not want psychotherapy because of the stigma attached to mental illness (Lebowitz & Niederehe, 1992). On the contrary, older people express surprisingly positive attitudes toward psychotherapy. Landreville, Landry, Baillargeon, Guerette, and Matteau (2001) investigated the acceptability of psychological and pharmacological treatments for late life depression. Using a series of case vignettes describing components of each treatment intervention, older people were asked their opinion about the acceptance of these methods. Older people considered both CBT and antidepressant medications as equally acceptable treatments for late life depression. For more severe depression symptoms, they rated CBT as more acceptable than antidepressant medication.

Cognitive behavior therapy is conceptualized as having three distinct phases: early, middle, and late (Laidlaw, Gallagher-Thompson, Thompson, & Siskin-Dick, 2003). Commonly, a full course of CBT is considered to last for about 16 to 20 sessions, but in many instances older people need many fewer sessions (Dick, Gallagher-Thompson, & Thompson, 1996). It is in the early part of therapy that patients are educated about the process of therapy and are socialized into a specific way of data gathering and self-monitoring. Socializing the patient into psychotherapy means addressing such issues as the patient's expectations for therapy, working collaboratively in a problem-solving way, planning for the end of therapy right at the start, establishing goals for treatment outcome, and planning on the use of homework out of session. In the early phase of treatment, setting up a working therapeutic relationship is essential. Ideally, by the end of the third session of therapy, an agreed problem list is drawn up by therapist and patient. The problem list should contain a maximum of three items that are then translated into goals and aims for therapy. Goals should be relevant, specific, measurable, time limited, and achievable.

It is in the middle phase of CBT treatment that most time is spent on dealing with negative automatic thoughts. The patient is taught self-monitoring skills to identify thoughts that are associated with negative mood and maladaptive behavioral response. The negative thoughts are examined for their reality and validity using simple questions, such as "What is the evidence for and against this thought?" "How does it help you to think this way?" "What is an alternative way to think about this situation?" and "If this thought were true, what would it mean to you?" By asking these questions, the negative thought is cognitively restructured so that patients are able to regulate their mood more easily even when they experience similar negative thoughts. Most cognitive restructuring is done using a dysfunctional thought record (DTR). The DTR has space for patients to record their thoughts and to record rational responses to these and to note the impact this has on their mood. As therapy proceeds, patients learn to challenge their negative thoughts using the DTR by themselves.

In the middle phase of therapy, it is important to take time to review progress. This review can be carried out by looking at copies of the weekly activity schedule completed over a number of sessions. If a DTR has been completed, this can be reviewed also. Patterns of behavior that a patient habitually engages in when mood is low are examined for their impact. It is not uncommon for people to distance themselves from others when they are depressed for fear of being a burden on others and an associated fear of contaminating another person's mood (bringing another person down). To produce behavior change, it is important to explore alternative strategies by utilizing behavioral experiments, such as making contact with friends when one's mood is low. It is usually illuminative for patients if they have made a prediction about the experiment before they engage in it. The middle phase of therapy sees the development of a shared conceptualization and potentially a discussion of hypothesizes underlying maladaptive beliefs.

In the final phase of therapy there are two main tasks to be accomplished: (1) to agree on an appropriate termination point for therapy and (2) to work out a relapse prevention plan with the patient prior to the end of therapy. It is important that the relapse prevention plan is at least role-played with patients before they are discharged. The role-play should investigate what the patient would do if he or she were facing a challenging crisis situation. An important means of promoting relapse prevention is to engage patients in actively reviewing what they have learned from therapy and to list what strategies work well for them. Prior to the end of therapy, fears are elicited from the patient about future challenges and a discussion centers around the elicitation of appropriate supports and utilization of appropriate coping strategies for anticipated future events.

At the end of treatment using a CBT approach, the therapist may have to consider gradual termination of contact. This is especially important if the client is isolated and has a less developed social network. If necessary, intermittent or booster sessions can be built into the treatment package. In CBT, a full course of treatment does not necessarily mean continuing treatment until the complete resolution of presenting problems has been achieved. Cognitive behavior therapy is, after all, a time-limited treatment, and it may be that once the patient is successfully able to assimilate new techniques, skills, and coping strategies into confronting his or her difficulties, then therapy may terminate with the agreement of the patient. If CBT aims to equip patients with skills and strategies, then we must have confidence that once essential skills and knowledge have been assimilated and consolidated by the patients and sufficient progress has been made, they can continue on the journey by themselves. By continuing to work with the patient all the steps of the way, one is inadvertently negatively reinforcing an implicit message that people cannot cope without their therapist by their side.

THE APPLICATION OF COGNITIVE BEHAVIOR THERAPY WITH OLDER ADULTS

Working with older people in therapy can be challenging, and it can be different from working with younger people in a number of important respects: the higher likelihood of physical comorbid conditions, changes in cognitive capacity, different cohort experiences (Glantz, 1989), and different understandings and expectations about psychotherapy (Knight, 2004). In many cases, the complex types of problems that older people bring to therapy can be daunting, even overwhelming, to therapists un-used to working with older clients. At the same time, there is great vari-ability in the aging process (Vaillant & Mukamal, 2001), with the result that adaptations and modifications of therapeutic procedures may not be necessary (Laidlaw, 2003). Unfortunately, all too often therapists see the age of the patient as an important defining characteristic; this can bias a therapist into expecting poorer outcomes, and therapy becomes much more passive and less directive. In turn, the slow pace and lack of struc-ture in sessions may make the process of therapy more confusing and less helpful to older persons, who may become disheartened and come to be-lieve that their problems really *are* unchangeable and their situation re-ally *is* hopeless. This can then affect the therapist, so that both parties are negatively reinforced about psychotherapy with older people.

In CBT with older adults, the pace and length of treatment may differ from that with younger clients. It may be that the treatment sessions are shorter because the patient is frail or because of mild cognitive impair-ment. This may result in patients being enrolled for a greater number of sessions. Sometimes the pace is different because older people just need longer to tell their story. As subclinical levels of depression are more com-mon than Major Depressive Disorder in later life (Blazer, 2002), this may mean that it will take more patience on the part of the cognitive therapist to gain an accurate picture of the level of the patient's problems. The longer time spent with the patient is not wasted as this builds the thera-peutic alliance.

Often older adults have become accustomed to adopting a passive re-cipient role in dealings with health professionals (Glantz, 1989). Often with older people, there is a pervasive notion that it is wrong to discuss problems outside the family unit, and they can often feel considerable guilt at their perceived inability to deal with their difficulties themselves (Glantz, 1989; Thompson, 1996; Yost, Beutler, Corbishley, & Allender, 1986). The therapist may have to highlight this as an issue from the first session onward and introduce the patient to the idea of solutions arising from shared discovery (Laidlaw et al., 2003). Cognitive behavior therapy maintains an emphasis that what the patient brings into the therapy ses-sion is important, so that patients are given a realistic sense of responsibil-ity and agency when solving their own problems. A supportive stance by the therapist can make an enormous difference to a nervous older person. Encouragement to talk may take the form of simply saying that you do not regard their problems as trivial, or that you do not think depression is a sign of weakness. It may also be helpful simply to say, "It sounds as if this is very difficult for you, but you are doing very well." The therapist may need to set aside time in initial sessions to take an educational approach and explain what depression is and what impact it has on the individual. Zeiss and Steffen (1996) emphasize the nonpathologizing stance of CBT and state that it makes this type of approach particularly helpful for use with older adults suspicious of being labeled mentally ill.

Communication styles of older people sometimes require CBT therapists to take a much more directive stance in therapy. Early in therapy, frequent use of summarizing statements to signal that you are following what the person is saying and that it is making sense can give patients tremendous encouragement to continue to reveal more about their personal circumstances. It is not uncommon for older people to wander off topic (Steuer & Hammen, 1983). In many cases, therapists mindful of being respectful to elders will allow their patients to talk without interruption, often losing the focus entirely. In CBT, the therapist is active and directive and often needs to interrupt patients to keep them focused on the topic being discussed. This can be done with some humor to avoid seeming to be rude. Older people sometimes experience short-term memory difficulties in staying on track with a particular focus, or they may be used to telling stories and will get sidetracked when relaying information to their therapist. As Zeiss and Steffen (1996) state, helping patients stay on track with information in session is often appreciated by older people, as long as it is done gently and with respect. Repeated presentation of information is also helpful for ensuring that older people stay on track with therapy procedures and topics being discussed (Glantz, 1989). When discussing new skills or tasks with older people, Zeiss and Steffen encourage a multimodal presentation of information that includes discussion, modeling, and practice in-session; this is termed: say it, show it, do it.

An important element in the application of CBT with older people is the translation of discussions and exploration of covert thoughts, feelings, and beliefs into actions in the form of behavioral experiments. Especially important is the use of problem-focused strategies for helping older people deal with their current concerns. In many instances, CBT techniques are used to assist an older adult in rediscovering old tricks rather than learning new ones (Thompson, 1996). In this way, CBT is respectful of the skills and talents that older people have and recognizes that a life lived is one that is seldom lived without having to learn to solve problems. In many cases, CBT doesn't teach older people new strategies, it merely serves to remind them to reuse old skills they have stopped using along the way (Thompson, 1996). Older people take to this approach readily and find it encourages optimism and a sense of independence.

SUITABILITY FOR COGNITIVE BEHAVIOR THERAPY

Novice therapists and those therapists unused to working with older people often ask what types of older people are suitable candidates for CBT. This question is difficult to answer with any precision. One could assume that because CBT has a cognitive focus, older people who are experiencing some degree of cognitive impairment may be less suitable candidates for therapy. More probably, one would wish to adopt a change in pacing in therapy and use cognitive aids such as tape recorders and encourage the use of note taking by patients rather than applying a blanket rule here. Teri and Gallagher-Thompson (1991) suggest that behavioral interventions should be adopted much more than cognitive interventions in such cases. Perhaps the reason this question is so difficult to answer is that skilled CBT therapists are not technicians applying a set of protocols in isolation from the needs of their patients. Instead, CBT is individually tailored to meet the patient's needs.

In terms of suitability, it is not necessary for patients to be convinced about the model of therapy. The model of collaborative empiricism encourages testing interventions to see if they are suitable for the patient. For many older people, CBT may be their first experience of psychotherapy, and they may be skeptical about the outcome of talking things over.

Safran and Segal (1990) have developed a set of guidelines that aim to predict which patients will be suitable for CBT interventions. The Suitability for Short-Term Cognitive Therapy Scale (Safran & Segal, 1990) is a therapist-rated short questionnaire providing a measure of suitability for CBT. The scale measures patients' suitability in terms of their ability to access thoughts, awareness and differentiation of emotions, acceptance of personal responsibility for change, compatibility with cognitive rationale, alliance potential, chronicity, security and safety-seeking operations, and ability to maintain problem focus.

Although this scale is very interesting and very thoughtfully developed within a sophisticated process model of therapeutic outcome, it may actually provide a barrier to older people being offered CBT if it is applied too rigidly. The scale was devised to be used in general adult settings and may be inappropriate for use with older people. For instance, when considering chronicity, older people may have a long history of depression but no history of receiving psychotherapy. Likewise, if older people are unused to psychotherapy, they may not wholeheartedly endorse the cognitive rationale.

The most straightforward answer to the question as to which candidates are suitable for CBT is to say that we simply do not know with any precision and there is no clear or accurate clinical algorithm that can be applied. What we do know is that many older people are denied access to psychotherapy. In the past, this has been for reasons that seemed factual but later proved to be erroneous. It is probably better to offer older people therapy and assess the outcomes frequently rather than to apply a blanket strategy.

MODIFYING COGNITIVE BEHAVIOR THERAPY WITH OLDER ADULTS

Knight (1996, 2004) states that there are two key questions for psychotherapists when working with older people: Can psychological interventions developed in adult settings be expected to work for older people, and does one need to make adaptations to these psychological interventions for use with older people? The answer to the first question for CBT with older people is a resounding yes (see Laidlaw, 2003, for review). The answer to the question of adaptation and therapy with older people is much more difficult and complex because adaptations suggest to clinicians that the treatment model they have chosen may be inadequate in some important respect for the patients they intend to treat (Laidlaw et al., 2003). This can lead to confusion, as one could reasonably ask in what important respect is CBT as a treatment intervention with older people deficient.

In most instances, however, modifications that are intended to enhance treatment outcome are sufficient for CBT with older people (Grant & Casey, 1995; Zeiss & Steffen, 1996). Modification of therapy may be required to take account of normal age-related changes and transitions (Grant & Casey, 1995; Knight, 1996, 2004; Laidlaw, Thompson, & Gallagher-Thompson, 2004). However, there is a great deal of individual variation in this section of the population (Laidlaw et al., 2003; Steuer, 1982; Steuer & Hammen, 1983; Zeiss & Steffen, 1996), so no modifications may be necessary. As CBT is idiosyncratically based and always aims to understand an individual's particular circumstances, this means that the standard intervention strategies in CBT are fully at the disposal of therapists, while the context of aging and the transitions experienced by older people may have to be conceptualized and understood with a broader framework (Knight, 2004; Laidlaw et al., 2004).

Knight (2004) notes that therapists unused to working with older people often believe that they are unlikely to benefit from psychotherapy. This is a commonly held belief, due in part perhaps, because of Freud's assertion that older people lack the mental plasticity to change or to benefit from psychotherapy (Lovestone, 1983; Steuer, 1982). Clinical psychologists have tended to ignore and avoid the needs of this population group with an expectation that psychological treatments are not applicable to older adults because of a pervasive notion that the complex presentations of psychological problems in later life result in less likelihood of meaningful clinical change and progress. Nonetheless, experience teaches those of us in this area to be more optimistic and enthusiastic about the range of benefits older people derive from psychotherapy.

A NEW CONCEPTUALIZATION FRAMEWORK FOR COGNITIVE BEHAVIOR THERAPY WITH OLDER ADULTS

Many experienced therapists working in the field consider standard CBT conceptualizations to be inadequate for describing the complexity of the issues facing their patients. When working with a depressed older client presenting with a range of physical illnesses, multiple loss experiences, and age-related negative cognitions (such as "It is depressing to be old"), cognitive therapists can feel underserved by the narrowness of the original CBT conceptualization model.

Laidlaw et al. (2004) developed a new comprehensive conceptualization framework for CBT with older people consisting of a developmental approach across the entire life span, where every individual is considered to be at a different transitional stage across his or her life trajectory. The conceptualization framework for CBT with older people takes account of aging issues and assesses the impact of cohort beliefs, role transitions, intergenerational linkages, the sociocultural context, and health status when understanding the overt and covert (Persons, 1989) nature of problems that older people bring with them into the clinic room. The framework is illustrated schematically in Figure 4.1.

The Importance of the Cohort

Cohort beliefs are those beliefs held by groups of people born in similar years or similar time periods (Neugarten & Datan, 1973). They are the shared beliefs and experiences (cultural and developmental) of age-specific generations (Smyer & Qualls, 1999). Laidlaw et al. (2003, p. 7) state, "Understanding cohort experiences, and taking these into account when working psychotherapeutically with older people, is no more difficult and no less important than when working with cohorts such as ethnic minority groups."

It follows that certain cohort beliefs may impact the process and outcome of psychotherapy. Knight (2004) emphasizes this when he states that working with older adults entails learning something of the folkways of people born many years before. In CBT, certain types of negative automatic cognitions overlap with cohort beliefs, and it can be useful for the therapist to point out to the patient that certain belief systems may have been appropriate in the past but are no longer relevant or useful now.

TRANSITIONS IN ROLE INVESTMENTS

Remaining invested and involved in activities and interests that are personally meaningful, purposeful, and relevant is likely to improve one's

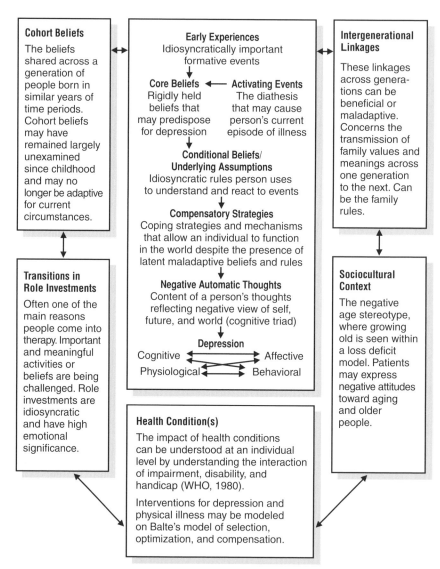

Cohort Beliefs

The beliefs shared across a generation of people born in similar years of time periods. Cohort beliefs may have remained largely unexamined since childhood and may no longer be adaptive for current circumstances.

Early Experiences
Idiosyncratically important formative events

Core Beliefs ← Activating Events
Rigidly held   The diathesis
beliefs that   that may cause
may predispose   person's current
for depression   episode of illness

Conditional Beliefs/ Underlying Assumptions
Idiosyncratic rules person uses to understand and react to events

Compensatory Strategies
Coping strategies and mechanisms that allow an individual to function in the world despite the presence of latent maladaptive beliefs and rules

Negative Automatic Thoughts
Content of a person's thoughts reflecting negative view of self, future, and world (cognitive triad)

Depression
Cognitive ⇄ Affective
Physiological ⇄ Behavioral

Intergenerational Linkages

These linkages across genera- tions can be beneficial or maladaptive. Concerns the transmission of family values and meanings across one generation to the next. Can be the family rules.

Transitions in Role Investments

Often one of the main reasons people come into therapy. Important and meaningful activities or beliefs are being challenged. Role investments are idiosyncratic and have high emotional significance.

Sociocultural Context

The negative age stereotype, where growing old is seen within a loss deficit model. Patients may express negative attitudes toward aging and older people.

Health Condition(s)

The impact of health conditions can be understood at an individual level by understanding the interaction of impairment, disability, and handicap (WHO, 1980).

Interventions for depression and physical illness may be modeled on Balte's model of selection, optimization, and compensation.

Figure 4.1   CBT Conceptual Framework for Older People

quality of life and maintain psychological health (Rowe & Kahn, 1998; Vaillant, 2002). The transitions in role investment experienced by people are therefore likely to be important variables to consider when working with older people. In later life, there may be transitions that an individual needs to navigate to successfully adapt to age-related changes. Champion and Power (1995) state that vulnerability to depression is related to the extent to which an individual invests in certain highly valued roles and goals. Overinvestment, that is, investment in certain roles and goals to the exclusion of all others, may constitute vulnerability for the development of depression. Champion and Power recognize a gender bias in the sorts of roles and goals that are invested in: Women are more likely to invest in interpersonal relationships, and men are more likely to invest in areas of achievement orientation such as work.

In CBT, the transitions in role investments that are commonly seen are when people try to adapt to a change in circumstances by rigidly adhering to unsuccessful coping strategies that may have served them well in the past. This may occur, for example, when losing independence because of a change in physical health status, or when taking on a new role, such as caregiving. The amount of investment one has in the roles that give life personal meaning may be an important determinant in how successfully one adapts to a change in circumstance.

Intergenerational Linkages

Older generations tend to value continuity and transmission of values, whereas younger generations tend to value autonomy and independence (Bengtson et al., 2000). The change in family and society demographics, such as increased longevity, reduction in family size, and the increased rate of divorce with subsequent reconstitutions of families, has meant that grandparents and great-grandparents often perform an important role in our societies, sometimes providing strong intergenerational linkages across families (Bengtson, 2001; Bengtson & Boss, 2000), often taking on caregiving roles for younger generations. Intergenerational relationships can create tensions, especially when older generations do not approve of or understand changes in family structures or marital relationships (Bengtson et al., 2000). Likewise, when elders provide important supports, such as caring for grandchildren so as to permit adult children to work, this can be a source of intergenerational tension. There may be disapproval from elders toward their adult children, especially daughters, or there may be a sense of frustration as elders may feel limited by their child-care duties.

For many older people, intergenerational linkages may be confusing and distressing as they clash with cherished cohort beliefs about the family. Neugarten and Datan (1973) introduced the concept of the social clock in which people have certain socially influenced (and hence cohort-related) notions about the timetable for accomplishing life's tasks. For example, older generations may express disappointment or disapproval of their adult children if they have not settled down and started a family by their 30s. The increase in longevity may result in certain life stages being reached at different ages for different cohorts, resulting in misunderstandings and tensions across generations.

In CBT, Thompson (1996) notes that marital breakdown affecting adult children can have a big impact on older people themselves who may feel responsible either that they did not raise their son or daughter correctly or that they should have done more to have prevented the breakup.

Sociocultural Context

Depressed older people often explicitly state that growing old is a terrible thing. Unfortunately, professionals may be swayed into believing such statements are factual and realistic appraisals of a difficult time of life (Unutzer, Katon, Sullivan, & Miranda, 1999). In fact, these statements reveal the internalization of sociocultural negative stereotypes about growing old. As Levy (2003, p. 204) states, "When individuals reach old age, the aging stereotypes internalized in childhood, and then reinforced for decades, become self-stereotypes." Many older people have an implicit assumption (that can be challenged with CBT cognitive restructuring techniques) that old age inevitably means loss and decrepitude. As one gets older, the growing sense of dread about what aging will bring can be accompanied by an increased vigilance for the first signs of the slippery slope. In CBT terms, the negative age stereotype can be considered a latent and maladaptive vulnerability about aging that has been reinforced and often endorsed by patients themselves and society for decades. Hence, older people may assume that if they are unhappy or depressed, this is a normal part of aging and is not therefore amenable to treatment. Especially in depression, beliefs such as these often prevent individuals from seeking treatment. In CBT, therapists ought to explore the sociocultural beliefs of the patient at the start of therapy.

Physical Health

Increasing age brings with it an increased likelihood of developing chronic medical conditions. However, it does not follow that all older people have a chronic medical condition that has a limiting functional effect (Zeiss, Lewinsohn, Rohde, & Seeley, 1996). It is equally important to inquire about patients' understanding about diseases and to examine what they think will be the outcome of any chronic condition. In the conceptualization framework for CBT with older people, health status is formulated using the World Health Organization (1980) classification of disease, where physical ill health is understood in terms of three simple components: impairment, disability, and handicap. *Impairment* refers to the loss or abnormality of body structure, appearance, organ, or system; an example is the presence of an infarct (i.e., an area of dead tissue in the brain) after a stroke. *Disability* is the impact of the impairment (e.g., infarct in a certain part of a person's brain) on the individual's ability to carry out normal activities. For example, following a stroke, a person may find it difficult to dress without assistance. *Handicap* can be thought of as the social impact that the impairment or disease has on the individual. Consequences of handicap are visible when a person interacts with the environment. Thus, a person who has experienced a stroke may find that other people now treat him or her differently, by excluding him or her from normal communications. The notion of handicap is useful for looking at the consequences of disease for an individual. It should be evident that in any physical illness, CBT therapists can usefully employ behavioral strategies and develop problem-solving skills to help the person minimize levels of disability so as to minimize handicap to the lowest level possible. The usefulness of this system to psychotherapists generally, however, is that it allows one to consider the consequences of impairment or disease for an individual.

SUMMARY OF CONCEPTUALIZATION FRAMEWORK FOR COGNITIVE BEHAVIOR WITH OLDER ADULTS

Each element of the conceptualization framework may either stand alone or be interconnected with other elements of the framework. For example, the physical domain of the conceptualization framework provides therapists with a mini-conceptualization by itself as it uses the World Health Organization (1980) system of classifying disease according to three simple components that can allow a therapist to focus and target interventions. Another important attribute of this conceptualization framework is that elements overlap and interact. For example, cohort beliefs may influence how an individual reacts to a change in health status ("I must not be a burden to my family") and may determine some aspects of an individual's sociocultural beliefs ("Growing older is growing weaker").

Cognitive behavior therapy therapists unfamiliar with working with older people are vulnerable to feeling deskilled in the midst of such complexities. The broader span of the conceptual framework prevents the focus in therapy from becoming too narrow and too unspecific to the problems encountered. For a fuller account of this model with clinical examples of its application in therapy, the interested reader is encouraged to consult Laidlaw et al. (2004).

Case Example: Understanding Helen in a Cognitive Behavior Therapy Framework

Cognitive behavior therapy is an active, directive, time-limited, and structured treatment approach whose primary aim is symptom reduction (Laidlaw et al., 2003). When working with Helen, *active* means listening actively as she describes her predicament and asking her whether she has been in a similar situation in the past. This is important to gain an understanding of how Helen deals with problems. Cognitive behavior therapy is *directive* in the sense that the therapist needs to work with Helen to keep her focused on current difficulties and specific aspects of her current situation. If at all possible, it is useful to gain examples of aspects of the situation Helen finds particular difficulty in dealing with. The therapist ought to expect that Helen will be feeling quite hopeless about the possibility for change in this situation. Likewise for the therapist, it may be very easy to become demoralized, as the problems are realistic, but in situations like these, when people become depressed, they often exaggerate the unchangeable nature of the problem (Glantz, 1989). Depressed persons are pessimistic in their outlook and tend to distort their experience in a negative way (Beck et al., 1979). In every situation, there are aspects that are changeable; some are more easily changeable than others.

In this situation, the therapist needs to maintain an active-directive stance to help Helen target aspects of this situation that are under her direct conscious control. In many situations like these, patients will expend much energy trying to bring about change in others, when ultimately this is a behavior they have less control over. Another potential difficulty here is the longitudinal nature of this problem. This is a potential minefield for any therapist. If one spends too much time on past issues, less session time is spent on symptom reduction. But if one ignores the premorbid nature of the problem, Helen could end up feeling devalued and not listened to.

An interesting way to view this problem that maintains the *time-limited* nature of the CBT sessions is to split the issue into two: historical factors and current problems. During the CBT intervention, most time will be focused on adopting an explicitly problem-focused approach to current depression symptoms, and some time is spent on historical issues so as to gain an accurate conceptualization and understanding of the issues. Understanding issues from the past may contribute to a greater understanding about causation of depression, but ultimately they are less important in understanding how depression symptoms are *maintained*. In Helen's case, although she may experience a great deal of anguish over unresolved issues, these feelings may become more accessible when her mood is low. These feelings and their associated thoughts can be considered mood state symptoms and treated as such. Encouraging Helen to take a more active approach to solving her current problems and becoming more active by scheduling in pleasant activities, such as meeting friends, may bring an improvement in her mood state. Once her mood state shows improvement, her sense of hopelessness and helplessness will be reduced. In the early stages of therapy, it is important to get an early win, and a behavioral approach at the start of therapy will often provide some evidence of movement. This can be encouraging and interesting to the patient, who sees that change is possible.

As the CBT intervention adopts a here-and-now focus on current difficulties and seeks a resolution of these, Helen may wish to seek a referral to a counseling service or a more psychodynamically oriented treatment program to gain some resolution of past issues once the CBT intervention has ended if these are still troubling her. This is not to suggest that Helen's case is an awkward fit for CBT; on the contrary, there are good grounds for optimism that CBT is very helpful in these situations. For example, an interesting study by Gallagher-Thompson and Steffen (1994) evaluated CBT in comparison to a brief psychodynamically oriented treatment targeted at depression in dementia caregivers. The results are fascinating: There were no differences overall between the two conditions in terms of treatment outcome, but there was an interaction in terms of length of caregiving. Those caregivers who had been caregivers for longer showed more benefit from the CBT intervention. In addition, Gallagher-Thompson and Steffen found that longer-term caregivers were much more likely to drop out of treatment prematurely if they had been assigned to the brief psychodynamic intervention. However, those participants who had been caregivers for less time made more gains with the brief psychodynamic intervention. This suggests that people are at different stages in terms of a caregiving career but also that different forms of psychotherapy are necessary to promote different coping strategies for an ever-changing situation. In the early stages of caregiving, having an opportunity to make sense of the illness and its impact is best achieved using a less structured and more verbal treatment such as psychodynamic psychotherapy, whereas later on in the caregiving process, the skills and problems-solving strategies that are part and parcel of CBT interventions are more helpful and welcomed.

Early sessions in therapy would focus on understanding Helen's view of her current situation in the context of past learning experiences. Of importance is the connection between thoughts, feelings, and behaviors that Helen habitually experiences during moments of stress and challenge in her current caregiving situation. It would be expected that during more severe bouts of low mood, Helen will view her situation much more negatively; therefore, a full assessment should be undertaken over the first two to three sessions.

Given that she had an episode of supposed suicide attempt, at the first session, the therapist needs to take a careful mood screen and ascertain *current* risk of self-harm. As there is the suggestion that suicidal impulses led Helen to being admitted to a psychiatric hospital after a visit to an ER, it would be very important for the therapist to make a careful postmortem analysis of this episode to ascertain what risk factors her current behavior shares with the previous episode. In reviewing her previous episode of self-harm, triggers are elicited for this behavior and alternative and more adaptive coping strategies substituted. It is important to realize that attempting to end one's life is still a taboo in our society, and if Helen has already broken this taboo, the social norms and restraints that may impact one who has never attempted to self-harm are not necessarily in place for her. Sensitively, the therapist will want to elicit Helen's experience of her episode of self-harming. Ellis and Newman (1996) suggest that the therapist should engage patients in a discussion of what they would have missed out on had they completed their suicide attempt. In Helen's case, this may make for an interesting discussion.

In the early phase of therapy, a problem list that is clearly specified with a maximum of three items needs to be drawn up collaboratively with Helen or else therapy will remain poorly focused and Helen will find her problems overwhelming. Targets for therapy in this case might entail the following:

- Reduce depression symptoms by increasing activities (pleasant event scheduling).
- Increase problem-solving skills.
- Reduce social isolation.

In this case, the early session homework tasks would be completion of standardized measures assessing depression severity levels, anxiety severity levels, and optimism and pessimism about the future. A weekly activity diary would also provide useful information about what things Helen is doing for others and what things she is doing for herself.

As the middle phase of therapy is reached, it is important to review what progress has been achieved on the original problem list and goals for therapy. This review can be carried out by looking at copies of the weekly activity schedule completed over a number of sessions. If DTRs have been completed, these can be reviewed so that Helen can see what progress she has made. As the therapist will have gathered a great deal of information about Helen, this may be the time to teach her to differentiate between *noxious* and *nurturant* behaviors. Noxious behaviors in this instance may be when she self-sacrifices and this leaves her feeling depressed, hopeless about the future, and out of control. Nurturant behaviors can best be taught by asking Helen to think about the advice she would give a very close friend who was dealing with a situation similar to her own. Further examples of nurturant behaviors are when she takes time out for herself. To care for her parents, Helen must also care for herself. This process can be supported with the use of DTRs as she may be vulnerable to developing a number of negative thoughts about placing her own needs on a par with those of her parents.

For the final phase of therapy, the focus turns increasingly toward a relapse-prevention strategy. This can be seen as avoiding engaging in noxious behaviors, such as the potential for self-harming and overeating, leaving herself feeling out of control. An important stage is to engage Helen in actively reviewing what she has learned from therapy and to list what strategies she has learned that work well for her. She may find that a symbolic box of helpful tricks may be useful for her to put together with the aid of the therapist. She might decorate a shoe box and place in it specific items that are significant reminders of skills learned. An alternative is that Helen write a letter to herself and in compassionate and understanding terms remind herself what she can do in the situation to make things better for herself. Helen could be referred to a social worker to discuss the possibility of seeking alternative accommodation near her parents. This strategy would need to be discussed in therapy as it has great potential for emotional reasoning errors such that Helen may see herself abandoning her parents when in fact she may paradoxically bring some stability to a situation that had the potential for breakdown in care.

As well as focusing on relapse-prevention strategies, Helen and the therapist need to agree on a discharge time; if necessary, booster sessions can be prearranged. An agreement about what Helen should do in the event that the situation changes and she needs to seek out rereferral is also important to discuss. This is not to encourage dependence, but it lessens anxiety that patients naturally experience at the end of therapy if they have a sense of understanding the system and have an increased sense of how they can access help if needed.

Conceptualization of Helen in the Cognitive Behavior Framework for Older People

The conceptualization of this case would be drawn up near the end of the first phase of therapy and the beginning of the middle phase and shared collaboratively and openly with Helen. As therapy proceeds, a continual and dynamic process or reconceptualization will take place as new understandings come to light.

Intergenerational Linkages

From the information supplied about Helen, it seems evident that negative intergenerational linkages will form an important part of therapy. Many CBT interventions may be required to deal with this issue because there may not be much sense of reciprocity of care given Helen's experience of being parented by her father. In addition, given her father's lifetime experience of depression, Helen may assume that her problems are inherited and unchangeable. The values of Helen and her parents may be at odds, and this may in part be due to intergenerational differences. Family rules are often transmitted across generations and are not always a comfortable fit for all family members. The family rules may be explicated and examined for their utility in the current caregiving situation.

Investment in Role Transitions

Clearly, Helen is also in the early stage of a major role transition, that of becoming the primary caregiver for both her parents. This is overlaid with a poor premorbid relationship with her father particularly. It is an important part of the therapy process to assess the impact on Helen of caring for someone she does not appear to care for. It would also be normalizing and validating for Helen to reframe her current difficulties as a transitional problem, in that she is trying to solve a new problem with old and outmoded sets of strategies. With her ability to learn new skills and employ new strategies, she can transition from her current role to one that is more comfortable and optimal for her.

Cohort Beliefs

Cognitive restructuring may be necessary with some cohort beliefs about caring that she would share with other members of her age group. For example, she may express cohort beliefs about providing care for her parents that are at odds with her emotional interactions with them, but with her father in particular. It would be important to investigate possible generational beliefs when discussing the guilt Helen has expressed at not providing more care for her parents and about her negative feelings toward her parents.

Sociocultural Context

As Helen is a relatively young-older adult and is exposed to her parents' poor experience of aging, she is likely to have a strong negative age stereotype and may have a strong negative expectation for her own old age, and this may be contributing to the maintenance of depressive symptoms. Helen has already expressed worries about her own mental abilities.

Physical Health

Although the history is unclear about any physical illnesses that Helen is dealing with, she may develop a number of chronic illnesses (such as diabetes) if she continues to overeat and put on weight as a response to her own depression.

CONCLUSION

In working with patients such as Helen, CBT can be very relevant and validating, adopting as it does a problem-focused, here-and-now stance. The CBT therapist working with Helen should always consider and take account of the broader context when understanding how she faces up to her difficulties. People come into therapy because of transitions in circumstance that are proving hard to navigate by recourse to habitual strategies. This would seem to be borne out by Helen's case profile. Later life is seen as another stage of life that shares similarities with all other stages of life, with transitions and challenges to be faced by the individual to maximize his or her emotional and physical independence. Adopting this perspective gives CBT therapists a rationale for treatment in any situation that an older person brings into the clinic. The psychoeducational perspective of CBT teaches older people dealing with a role transition that it is more than a single isolated event: It is a process, and CBT assists in this process by teaching or tuning up skills to cope with changed circumstances. One can be optimistic that Helen will be able to move from this transitional stage as long as she has access to appropriate supports such as those provided by a CBT intervention.

Cognitive behavior therapy with older people is often thought to require conceptual, procedural, and technological (in the form of interventions) adaptations to render it applicable for use with older people. This is a misconception, as shown by the fact that randomized controlled trials of standard CBT with older people record outcomes similar to those of younger adults (Laidlaw, 2001). The application of CBT with older people leaves the therapist with the same challenges as those faced by any other psychotherapist working with older people: of applying psychology in the face of often long-term problems, problems of physical health co-morbidity, and realistic and challenging life transitions. The collaborative stance of CBT is particularly helpful when working with older people because it encourages respect for the life-years' experience of the individual.

REFERENCES

Beck, A. T. (1987). Cognitive models of depression. *Journal of Cognitive Psychotherapy: An International Quarterly, 1,* 5–37.

Beck, A. T., Rush, A. J., Shaw, B. F., & Emery, G. (1979). *Cognitive therapy of depression.* New York: Guilford Press.

Bengtson V. L. (2001). Beyond the nuclear family: The increasing importance of multigenerational bonds. *Journal of Marriage and the Family, 63,* 1–16.

Bengtson, V. L., Biblarz, T., Clarke, E., Giarusso, R., Roberts, R., & Richlin-Klonsky, J. (2000). Intergenerational relationships and aging: Families, cohorts, and social change. In J. M. Clair & R. Allman (Eds.), *The gerontological prism: Developing interdisciplinary bridges* (pp. 115–147). New York: Baywood Publishing.

Bengtson, V. L., & Boss, P. (2000). What living longer means to families. *Public policy through a family lens: Sustaining families in the 21st century.* Minneapolis, MN: NCFR.

Blazer, D. G. (2002). The prevalence of depressive symptoms. *Journals of Gerontology: Biological Sciences and Medical Sciences, 57,* M150–M151.

Chambless, D. L., Sanderson, W. C., Shoham, V., Johnson, S. B., Pope, K. S., Crits-Cristoph, P., et al. (1996). An update on empirically validated therapies. *Clinical Psychologist, 49,* 5–18.

Champion, L. A., & Power, M. J. (1995). Social and cognitive approaches to depression: Towards a new synthesis. *British Journal of Clinical Psychology, 34,* 485–503.

Clark, D. A., Beck, A. T., & Alford, B. A. (1999). *Scientific foundations of cognitive theory and therapy of depression.* New York: Guilford Press.

DeRubeis, R. J., Hollon, S. D., Amsterdam, J. D., Shelton, R. C., Young, P. R., Salomon, R. M., et al. (2005). Cognitive therapy versus medications in the treatment of moderate to severe depression. *Archives of General Psychiatry, 62,* 409–416.

Dick, L. P., Gallagher-Thompson, D., & Thompson, L. W. (1996). Cognitive-behavioral therapy. In R. T. Woods (Ed.), *Handbook of the clinical psychology of aging.* Chichester, West Sussex, England: Wiley.

Ellis, T., & Newman, C. (1996). *Choosing to live: How to defeat suicide through cognitive therapy.* Oakland, CA: New Harbinger Publications.

Gallagher-Thompson, D., & Steffen, A. (1994). Comparative effects of cognitive-behavioral and brief psychodynamic psychotherapies for depressed family caregivers. *Journal of Consulting and Clinical Psychology, 62,* 543–549.

Gatz, M., Fiske, A., Fox, L. S., Kaskie, B., Kasl-Godley, J. E., & McCullum, T. J. (1998). Empirically validated psychological treatments for older adults. *Journal of Mental Health and Aging, 4,* 9–46.

Gerson, S., Belin, T. R., Kaufman, M. S., Mintz, J., & Jarvik, L. (1999). Pharmacological and psychological treatments for depressed older patients: A meta-analysis and overview of recent findings. *Harvard Review of Psychiatry, 7,* 1–28.

Glantz, M. (1989). Cognitive therapy with the elderly. In A. Freeman, K. M. Simon, L. E. Beutler, & H. Arkowitz (Eds.), *Comprehensive handbook of cognitive therapy* (pp. 467–489). New York: Guilford Press.

Grant, R. W., & Casey, D. A. (1995). Adapting cognitive behavioral therapy for the frail elderly. *International Psychogeriatrics, 7,* 561–571.

Hollon, S. D., DeRubeis, R. J., Sherlton, R. C., Amsterdam, J. D., Salomon, R. M., O'Reardon, J. P., et al. (2005). Prevention of relapse following cognitive therapy vs. medications in moderate to severe depression. *Archives of General Psychiatry, 62,* 417–422.

Knight, B. G. (1996). Psychodynamic therapy with older adults: Lessons from scientific gerontology. In R. T. Woods (Ed.), *Handbook of the clinical psychology of aging.* Chichester, West Sussex, England: Wiley.

Knight, B. G. (2004). *Psychotherapy with older adults* (3rd ed.). London: Sage.

Knight, B. G., & Satre, D. D. (1999). Cognitive behavioral psychotherapy with older adults. *Clinical Psychology, 6,* 188–203.

Koder, D. A., Brodaty, H., & Anstey, K. J. (1996). Cognitive therapy for depression in the elderly. *International Journal of Geriatric Psychiatry, 11,* 97–107.

Laidlaw, K. (2001). An empirical review of cognitive therapy for late life depression: Does research evidence suggest adaptations are necessary for cognitive therapy with older adults? *Clinical Psychology and Psychotherapy, 8,* 1–14.

Laidlaw, K. (2003). Depression in older adults. In M. J. Power (Ed.), *Mood disorders: A handbook of science and practice* (pp. 137–152). Chichester, West Sussex, England: Wiley.

Laidlaw, K., Gallagher-Thompson, D., Thompson, L. W., & Siskin-Dick, L. (2003). *Cognitive behavioural therapy with older people*. Hoboken, NJ: Wiley.

Laidlaw, K., Thompson, L., & Gallagher-Thompson, D. (2004). Comprehensive conceptualisation of cognitive behavior therapy for late life depression. *Behavioral and Cognitive Psychotherapy, 32*, 389–399.

Landreville, P., Landry, J., Baillargeon, L., Guerette, A., & Matteau, E. (2001). Older adults' acceptance of psychological and pharmacological treatments for depression. *Journal of Gerontology; Psychological Sciences, 50B*, P285–P291.

Lebowitz, B. D., & Niederehe, G. (1992). Concepts and issues in mental health and aging. In J. E. Birren, R. B. Sloane, & G. D. Cohen (Eds.), *Handbook of mental health and aging* (2nd ed., pp. 3–26). San Diego, CA: Academic Press.

Levy, B. R. (2003). Mind matters: Cognitive and physical effects of aging self-stereotypes. *Journal of Gerontology: Psychological Sciences, 58B*, P203–P211.

Lovestone, S. (1983). Cognitive therapy with the elderly depressed: A rational and efficacious approach. In R. Levy & A. Burns (Eds.), *Treatment and care in old age psychiatry* (pp. 183–189). New York: Biomedical Publishing.

Morris, R. G., & Morris, L. W. (1991). Cognitive and behavioural approaches with the depressed elderly. *International Journal of Geriatric Psychiatry, 6*, 407–413.

Neugarten, B. L., & Datan, N. (1973). Sociological perspectives on the life cycle. In P. B. Baltes & K. W. Schaie (Eds.), *Lifespan developmental psychology: Personality and socialization* (pp. 53–79). London: Academic Press.

Persons, J. B. (1989). *Cognitive therapy in practice: A case formulation approach.* New York: Norton.

Rowe, J. W., & Kahn, R. L. (1998). *Successful aging.* New York: Pantheon Books.

Safran, J., & Segal, Z. (1990). *Cognitive therapy: An interpersonal process perspective.* New York: Basic Books.

Scogin, F., & McElreath, L. (1994). Efficacy of psychosocial treatments for geriatric depression: A quantitative review. *Journal of Consulting and Clinical Psychology, 62*, 69–74.

Smyer, M. A., & Qualls, S. H. (1999). *Aging and mental health.* Oxford: Blackwell.

Steuer, J. L. (1982). Psychotherapy with the elderly. *Psychiatric Clinics of North America, 5*, 199–213.

Steuer, J. L., & Hammen, C. L. (1983). Cognitive-behavioral group therapy for the depressed elderly: Issues and adaptations. *Cognitive Therapy and Research, 7*, 285–296.

Teri, L., & Gallagher-Thompson, D. (1991). Cognitive behavioral interventions for the treatment of depression in Alzheimer patients. *Gerontologist, 31,* 413–416.

Thompson, L. W. (1996). Cognitive-behavioral therapy and treatment for later life depression. *Journal of Clinical Psychiatry, 57,* 29–37.

Unutzer, J., Katon, W., Sullivan, M., & Miranda, J. (1999). Treatment of depressed older adults in primary care: Narrowing the gap between efficacy and effectiveness. *Midbank Quarterly, 77,* 225–256.

Vaillant, G. E. (2002). *Aging well: Surprising guideposts to a happier life from the landmark Harvard study of adult development.* Boston: Little, Brown.

Vaillant, G. E., & Mukamal, K. (2001). Successful aging. *American Journal of Psychiatry, 158,* 839–847.

World Health Organization. (1980) *International classification of impairments, disabilities and handicaps: A manual of classification relating to the consequences of disease.* Geneva, Switzerland: Author.

Yost, E. B., Beutler, L. E., Corbishley, M. A., & Allender, J. R. (1986). *Group cognitive therapy: A treatment approach for depressed older adults.* New York: Pergamon Press.

Zeiss, A. M., Lewinsohn, P. M., Rohde, P., & Seeley, J. R. (1996). Relationship of physical disease and functional impairment to depression in older people. *Psychology and Aging, 11,* 572–581.

Zeiss, A. M., & Steffen, A. (1996). Treatment issues with elderly clients. *Cognitive and Behavioral Practice, 3,* 371–389.

5

Interpersonal Psychotherapy with Older Adults

GREGORY A. HINRICHSEN

Interpersonal psychotherapy (IPT) is a psychotherapeutic modality that has been in existence for more than 30 years (Klerman, Weissman, Rounsaville, & Chevron, 1984). Interpersonal psychotherapy was originally developed by Gerald Klerman, Myrna Weissman, and their associates as a treatment for depression. Theoretically, IPT was nested in the interpersonal school of psychiatry best known through the work of Harry Stack Sullivan (1953) that emphasized the role of interpersonal factors in the genesis and amelioration of mental disorders. Empirically, IPT rested on the foundation of a then growing number of research studies that demonstrated that social and interpersonal factors were related to increased or decreased risk for the onset of mental disorders. In a seminal study, Weissman and Paykel (1974) found that depression also impaired depressed women's ability to function in a variety of social roles. Even after the end of a depressive episode, social role dysfunction persisted in women, notably problems in marital relationships. In the years since the development of IPT, a large body of research on interpersonal issues and depression has continued to demonstrate the importance of interpersonal factors in vulnerability to depression as well as recovery from and relapse into depression (Butzlaff & Hooley, 1998; Kawachi & Berkman, 2001; Mazure, 1998). Further, depression is now known to damage social relationships, in part because of the complicated interpersonal dynamics of this disorder (Joiner, 2000; Judd et al., 2000).

Research has demonstrated that IPT is an effective treatment for major depression (DiMascio et al., 1979; Elkin et al., 1989; Weissman et al., 1979). Interpersonal psychotherapy has also been found to reduce the likelihood of depressive relapse (Frank et al., 1990; Klerman, DiMascio, Weissman, Prusoff, & Paykel, 1974; Kupfer, Frank, Perel, Cornes, & Mallinger, 1992). Interpersonal psychotherapy has been adapted to treat depression in specific populations and other psychiatric disorders. Some of these studies include treatment of depression in adolescents (Mufson, Pollack Dorta, Moreau, & Weissman, 2004), women with postpartum depression (Spinelli & Endicott, 2003), HIV-positive persons (Markowitz et al., 1999), and older adults (Reynolds et al., 1999). In the first randomized, controlled psychotherapy treatment study in Africa, IPT was found to be highly successful in the treatment of depression in Ugandans (Bolton et al., 2003). Interpersonal psychotherapy has found international appeal and is currently used and studied in Canada, the European Union, Australia, and elsewhere.

THE STRUCTURE AND ETHOS OF INTERPERSONAL PSYCHOTHERAPY

In the treatment of acute major depression, IPT is typically conducted in 16 weekly individual sessions (Klerman et al., 1984; Weissman, Markowitz, & Klerman, 2000). There are three phases of IPT: the initial sessions (weeks 1 to 3), the intermediate sessions (weeks 4 to 13), and termination (weeks 14 to 16). The original IPT manual is in Klerman et al.'s (1984) *Interpersonal Psychotherapy of Depression.* This volume was revised and updated along with reviews of relevant IPT research studies in Weissman et al.'s (2000) *Comprehensive Guide to Interpersonal Psychotherapy.*

The Initial Sessions

There are four foci of the initial sessions. First, a diagnosis of depression is made and discussed with the client. As part of the diagnostic process, depressive symptoms are reviewed and are rereviewed throughout the treatment. Depression is characterized as an illness. The client is educated about the emotional, cognitive, and physical symptoms of major depression and their deleterious impact on functioning. The client is encouraged to take a temporary reprieve from some life responsibilities, which is called giving the client the "sick role." Education about treatments for and usual treatment outcomes of depression is provided. An evaluation of the need for psychiatric medication is also conducted, and, if necessary, a referral made to a prescribing mental health professional. Second, an inventory of relevant interpersonal relationships is conducted. The likely connection between an interpersonally relevant life circumstance(s) and depression is identified. Third, the major problem area(s) that will be the focus of the intermediate sessions is determined. The four IPT problems areas are grief, interpersonal role disputes, role transitions, and interpersonal deficits. Fourth, an interpersonal formulation is provided to the client by the therapist. The formulation conveys the therapist's understanding of the problem(s) and its relationship to depression. The therapist also works with the client to identify treatment goals and clarify practical issues in the implementation of IPT (e.g., 50-minute weekly meetings, policy for missed appointments).

The Intermediate Sessions

During the intermediate sessions, therapist and client work to achieve goals tied to one or possibly two of the four IPT problem areas. Goals and strategies are articulated for each of the problem areas (Weissman et al., 2000). The first IPT problem area is grief—the treatment of complicated bereavement. Interpersonal psychotherapy goals in the treatment of grief are to facilitate the mourning process and help the client to reestablish interests and relationships. The second area, interpersonal role disputes, involves conflicts with a significant other. Common examples include conflict with a spouse/partner or parent. Goals for role disputes include identification of the dispute, establishment of a plan of action to address issues in the dispute, and modification of expectations toward or poor communication with the party to the dispute. The third area, role transitions, involves change in a life role(s) or life situation. Common examples include beginning college, a residential move, job change or retirement, and onset of parenting. The goals of role transitions include mourning and accepting the lost role or life situation, regarding the new role or life situation as more positive, and restoring client self-esteem by the development of mastery associated with the new role or life situation. The fourth area, interpersonal deficits, refers to persons who want more or better connections with others but who lack the skills to initiate or sustain relationships. Goals for this problem area include reduction of the client's social isolation and encouragement of the formation of new relationships.

Termination

The final phase of IPT is termination. In the termination phase there is a discussion of the upcoming end of psychotherapy, acknowledgment that termination can be a time of grieving, movement of the client toward recognition of independence, and a review of whether IPT maintenance treatment is needed. Consideration of maintenance IPT is made as studies have found that after completion of weekly IPT in the treatment of acute depression, monthly maintenance IPT treatment reduces the likelihood of recurrence of another depressive episode (Frank et al., 1990; Klerman et al., 1974; Kupfer et al., 1992). For clients who have not shown a substantive clinical response to IPT, this fact is discussed and future therapeutic options are discussed (e.g., continue IPT, change to another therapeutic modality, change therapist).

Techniques and Therapeutic Ethos of Interpersonal Psychotherapy

Common techniques used in IPT include exploration, encouragement of affect, clarification, communication analysis, use of the therapeutic relationship, and behavior change techniques (therapeutic direction, decision analysis, role-play). The therapist's role in IPT is one of being active and, as needed, advocating for the client. The therapist does not interpret the therapeutic relationship as transference, as in some psychotherapies.

The ethos of IPT is one of collaborative empowerment. Major depression often engenders hopelessness and helplessness, a narrowed perspective on what can be done to address life problems, and reduced activity. Therapist and client work together to understand the nature of the depressive illness and develop a plan to address a central problem(s) that appears tied to the onset of depression or that was seeded by the depression. The primary focus of IPT is on current problems. The link between mood and daily events is frequently pointed out to the client because the therapist can then help the client to better address life events that promote depressive symptoms. Interpersonal psychotherapy's therapeutic mantra is "options." When a client feels stuck around a life issue, the therapist asks, "What are your options to deal with this problem?" If the client replies that there are no options, the therapist might respond, "There are always options. You don't feel there are options because of your depression."

INTERPERSONAL PSYCHOTHERAPY IN THE TREATMENT OF LATE LIFE DEPRESSION

Historically, gerontologists have had concerns about the social well-being of older adults. Social gerontologists examined the nature and impact of loss of social roles in later life (Rosow, 1967) and possible tensions in intergenerational relationships (Bengtson & Cutler, 1976). Psychologists have been concerned about the effects of multiple personal losses for older adults (Kastenbaum, 2000). Overall, gerontologists have documented considerable resilience in the aged to contend with late life social and interpersonal stresses (APA Working Group on the Older Adult, 1998; Shanas, 1979). Yet a minority of older adults become depressed, in part because of the social stresses of later life.

A respectable body of both cross-sectional and longitudinal studies has found that psychosocial factors are linked to depression in older adults (Bruce, 2002). Depression is associated with problems in daily functioning and social functioning in older adults (Lenze et al., 2001). Family members providing care to seriously depressed older adults report many stresses associated with this care, including interpersonal tensions with and criticism directed toward the depressed relative

(Hinrichsen, Adelstein, & McMeniman, 2004; Hinrichsen, Hernandez, & Pollack, 1992). Spouses of depressed older adults are themselves more likely to experience depression (Tower & Kasl, 1996). Although the evidence is mixed, interpersonal factors have been tied longitudinally to clinical outcomes in older persons with major depression (Bosworth, McQuoid, George, & Steffens, 2002; Hinrichsen & Hernandez, 1993).

Why Interpersonal Psychotherapy Makes Sense in the Treatment of Late Life Depression

The link between interpersonal factors and outcomes in late life major depression led to my own interest in the use of IPT with my older clients. Interpersonal psychotherapy appeared especially well suited to older adults. The four problem areas broadly reflect the kinds of difficulties confronted by older adults. Interpersonal psychotherapy's problem area role transitions encompasses not only the loss of social roles associated with aging (e.g., work, parenting) but also the often stressful acquisition of roles (e.g., caregiving, becoming a person with health problems). In clinical practice, interpersonal role conflicts in older adults often involve adult children and spouses. The onset of health problems in self or spouse may put pressure on marriages or partnerships, especially those that have had long-standing problems. Grief is a common experience for older people as they contend with the loss of spouse, family, and friends. Further, loss of established social relationships confronts older adults with the need to initiate new relationships for which they may lack the requisite interpersonal skills. The collaborative, present-focused stance of IPT is consistent with general recommendations for doing psychotherapy with older adults (Knight, 2004).

Research on Interpersonal Psychotherapy and Older Adults

Early in the development of IPT, some authors suggested that with adaptation IPT might be useful for depressed older adults (Sholomskas, Chevron, Prusoff, & Berry, 1983). Despite the corpus of studies that have demonstrated the utility of IPT in the treatment of different disorders and different populations, there are only a few studies of IPT in the acute treatment of late life major depression. Although these studies provided hopeful findings about the utility of IPT for older people, they are basically pilot work (Rothblum, Sholomskas, Berry, & Prusoff, 1982; Sloane, Staples, & Schneider, 1985). Convincing data on the utility of IPT in the treatment of recurrent major depression in older adults come from a major study conducted at the University of Pittsburgh by Charles Reynolds, Ellen Frank, and their colleagues (Reynolds et al., 1999). The chief goal of their IPT and Late Life Study was to find out which treatment or treatments were useful in preventing or delaying another episode of major depression in older adults with histories of recurrent depression. Interpersonal psychotherapy was modified for older adults and called IPT-Late Life Maintenance (IPT-LLM). In our judgment, the modifications were minor and reflected the kind of flexibility that is generally recommended in doing psychotherapy with older adults. Experience during the conduct of this study, in fact, was that IPT could be conducted in a fashion that was parallel to its use with younger adults (Miller & Silberman, 1996). In the IPT and Late Life Study, older adults with recurrent major depression were treated with the combination of weekly IPT and antidepressant medication. Those who improved were then randomized into several groups for the continuation/maintenance phase of the study. Study groups included medication, monthly maintenance IPT, and the combination of medication and IPT, or no treatment. Study subjects were followed for up to 3 years. There were several notable results from the study. Over three-quarters of older adults initially treated with the combination of IPT and antidepressant medication evidenced remission of major depression. Rates of a recurrence of another episode of major depression were the following: antidepressant medication plus IPT, 20%; antidepressant medication alone, 43%; IPT alone, 64%; no treatment, 90%. The researchers concluded that in clinical practice, older adults with recurrent depression should be treated with the combination of IPT and antidepressant medication. One other well-designed study treated medically ill older adults with depressive symptoms with a brief version of IPT. After 6 months, older people treated with brief IPT had lower rates of depressive symptoms than those not treated with IPT (Mossey, Knott, Higgins, & Talerico, 1996).

Clinical Experience in Using Interpersonal Psychotherapy with Depressed Older Adults

For 10 years, my colleagues, students, and I have conducted IPT with depressed older adults in the geriatric psychiatry outpatient clinic at our hospital. We have generally found that IPT can be applied as originally developed by Klerman, Weissman, and colleagues (Klerman et al., 1984). Clinical outcomes have been favorable. Almost three-quarters of older adults treated with IPT have shown a significant reduction in depressive symptoms (as judged by at least a 50% reduction on scores on the Hamilton Depression Rating Scale) from the beginning to the end of treatment (Hinrichsen, 2004), results comparable to those found in the acute treatment phase of the University of Pittsburgh IPT and Late Life Study (Reynolds et al., 1999). During IPT, some clients have been on psychiatric medication and some have not been. The most common focus of IPT is on role transitions and interpersonal disputes. We have had very few treatment dropouts from IPT. Many of our older IPT clients find the time-limited, problem-focused, collaborative frame of IPT appealing.

ISSUES IN THE APPLICATION OF INTERPERSONAL PSYCHOTHERAPY TO DEPRESSED OLDER ADULTS

Although we have found that IPT can be used generally with depressed older adults as it was originally developed (Klerman et al., 1984; Weissman et al., 2000), the treatment must be informed by a broader understanding of later adulthood. Knight's (2004) framework for conducting psychotherapy with older adults, "the contextual, cohort-based, maturity, specific-challenge model," is especially useful. More broadly, individuals providing psychological services to older adults are well served by substantive familiarity with late life issues (American Psychological Association, 2004). Familiarity with late life issues arms the IPT therapist with facts about aging that build therapeutic credibility with the older client and helps the therapist to more ably assist in problem-solving specific issues of concern. What follows is a summary of common issues that we have found for those learning how to conduct IPT with older adults (Hinrichsen & Clougherty, 2006). Some of the issues are age specific and others are general issues of concern to therapists less familiar with conducting time-limited psychotherapy.

General Issues

• *The therapist wonders whether substantive therapeutic work can be done with brief therapy, especially with older adults.* For therapists who provide typically long-term psychotherapy, a time-limited therapy seems too brief to have substantive results. This may be especially the case with older adults who may have several life problems. However, the goals of IPT are circumscribed: significant reduction of depressive symptoms and improvement in one or two relevant problem areas. In this manner IPT differs from other psychotherapies, notably psychodynamic psychotherapy, that broadly aim for characterological change. Confidence about the usefulness of IPT can be increased for the therapist by familiarity with research studies that document that most depressed clients get better.

• *The therapist is uncomfortable with IPT's conceptualization of depression as an illness.* Some nonmedical psychotherapists complain that there is an overemphasis on the medical model of human problems and that calling depression an illness further perpetuates this emphasis. However, the affective, cognitive, and physical debilitation of depression attests to the power of this syndrome. The fact that depression is as functionally impairing as physical health problems such as heart disease further attests to this reality (Wells et al., 1989). Many persons with depression are prone to blame themselves for the depression. This is especially the case for older adults, who have less familiarity than many younger adults who were raised in a society more conscious of mental health. Viewing depression as an illness and not a personal failing generally reduces self-blame. We find that IPT's illness conceptualization of depression makes sense to many older adults, the majority of whom have one or more physical health problems.

- *The therapist finds it difficult to take a directive role in therapy, especially with very verbal older adults.* Some older adults have difficulty staying on target in therapy; that is, they may become tangential and circumstantial. Therapists may find that redirection of these clients breaks the flow of therapy and may offend the older person. Given that IPT is time limited, one important role of the IPT therapist is to keep therapeutic sessions focused on the goals and strategies of the problem area. Studies have shown that failure of the therapist to adhere to IPT goals and strategies results in poorer treatment outcomes (Frank & Spanier, 1995). We find that the majority of older adults who have difficulty focusing on agreed-on therapeutic goals can be engaged in a discussion of this issue and redirected. Sometimes the reasons older adults have interpersonally relevant problems are, in fact, because they are prone to avoid thinking about and problem-solving these problems.

- *The therapist wonders who is a good candidate for IPT.* Interpersonal psychotherapy is a versatile therapy, yet we generally find that the best candidates are older adults with depressive symptoms (as evidenced in Major Depressive Disorder and Adjustment Disorder with depressive symptoms) with an interpersonally relevant problem. We find that older adults with prominent anxiety are better candidates for cognitive-behavioral therapy. Interpersonal psychotherapy is unlikely to be useful for an older adult who does not have a problem relevant to one of the four IPT problem areas. Older adults with personality disorders are usually better treated with dialectical behavior therapy or long-term psychodynamic psychotherapies.

- *The older client is pessimistic that any change is possible.* We sometimes hear older clients comment, "I'm too old to change." Pessimism about change usually reflects the discouragement that accompanies depression. The client is educated about this: "It's common that depressed people feel the way you do. It's the depression talking." Older clients can be told that studies show that depressed older as well as younger adults typically improve when treated with psychotherapy. As noted earlier, sometimes therapists must also contend with their own doubts about the usefulness of time-limited therapy, doubts that might be communicated indirectly to the client.

The Initial Sessions

- *The therapist does not feel there is enough time to cover all the issues that need to be covered in the initial sessions.* A review of relevant current and past relationships (i.e., "the interpersonal inventory") may be especially challenging as most older clients have a larger aggregate of relationships than do most younger adults. For the beginning IPT therapist, it is useful to review the outline of IPT (Weissman et al., 2000) in advance of the meeting with the client, advise the client of the issues that need to be covered during the initial sessions, and keep in mind the fact that a major goal of the initial sessions is information gathering. Most of the IPT sessions will be devoted to an in-depth examination of problems and issues that are identified in the initial sessions. For very verbal older adults, the initial sessions are an opportune time to address problems they may have in maintaining focus.

- *The older client has many different life problems and it is hard to judge which one or two will be the focus of IPT.* A critical issue for the therapist is to try to discern which interpersonally relevant problem appears to be associated with the onset of the depression or was seeded by the depression. Some clients have not made a connection between life circumstances and depression. Simple inquiries such as "What was going on in your life before or around the time you became depressed?" or "Have there been more problems in your relationships since you became depressed?" can be useful.

- *The therapist is not sure which IPT problem area best fits the older client's problems.* Common late life problems include onset of medical illness in self and others (i.e., caregiving issues) and are best conceptualized within the role transitions problem area. Novice IPT therapists tend to identify more problem areas than are needed. For example, the therapist may identify both role transitions and grief as problem areas for a dementia caregiver who is engaging in anticipatory grieving over loss of the relationship with the relative with dementia. As noted, the grief problem area is only for complicated bereavement; part of the confusion lies in the fact that feelings of loss and grief are part of making a role transition. Some therapists identify both interpersonal role disputes and interpersonal deficits for an individual who has conflict with a significant other. Improvement in interpersonal skills is part of all four problem areas, but the problem area of interpersonal deficits is reserved for individuals who have long-standing problems in initiating and sustaining human relationships.

The Intermediate Sessions

• *The therapist does not continue to discuss depressive symptoms or the client's depressive illness.* After the initial sessions, some therapists do not continue to actively inquire about depression. The status of depressive symptoms should be ascertained at the beginning of each session. The relationship between exacerbation or improvement of depressive symptoms and recent events also should be pointed out. The connection between interpersonally relevant life events and depression lays the groundwork for helping clients to problem-solve better ways to handle those events. Some older clients need to be continually educated that depression impairs functioning.

• *The therapist does not remind the client of the number of remaining sessions.* Part of the power of brief therapy is that both therapist and client are aware that the number of psychotherapeutic sessions is predetermined and they need to actively work to achieve goals during this time frame. Some therapists fail to keep this issue in the therapeutic discourse because of lingering doubts about whether therapeutic goals will be achieved or concern that the client may feel uncomfortable being reminded of the planned end to therapy.

• *The therapist loses therapeutic focus.* Some therapists begin to lose sight of the goals and strategies associated with the problem area. Older clients begin to discuss topics that are unrelated to the problem area and the therapist does not redirect them. We sometimes tell IPT supervisees that if they cannot find a clinical rationale for what is being discussed in a given session, particularly as the discussion relates to goals and strategies of the IPT problem area, then they are probably not being faithful to IPT as a treatment.

Termination

- *The therapist is not comfortable with ending treatment at 16 weeks.* More generally, it is challenging for psychotherapists working with older adults to end therapy. Many older adults have ongoing problems in their lives, and some therapists feel they are abandoning older clients if therapy is ended. Some novice IPT therapists prejudge that older clients will necessarily want to continue beyond 16 weeks and signal to clients that they would be happy to continue to see them. Assuming that clients will want to continue violates the treatment contract and conveys to them that they have not achieved goals or are too fragile to handle problems on their own. We find that some older adults handle termination better than the therapist!

- *The therapist is not sure which clients may need ongoing psychotherapy after completion of 16 weeks.* Some clients may need continued treatment, but this should be determined by clinical necessity and client interest. For older clients who have not shown substantive improvement in depression symptoms and/or the identified problem area(s), treatment options should be discussed. These options typically include continuation of IPT for a specified period of time, use of another psychotherapeutic modality, change of therapist, or addition or change of psychiatric medication. For clients who have shown considerable improvement but yet appear to need and desire additional psychotherapy, frequency of IPT sessions can be reduced with the goal of ending therapy. As noted earlier, research studies have found that monthly maintenance IPT reduces the likelihood of recurrence of depression in older adults with histories of recurrent depression (Reynolds et al., 1999). Since the publication of these study results, we have been more likely to provide maintenance IPT to older clients. A critical issue, however, is that the end of the contracted 16 weeks of IPT is discussed with the client during the termination phase. Sometimes clients want to continue IPT even if they have made substantive clinical progress because they want to continue the relationship with the therapist or they mistakenly confuse feelings of sadness about ending therapy with recurrence of depression. The therapist must also sort out whether a desire to continue therapy with the client reflects personal discomfort with ending therapy and not a well-reasoned rationale for why some form of therapy is clinically indicated.

Assessment of Treatment Outcomes

Status of the client's depressive symptoms is evaluated clinically throughout IPT. We administer the Hamilton Depression Rating Scale (Hamilton, 1960) in the initial sessions, at week 8, and at week 16. Other clinician-administered or patient self-report questionnaires can be used. It is also useful at the end of treatment to make an assessment of whether the client continues to meet criteria for the depressive disorder. Assessment information is provided directly to the client and is a fruitful focus of discussion throughout IPT. When older clients demonstrate notable improvement in depressive symptoms, many find quantification of the reduction of their depressive symptoms appealing. One reason is that most older people are familiar with numerical indices of their health (e.g., blood pressure, cholesterol). For example, the therapist might say, "At the beginning of psychotherapy you had a score of 24, which indicated severe depression. Now you have a score of 6, which means you are virtually without depressive symptoms." If the client has not shown clinical improvement, a discussion of the lack of change in scores addresses this fact.

One tool for evaluating improvement in social functioning is the Social Adjustment Scale (SAS). The SAS has been used in numerous studies, including early IPT studies. As originally developed, the SAS is clinician administered, but there is also a paper-and-pencil self-report client version (Weissman & Bothwell, 1976) and a version of the SAS adapted for older adults (Zweig et al., 2001). It may also be useful to use the Global Assessment of Functioning (GAF), which is frequently used in conjunction with the DSM multiaxial diagnostic scheme (American Psychiatric Association, 1994). The GAF provides a numerical summary of the degree to which client functioning is impaired by depression and can be cited as another source of evidence demonstrating improvement. Clinically, we find that it is most useful to verbally review with clients their own progress in addressing the problem area or areas that have been the focus of IPT. I have found that I am usually in accord with the client's own assessment of how much improvement in depressive symptoms has been made as well as in the IPT problem area.

COMMENTS ON THE CASE OF HELEN

From an IPT perspective, Helen is suffering from a major depressive episode that has impaired her ability to function in her role as a caregiver to her parents. The onset of the depressive episode appears tied to retirement, the move to live with her parents, acquisition of the caregiving role, or some combination of these factors. The fact that her father is depressed may be another contributor to her depression. Research has demonstrated that living with a depressed person increases risk for depression for coresidents (Tower & Kasl, 1996). Further, it is likely she is in less frequent contact with friends since the move to her parent's home, thus depriving her of social supports.

During the initial sessions of IPT, Helen's depressive symptoms will be reviewed, quantified on a rating scale, and discussed with her. Her psychiatric diagnosis also will be discussed with her. The case material suggests that Helen has unipolar major depression, but given her past use of lithium the therapist will be alert for any signs of hypomanic behavior. She will be educated about the functional impairment associated with major depression and why depression makes it much more difficult for her to function in her role as caregiver to her father with depression and mother with dementia. If feasible, she will be encouraged to temporarily reduce some of her caregiving responsibilities. In view of her fear that she may be experiencing the first signs of dementia, she will also be told that it is common that concentration is impaired in major depression. The therapist will be especially interested in understanding when the depressive episode began and which interpersonally relevant circumstance(s) may have preceded the episode. Likely interpersonal antecedents or interpersonally relevant problems seeded by the depression will inform the therapist as to which IPT problem area will be the focus of treatment. The therapist will also inquire about events associated with Helen's prior episodes of major depression, as they may be a clue to interpersonally relevant vulnerabilities to depression for her. The therapist will conduct a broad review of positive and negative aspects of important current and past relationships, including those with her parents and her child. From this review the therapist will gain not only a sense of Helen's interpersonal strengths and weaknesses, but also discern whether other interpersonally relevant issues may have a bearing on the genesis or maintenance of the current episode of major depression. The therapist will regularly inquire about suicidal thoughts as well as other symptoms associated with major depression.

It is likely that in this case the problem area that will be the focus of IPT is role transitions. Helen has transitioned from the role of a working woman living alone to a caregiver coresiding with her parents. Implementation of goals in this problem area for Helen will involve coming to terms with the loss of her life circumstances prior to taking on the caregiving role for her parents, helping her to see her caregiving role as more positive (or at least more tolerable), and helping her build a sense of mastery and associated enhancement of self-esteem in her role as caregiver. The therapist will help Helen identify aspects of her caregiving role that are especially challenging and then review options to better contend with these difficulties. Possible options to better deal with her caregiving responsibilities include hiring a paid caregiver to help her; getting help from neighbors, other family, or friends; enrolling her mother in a day program for persons with dementia; exploring strategies to get mental health care for her father; and trying out new ways of handling issues with her parents that have been triggers for discord. It appears that providing care to her parents is complicated by a prior history of difficulties with each of them. This fact will be acknowledged and the therapist will encourage Helen to think about ways she can provide care to her parents and manage strong negative feelings toward them that likely have historical antecedents. Helen will be encouraged to find social supports for herself, which might include reconnecting with old friends, finding new relationships, or taking part in a caregiver support group.

In the middle and end of therapy the therapist will formally assess improvement in depressive symptoms as well as progress in achievement of goals associated with the IPT problem area, role transitions. As Helen will likely remain in her role as caregiver to her parents, like other caregivers she would likely benefit from ongoing support after the end of therapy. Support may come from a caregiver support group. Because Helen has had recurrent depressions, one option at the end of treatment would be monthly maintenance IPT. As noted earlier, studies have found that monthly maintenance IPT (alone or in combination with antidepressant medication) significantly reduces the likelihood of depressive relapse among older adults with recurrent major depression (Reynolds et al., 1999).

CONCLUSION

In clinical practice we have found that IPT is well suited to many of the problems that are a common focus of psychotherapy with older adults. A large body of research has demonstrated that IPT is useful in the treatment of depression and other psychiatric disorders in adolescents and adults (Frank & Spanier, 1995). A smaller body of clinical research suggests IPT is likely useful in the treatment of acute depression in older adults (Sloane et al., 1985) and is useful in reducing depressive symptoms in medically ill older adults (Mossey et al., 1996). Alone or in combination with antidepressant medication, IPT reduces the likelihood of recurrence of another episode of major depression in older adults with recurrent major depression (Reynolds et al., 1999).

Those interested in learning more about IPT are encouraged to read *Comprehensive Guide to Interpersonal Psychotherapy* (Weissman et al., 2000) and other books and articles relevant to the application of IPT to older adults (Hinrichsen & Clougherty, 2006; Miller & Silberman, 1996). The International Society for Interpersonal Psychotherapy is a resource for information and possible supervision for those interested in learning how to conduct IPT. The Society's web site contains a listing of IPT-relevant publications, clinical applications of IPT, training, and events, as well as information on membership: http://www.interpersonalpsychotherapy.org.

REFERENCES

American Psychiatric Association. (1994). *Diagnostic and statistical manual of mental disorders* (4th ed.). Washington, DC: Author.

American Psychological Association. (2004). Guidelines for psychological practice with older adults. *American Psychologist, 59*, 236–260.

APA Working Group on the Older Adult. (1998). What practitioners should
know about working with older adults. *Professional Psychology: Research and
Practice, 29*, 413–427.

Bengtson, V. L., & Cutler, N. E. (1976). Generations and intergenerational rela-
tions: Perspectives on age groups and social change. In R. H. Binstock & E.
Shanas (Eds.), *Handbook of aging and the social sciences* (pp. 130–159). New
York: Van Nostrand Reinhold.

Bolton, P., Bass, J., Neugebauer, R., Verdeli, H., Clougherty, K. F., Wickramaratne, P. J., et al. (2003). A clinical trial of group interpersonal psychotherapy
for depression in rural Uganda. *Journal of the American Medical Association,
289*, 3117–3124.

Bosworth, H. B., McQuoid, D. R., George, L. K., & Steffens, D. C. (2002). Time-
to-remission from geriatric depression: Psychosocial and clinical factors.
American Journal of Geriatric Psychiatry, 10, 551–559.

Bruce, M. L. (2002). Psychosocial risk factors for depressive disorders in late life.
Biological Psychiatry, 52, 175–184.

Butzlaff, R. L., & Hooley, J. M. (1998). Expressed emotion and psychiatric relapse: A meta-analysis. *Archives of General Psychiatry, 55*, 547–552.

DiMascio, A., Weissman, M. M., Prusoff, B. A., Neu, C., Zwilling, M., & Klerman, G. L. (1979). Differential symptom reduction by drugs and psychotherapy in acute depression. *Archives of General Psychiatry, 36*, 1450–1456.

Elkin, I., Shea, M. T., Watkins, J. T., Imber, S. D., Sotsky, S. M., Collins, J. F.,
et al. (1989). National Institute of Mental Health treatment of depression collaborative research program: General effectiveness of treatments. *Archives of
General Psychiatry, 46*, 971–982.

Frank, E., Kupfer, D. J., Perel, J. M., Cornes, C., Jarrett, D. B., Mallinger, A. G.,
et al. (1990). Three-year outcomes for maintenance therapies in recurrent depression. *Archives of General Psychiatry, 47*, 1093–1099.

Frank, E., & Spanier, C. (1995). Interpersonal psychotherapy for depression:
Overview, clinical efficacy, and future directions. *Clinical Psychology: Science
and Practice, 2*, 349–369.

Hamilton, M. (1960). A rating scale for depression. *Journal of Neurology and Neurosurgical Psychiatry, 23*, 56–62.

Hinrichsen, G. A. (2004, June). *Training in and application of IPT in a geriatric
outpatient setting.* Paper presented at the first International Conference on Interpersonal Psychotherapy, Pittsburgh, PA.

Hinrichsen, G. A., Adelstein, L., & McMeniman, M. (2004). Expressed emotion in family members of depressed older adults. *Aging and Mental Health, 8,* 343–351.

Hinrichsen, G. A., & Clougherty, K. F. (2006). *Interpersonal psychotherapy for depressed older adults.* Washington, DC: American Psychological Association.

Hinrichsen, G. A., Hernandez, N. A., & Pollack, S. (1992). Difficulties and rewards in family care of the depressed older adult. *Gerontologist, 32,* 486–492.

Joiner, T. E. (2000). Depression's vicious scree: Self-propagating and erosive processes in depression chronicity. *Clinical Psychology: Science and Practice, 7,* 203–218.

Judd, L. L., Akiskal, H. G., Zeller, P. J., Paulus, M., Leon, A. C., Maser, J. D., et al. (2000). Psychosocial disability during the long-term course of unipolar major depressive disorder. *Archives of General Psychiatry, 57,* 375–380.

Kastenbaum, R. (2000). *The psychology of death.* New York: Springer.

Kawachi, I., & Berkman, L. F. (2001). Social ties and mental health. *Journal of Urban Health: Bulletin of the New York Academy of Medicine, 78,* 458–467.

Klerman, G. L., DiMascio, A., Weissman, M., Prusoff, B., & Paykel, E. (1974). Treatment of depression by drugs and psychotherapy. *American Journal of Psychiatry, 131,* 186–191.

Klerman, G. L., Weissman, M. M., Rounsaville, B. J., & Chevron, E. S. (1984). *Interpersonal psychotherapy of depression.* Northvale, NJ: Aronson.

Knight, B. (2004). *Psychotherapy with older adults* (3rd ed.). Thousand Oaks, CA: Sage.

Kupfer, D. J., Frank, E., Perel, J. M., Cornes, C., & Mallinger, V. J. (1992). Five-year outcome for maintenance therapies in recurrent depression. *Archives of General Psychiatry, 49,* 769–773.

Lenze, E. J., Rogers, J. C., Martire, L. M., Mulsant, B. H., Rollman, B. L., Dew, M. A., et al. (2001). The association of late-life depression and anxiety with physical disability: A review of the literature and prospectus for future research. *American Journal of Geriatric Psychiatry, 9,* 113–134.

Markowitz, J. C., Kocsis, J. H., Fishman, B., Spielman, L. A., Jacobsberg, L. B., Frances, A. J., et al. (1999). Treatment of HIV-positive patients with depressive symptoms. *Archives of General Psychiatry, 55,* 452–457.

Mazure, C. M. (1998). Life stressors as risk factors in depression. *Clinical Psychology: Science and Practice, 5,* 291–313.

Miller, M. D., & Silberman, R. L. (1996). Using interpersonal psychotherapy with depressed elders. In S. H. Zarit & B. G. Knight (Eds.), *A guide to psychotherapy and aging* (pp. 83–99). Washington, DC: American Psychological Association.

Mossey, J. M., Knott, K. A., Higgins, M., & Talerico, K. (1996). Effectiveness of a psychosocial intervention, interpersonal counseling, for subdysthymic depression in medically ill elderly. *Journal of Gerontology: Medical Sciences, 51A,* M172–M178.

Mufson, L., Pollack Dorta, K., Moreau, D., & Weissman, M. M. (2004). *Interpersonal therapy for depressed adolescents* (2nd ed.). New York: Guilford Press.

Reynolds, C. F., III, Frank, E., Perel, J. M., Imber, S. D., Cornes, C., Miller, M. D., et al. (1999). Nortriptyline and interpersonal psychotherapy as maintenance therapies for recurrent major depression: A randomized controlled trial in patients older than 59 years. *Journal of the American Medical Association, 281,* 39–45.

Rothblum, E. D., Sholomskas, A. J., Berry, C., & Prusoff, B. A. (1982). Issues in clinical trials with the depressed elderly. *Journal of the American Geriatrics Society, 30,* 694–699.

Rosow, I. (1967). *Social integration of the aged.* New York: Free Press.

Shanas, E. (1979). Social myth as hypothesis: The case of family relations of old people. *Gerontologist, 19,* 3–9.

Sholomskas, A. J., Chevron, E. S., Prusoff, B. A., & Berry, C. (1983). Short-term interpersonal therapy (IPT) with the depressed elderly: Case reports and discussion. *American Journal of Psychotherapy, 37,* 552–566.

Sloane, R. B., Staples, F. R., & Schneider, L. S. (1985). Interpersonal psychotherapy versus nortriptyline for depression in the elderly. In G. Burrows, T. R. Norman, & L. Dennerstein (Eds.), *Clinical and pharmacological studies in psychiatric disorders* (pp. 344–346). London: John Libbey.

Spinelli, M. G., & Endicott, J. (2003). Controlled clinical trial of interpersonal psychotherapy versus parenting education program for depressed pregnant women. *American Journal of Psychiatry, 160,* 555–562.

Sullivan, H. S. (1953). *The interpersonal theory of psychiatry.* New York: Norton.

Tower, R. B., & Kasl, S. V. (1996). Depressive symptoms across older spouses: Longitudinal influences. *Psychology and Aging, 11,* 683–697.

Weissman, M. M., & Bothwell, S. (1976). Assessment of social adjustment by patient self-report. *Archives of General Psychiatry, 33,* 1111–1115.

Weissman, M. M., Markowitz, J. C., & Klerman, G. L. (2000). *Comprehensive guide to interpersonal psychotherapy.* New York: Basic Books.

Weissman, M. M., & Paykel, E. (1974). *The depressed woman.* Chicago: University of Chicago Press.

Weissman, M. M., Prusoff, B. A., DiMascio, A., Neu, C., Goklaney, M., & Klerman, G. L. (1979). The efficacy of drugs and psychotherapy in the treatment of acute depressive episodes. *American Journal of Psychiatry, 134*, 555–558.

Wells, K. B., Stewart, A., Hays, R. D., Burnam, A., Rogers, W., Daniels, M., et al. (1989). The functioning and well-being of depressed patients: Results from the Medical Outcomes Study. *Journal of the American Medical Association, 262*, 914–919.

Zweig, R. A., Turkel, E., Siskin, L., Rosendahl, E., Dekel, N., & Liss-Bialik, A. (2001, November). *Validity of the Social Adjustment Scale Self-Report in older adults.* Poster presented at the 54th annual Scientific Meeting of the Gerontological Society of America, Chicago.

6

Problem-Solving Therapy with Older Adults

PATRICIA A. AREÁN AND TERRI HUH

Social problem-solving therapy (PST) is a learning-based psychotherapy that is an effective treatment for depression in young adults (Nezu & Perri, 1989), older adults (Alexopoulos, Raue, & Areán, 2003; Areán et al., 1993), and medical patients (Mynors-Wallis, Gath, Day, & Baker, 2000). According to this model, depression is multifaceted, the result of an interaction among daily stress, major life events, weak coping skills, and depressive affect (Nezu, 1986; see Figure 6.1). People most vulnerable to depression are those who have inadequate problem-solving skills or those whose skills are not being used because of poor self-efficacy. According to PST, the ideal way to intervene in this depressogenic cycle is to teach patients how to mobilize their coping resources and begin tackling the problems in their lives. Once they begin to successfully solve problems, depression lifts and the motivation to face other problems increases. The principal goal of PST is to teach clients that life is not problem free, that they can effectively manage the problems in their lives, and that there is a systematic way to approach these problems so that they can be better managed. The problem-solving process is designed to specifically address those goals in a highly explicit way by helping clients solve problems.

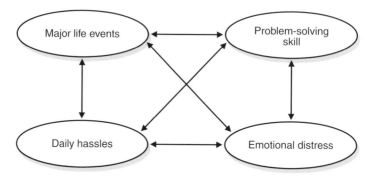

Figure 6.1   The Interactive Model of Negative Life Events, Problem Solving, and Depression

Two versions of PST exist, one that was developed for mental health settings (social PST; Nezu & Perri, 1989) and one for primary care settings (PST-primary care; Mynors-Wallis, 1996; Mynors-Wallis, Davies, Gray, & Barbour, 1997). The two models are alike in several ways, including the specific skills that are taught to clients and the theoretical underpinnings of the treatment. In both models, PST consists of seven steps. The first is *problem orientation,* which is concerned with how one views one's ability to cope with a problem. The second step is *problem definition,* which is concerned with the specific and concrete definition of the problem. The third step is *goal definition,* which concretely defines achievable outcomes. The fourth step, *generation of alternative solutions,* involves creative production of various methods for solving problems and meeting one's goals, while withholding judgment on their effectiveness. The fifth step, *decision making,* involves a systematic process to select the best solution for a problem from the list generated. The sixth step is *solution implementation,* which involves planning and initiation of solutions. The seventh and final step is *solution verification,* which involves evaluating the success of the solution and detailing what the client learned about the problem and his or her ability to solve problems by implementing the solution. Although not a final step in the problem-solving process, an important aspect of the therapy is engagement in *pleasant activities.* Because older clients will be focusing so much attention on solving problems, it is important to plan activities in the week that are not specifically related to solving problems. These can be considered mini-respites from struggling with daily hassles. PST-primary care and social PST differ only in their length and in the process by which the steps are taught. Social PST requires 10 to 12 sessions of treatment and presents each step over a series of visits. For instance, problem orientation is presented in the first session, problem definition in the second, and so forth (D'Zurilla & Nezu, 1999). PST-primary care is 6 to 8 sessions and presents all seven skills in the first session, using the remaining sessions to reinforce clients' use of the model (Hegel & Areán, 2004). Both versions have been studied in older depressed clients and have had positive results. The decision as to which to use depends largely on the setting in which treatment is delivered (primary care versus mental health) and cognitive features of the older client, which we discuss later.

SUPPORT FOR PROBLEM-SOLVING THERAPY IN OLDER ADULTS

Four empirical studies have evaluated the efficacy of PST in older depressed adults. The first study was conducted by Hussain and Lawrence (1981) on older nursing home patients. In this study, patients received either PST or supportive therapy. Patients who received PST showed fewer symptoms of depression after treatment than those who received the supportive care. The second study, conducted by Areán et al. (1993), compared PST to reminiscence therapy (RT), a treatment that at the time of the study was a common geriatric intervention. Although both interventions were superior to no treatment, PST resulted in far fewer symptoms and more remission of depression than RT. In 2002, Alexopoulos, Raue, and Areán published a randomized trial of PST compared to supportive therapy for major depression in older adults with executive dysfunction. Older clients with comorbid Major Depressive Disorder and executive dysfunction tend to have poor and unstable response to antidepressant medication (Alexopoulos et al., 2005). This study found that PST was superior to supportive therapy in treating depression and that depression outcome was mediated by acquisition of problem-solving skills related to executive impairments, specifically planning and initiation. Finally, data from the Hartford Foundation IMPACT study found that older primary care patients who received PST-primary care for depression had far better depression and functional outcomes than did older primary care patients who received community-based psychotherapy (Areán, Hegel, Vannoy, Unutzer, & Fan, 2006). Despite the presence of four trials, PST is still considered an emerging best practice for late life depression according to the Chambless and Hollon criteria (Mackin & Areán, 2005). All but one study was conducted by the same investigator, although two of those studies were multisite projects.

MODIFYING PROBLEM-SOLVING THERAPY FOR OLDER ADULTS

In the research just presented, PST for late life depression is very much like PST for depression in younger samples. There has been relatively little change in the content of PST. Most of the modifications are primarily related to *how* PST is presented. For instance, PST is a learning-based therapy, and because of its emphasis on acquiring new behavioral skills, the major process modifications made to PST take into account the typical age-related cognitive changes that affect learning and the common mild cognitive impairments that have been associated with late life depression (Lyketsos et al., 2005; see Chapter 4). The PST process is also modified to account for disability and for the number of socioeconomic issues many older depressed patients face. Problem-solving therapy is also modified to account for positive aspects of aging, such as greater experience in solving problems and reliance on a crystallized fund of information. We classify the modifications into cognitive modifications, system modifications, environmental modifications, and positive aging modifications.

Cognitive Modifications

As individuals age, the risk for developing cognitive difficulties increases (Buckner, 2004). One current theory of aging and depression specifies that age-related neurological changes may affect executive function abilities such as planning, organization, sequencing, and decision making. Typically, researchers refer to age ranges, starting at 65 and older as a particularly vulnerable period for expression of age-associated pathophysiological changes (Buckner, 2004). For example, studies demonstrate that older adults have more difficulty with the executive function tasks of shifting attention (Ridderinkhof, Span, & van der Molen, 2002), initiating and inhibiting their responses (Chao & Knight, 1997), and processing abstract concepts (Hartman, Nielsen, & Stratton, 2004) compared to younger adults. In older adults, these changes in executive function may influence the efficacy of psychosocial approaches that have been conducted in younger populations.

We have found that these changes, and deficits in some cases, can influence the success of PST. Problems with sequencing can influence some older clients' ability to organize stepped tasks such as problem solving. For these clients, the social PST model may be more helpful than the PST-primary care model, because the process is taught very slowly, in a stepwise fashion. Clients do not progress through the process until a step is mastered. For clients who have mild memory impairments, we find the PST-primary care process easier to manage. Social PST uses several forms that clients utilize to solve problems, whereas PST-primary care uses one form. Thus there are fewer papers to keep track of and the process is presented more clearly, with each step prompting the next on one form. In addition, presenting the steps at once and repeating the process over several meetings facilitate knowledge acquisition better than presenting new concepts each week.

Cognitive changes in knowledge acquisition can also influence each step in PST. The *problem orientation* phase, for instance, requires the ability to make abstractions regarding self-worth and its effect on solving problems. Some clients can grasp this concept easily; without concrete application, others struggle with learning that how one views one's ability to cope with a problem affects how one solves a problem. D'Zurilla and Nezu (1999) have found that in younger clients, mastery of the problem orientation phase is essential to the success of PST; however, in our practice, we have found that unless the client grasps this concept in the first and second session, focusing on this step will stall the therapeutic process. When we encounter difficulty with this step, we move on to the more behavioral steps, and when negative thinking begins to interfere with implementation, we use the in vivo experience to educate the client about how problem orientation works.

In the *problem definition* and *decision making* stages, the original forms developed by D'Zurilla and Nezu (1999) use a great deal of text and information. The amount of text tends to be overwhelming for older adults to navigate on their own because of sequencing problems or difficulties with organizing the information. For instance, in D'Zurilla and Nezu's model, solutions are evaluated in a grid with several criteria, such as short-term goals, long-term goals, societal impact, impact on others, and impact on self. We have simplified this form to include only three categories: meets goal, impact on others, is feasible.

Solution Implementation

Solution implementation involves additional executive function abilities such as planning and strategizing. This step can be more difficult for an older adult who already has age-related problems with planning and organization, in addition to initiation difficulties induced by depression. In this step, for clients with impairments in these areas, we often create plans that include environmental cuing, such as merging a step in the plan to an already planned event, like a meal or activity.

Memory complaints are one of the most common complaints among depressed elderly (Lyketsos et al., 2005). Memory impairment does not necessarily preclude the use of learning-based therapies. Environmental cuing is helpful for homework completion; a memory book in which the client and therapist record what they learned in the session that day can serve as a memory trigger for the problem-solving process; therapist-initiated telephone reminders can also serve as memory prompts for homework activities or use of the problem-solving process; in sessions, the use of "cue and review" techniques facilitate learning. This task, developed by Hegel and Areán (2004), organizes the therapy session in a way that promotes in-session recall of the new skill by first introducing the step, using the step two to three times in the session, and then reviewing the step after it has been implemented. Finally, tying the problem-solving process to past behavior can also facilitate skill acquisition. As an example, a client who had previously been struggling with the terms used in PST and hence was unable to implement the process began to better understand it when his therapist pointed out to him that the process was similar to the process he used as an engineer. Once he and the therapist established a common language for the problem-solving process, the client was better able to understand and implement it.

Socioeconomic Modifications

We encounter in our work many older clients who are depressed because of either health- or financial-related issues. At times, some of the problems raised, such as housing issues, caregiving issues, or poor response to medications, cannot be easily solved by the client alone. In these cases, we have added case management as a component to PST. Case management is a service that is typically provided by social work, nursing, and gerontology; it focuses on linking clients to needed services. The case manager and the client work together to identify problems, and the social worker then assists the client in finding and accessing appropriate services. This notion of problem solving being done by a third party is somewhat counterintuitive to a key principle of PST, that is, helping clients learn that they can solve problems themselves. However, the truth is that there are some problems older clients cannot solve on their own, and a knowledgeable person who is familiar with senior services can. In our research combining cognitive behavior therapy with case management in low-income elderly with depression, we found that the combination of the two interventions was superior in overcoming depression compared to each intervention alone (Areán et al., 2005). It should be noted here that in combining the two approaches (case management and PST), the therapist is responsible for both services, training in PST and case management services. The combined approach, therefore, requires a paradigm shift for many mental health specialists who are not familiar with or experienced in case management procedures. However, providing both services in one treatment facilitates treatment adherence and better coordination of care and reduces the time burden on the older client.

The process of combining PST with case management involves separating the list of problems into those that clients can focus on themselves and those that require the therapist's assistance. Thus, one list consists of problems that require case management services that the therapist provides, and the other list consists of problems the client has primary responsibility for solving. Therapists and clients use the problem-solving process for both problem lists. An advantage to the client is that the therapist models problem solving by showing the client how the process is employed in solving case management problems; in this way, the client learns the problem-solving approach by watching the therapist employ it for pressing problems.

Finally, encouraging participation in pleasant activities during the week can be complicated for low-income older clients on fixed incomes. Often when we think of doing something pleasant, we think of going to the movies, going out for coffee with friends, and other activities that have a financial cost. Even for middle-income older adults on fixed incomes, a night out at the movies can be more expensive than desirable. It is therefore important to help older clients on fixed or low incomes to consider activities that are free or low cost. Examples our clients have come up with are free museum Wednesdays, going to the library, listening to jazz on the radio, soaking in the bath, getting massages or facials at the cosmetic schools, working on the car, and playing with the grandkids.

Environmental Modifications

Many older adults have physical limitations that complicate regular attendance in therapy and the therapeutic process. Problem-solving therapy relies on the use of reading materials and forms, and thus clients with vision impairments are at a disadvantage. Rovner (submitted) has adapted PST for clients with macular degeneration by using aids such as tape recorders, Braille-based forms, and large dark print forms. Clients who have difficulty getting round or have many demands at home may find travel to therapy burdensome. We have often provided in-home PST to more frail patients, and a study of PST in the treatment of depression in home-bound elderly is under way by Ell and colleagues. Because older clients are learning new skills, continued and frequent sessions are necessary for reinforcement. Even mild illnesses can make regular attendance complicated and hence interfere with skill acquisition. Home visits and intermittent telephone contact to reinforce the newly learned material are helpful in this regard.

Positive Aging Modifications

Not all aspects of aging negatively influence the process of PST; thus, we would be remiss in neglecting to discuss the advantages age has in the PST process. The most obvious advantage older clients have in learning PST is a long history of solving problems, making mistakes, learning from them, and having had success with overcoming adversity. Even older clients with lifelong chronic depression have survived the illness and have developed strategies to manage their lives despite their depression. In teaching older clients PST, it is very important to point out that although the problem-solving structure that is imposed by the therapy is new to the client, the actual process of solving problems is not. Therefore, in participating in this therapy, clients are simply reactivating an existing skill, perhaps improving on it, and thus their past expertise in solving their problems is very helpful. Additionally, the use of reminiscence-type techniques can be very helpful for clients who are having trouble understanding the process or who are having trouble overcoming a particular problem. In the former instance, we often have older clients talk about their typical strategies for coping with problems throughout the life span; for instance, it is not uncommon to ask an older client how he or she solved work problems in the past, or how he or she overcame problems when going through other life transitions, such as going to a new school, starting a new job, or starting a family. In the latter instance, the same process can help an older client think through a particularly difficult problem; asking how similar problems in one's life were dealt with can help provide a fresh perspective on a vexing new problem.

Case Example: Helen, an Illustration of PST

PST Assessment

Based on the model of depression described by Nezu (1986; see Figure 6.1), there are several components contributing to Helen's depression. Helen experienced several *significant life changes,* including unemployment, becoming a primary caregiver for her parents, and moving away from friends and a familiar city. She also experiences numerous *daily hassles* that are related to these life changes: (a) difficulties with finances and dependency on her parents for financial support; (b) caregiving responsibilities for a mother with dementia and a depressed father, which may involve daily chores (such as managing their medical appointments and medication, shopping, and cooking); (c) managing psychiatric problems in both parents (mother's paranoia, father's depression) and other difficult behaviors from both parents; and (d) dealing with existential issues around changes in roles and changing relationships with her parents. The combination of these major life changes and daily hassles have contributed to her *depression symptoms* of hopelessness, fatigue, guilt, passive suicidal ideation, and cognitive complaints. Finally, assessment of current coping suggests both *poor coping skills* (e.g., overeating or just sitting in a chair for most of the day when depressed and feelings of being overwhelmed) and a negative problem orientation that she is unable to change her situation. This assessment indicates that Helen would benefit from a therapy focused on training in problem-solving-oriented coping skills.

Problem-Solving Therapy Strategy

There are several ways PST could be used for Helen given several factors: her age (65), her complaints (e.g., depression with cognitive complaints), and her issues (e.g., caregiving for parents). As is the case with older individuals, where health becomes more of an issue, it would be important to collaborate with Helen's psychiatrist because she is on an antidepressant and has a history of poor experience with lithium. It may be important to know when side effects from the medication may impact her ability to practice her assignments and to discuss other possible influences on her ability to engage in the treatment. Because she complains about concentration and decision-making difficulties, the skills would be presented in sequence over the course of five to six sessions, with another five to six sessions of guided practice. These cognitive problems are commonly seen in depression as well, but given her age, these complaints take on more significance and should be considered throughout her treatment. Finally, because of the increased demand on her time, the therapist would offer to do the therapy at home or in a convenient setting. If this is not acceptable, then scheduling sessions around respite care or other appointments may be necessary. If Helen has no respite care, the therapist should help her link to those services first.

The initial session would begin with an introduction of and education about depression and PST. A specific problem list would be generated. The possibility of case management to address the significant issues of accessing services for her mother and father would be discussed, and any problems that required case management intervention would be used as a demonstration of PST by the therapist. She would be asked to prioritize and order the problems on her list. It seems that there are two overall categories to Helen's situation, and so she may need to make two problem lists: one involving self-care and one specific to caregiving for her parents.

It would be important to separate out problems related to caregiving from difficulties she faces in her own self-care to help her develop a sense of mastery over her own issues. For many caregivers, caregiving easily becomes the most pressing priority, to the detriment of their own physical, mental, and emotional health (Schulz & Martire, 2004). Her needs must be raised as an important and separate issue from her parents', and the importance of attending to caregiving issues in the context of her own self-care should be discussed. However, the caregiving aspect of her situation may take initial priority because she consistently indicated feelings of hopelessness and of being overwhelmed in coping with her mother's dementia and her father's depression. Caregiving issues may also be at the forefront of her daily hassles and pull at her time and attention so that she feels she has even less control than over other problems (e.g., mother and father fighting). She also indicated negative problem-solving views and negative feelings toward her parents. These views

and feelings suggest that she would benefit from developing more effective problem-solving skills regarding caregiving and learning to
use her emotions to facilitate her ability to problem-solve. The next
sections use caregiving issues to provide more specific examples of
how PST might apply to Helen's situation.

Problem Orientation

Problem orientation will first be introduced. During this session
Helen will be encouraged to use her negative emotions to recognize
when there is a problem. However, separating out negative emotions
from her thoughts and behavior may be too abstract for her. What
is important is for her to be able to recognize when she is experiencing something that feels or seems difficult and to use this information as a signal that there is a problem to solve. It is possible that this
skill will continue to be difficult for her to acquire. Continuing
with the next skills may allow better understanding and facilitate
the problem-solving process for her because they will involve more
concrete applications.

In the next step, *problem definition*, she will learn how to define
her problems by gathering information, for example, "What are the
specific difficulties you face with your mother or father?" "What
makes these interactions difficult?" and "When do you feel particularly overwhelmed?" Although the therapist can introduce the use of
a general set of template questions involving who, what, where,
when, and why, for many older adults these questions may not be relevant and may even be confusing due to the amount of questions
written on the sheet. Simplifying this form and getting Helen to become curious about her problems by modeling a curious attitude and
encouraging her to be more concrete about her problems can be
helpful. A concrete problem definition might be "How to cope with
mother's (or father's) difficult behaviors." She would then be encouraged to identify some specific and concrete goals to work toward, such as learning more about dementia or how to manage
difficult behaviors. Helen would also need to learn to differentiate
between factual information and gut feelings. For instance, she may

feel that her mother is intentionally being difficult in certain situations. By having her learn more about dementia and the cause of repetitive or agitated behavior, Helen can set more realistic goals and minimize the emotionality of the situation.

Goal Setting

In the *goal setting* stage, Helen would be encouraged to review the aspects of her problem and to define a concrete and achievable goal. "Having my life back" is commonly a caregiver's first goal, often facetiously. So that Helen can develop a measurable outcome of her plan, the therapist should ask her what she misses in her life and how this particular problem gets in the way of her achieving this goal. Common examples we encounter include "More time to socialize with friends" and "One hour a day to do something for myself." These goals are far more concrete, measurable, and obtainable than "Having my life back."

Solution Generation

In *solution generation*, Helen may need additional help given her concentration difficulties. It may be necessary to refocus her on the specific problem and goal, because difficulties in concentration could lead to generating solutions that are unrelated to the problem and therefore not effective in solving it. The therapist could help her to generate possible solutions with more guided questions, such as "What would you like to see happen to help solve this problem?" and "What kind of advice would you give a friend to solve this problem?" Possible solutions may involve gaining better understanding of dementia by reading relevant literature and talking to a neurologist, attending support meetings for children of parents with dementia, and finding out about hiring a case manager or social worker. Important in this process is that she not reject solutions before they can be evaluated. Many depressed clients who are particularly negative struggle with this step because of the tendency to feel that no solution is helpful. It will be important for Helen to write down every solution that comes to mind, even some she has tried that did not work, so that a thorough evaluation of all her options can take place.

Decision Making

In the *decision-making* step, given Helen's negativity, it will be important for her to evaluate each solution by first focusing on its positive aspects. This strategy prevents her from rejecting solutions automatically. It is common for older clients to find one solution on the list that sounds like the ideal one and to stop the evaluation process then. We would encourage Helen to review the others, too, so that she can practice the process and also select a backup plan, should the solution she feels is best not work. A positive aspect of this step for Helen is that the decision-making process is externalized. She already complains of trouble with decisions, and that problem will be an issue here. Because the decision-making process allows for ranking solutions based on the number of positive ratings for each area on the grid (e.g., meets short-term goals, has no adverse impact on others, is feasible; total score 0 to 3), Helen can simply chose the solution with the best score.

Solution Implementation and Evaluation

When creating the steps necessary to implement and evaluate her plan, Helen may need the therapist to ask her for each step: "What do you need to do first? Second? . . ." In evaluating the solution, it is important for the therapist to help Helen review the success of the solution. Negative clients like Helen can have a tendency to report successes as "luck" or as a function of the therapist's help. Therapists working with Helen will need to reinforce that it was she who decided on the solution and implemented it, so the success is real.

At times solutions will not work. This is actually a very important lesson for clients: to not give up simply because the plan didn't work out. The therapist should help Helen review why the solution did not work and use the failure as an opportunity to learn more about her problem. For instance, a client with caregiver issues implemented a respite plan of having her brother-in-law stay with her demented mother for 30 minutes while the client went for a walk. The plan did not work because her mother became very agitated and broke several dishes by throwing them at the client's brother-in-law. Rather than taking this as a failure, the therapist asked the client to think about what she could learn from this situation. The client was able to recognize that her mother had done this a few times before when men were in her house. This led the client to modify the respite solution to finding a female family member to watch her mother.

Helen may experience difficulty with initiating the homework on her own given her tendency to become lethargic and overwhelmed when faced with problems. Her cognitive problems may also interfere with her ability to initiate and attend to her homework. In the early sessions, the therapist should work with her to set up a contingency plan, such as making sure she calls the therapist after completing her first homework assignment to discuss it.

Finally, Helen is socially isolated and is without support from her friends and appears to have very few, if any, positive activities. Several research studies suggest that increasing pleasant activities as part of an intervention plan may be helpful in alleviating depressed mood (Teri, Logsdon, Uomoto, & McCurry, 1997; Thompson, 1996). For many older adults, that one must put forth effort to incorporate pleasant activities into one's schedule is a foreign concept. Therefore, she may need strong encouragement to identify a pleasant activity to reward herself and to also incorporate these activities into her solution evaluation stage or whenever she completes a session or homework assignment. Identifying pleasant activities for herself would also serve to distinguish her needs from that of her parents' and address self-care needs.

CONCLUSION

Problem-solving therapy is a depression intervention with an emerging evidence base as a successful treatment for late life depression. It has been found to be successful in treating depression in older adults with mild cognitive impairments and physical disabilities and can be provided in nonspecialty settings. Special considerations in providing PST to older adults are important, such as altering the pace of treatment and making use of the fund of knowledge older clients bring to treatment. As noted in the case of Helen, PST can help clients who are facing several different social problems feel less overwhelmed by breaking problems down into doable and concrete steps, thus helping clients learn that slowing down and thoughtfully considering the problem and its solutions will yield better results.

It is important to note here that PST is a full treatment intervention; our anecdotal experience, from discussions with other colleagues, has shown that when added as an adjunct intervention to another treatment (e.g., Cognitive behavior therapy for anxiety, CBT for caregiver distress), the effect of PST is dampened. We suspect that our colleagues' findings are likely due to the fact that Problem-solving therapy was provided over a two-session period in conjunction with other mood regulation techniques. Problem-solving therapy can be learned over a brief period of time, but only when it is the sole focus of treatment. Therefore, although therapists may be tempted to use PST as part of a set of tools in treatment, they may be disappointed by the results.

It is also important to note that although PST is a relatively straightforward intervention, training by a PST expert is necessary, as implementation of the model in older depressed adults can be more complex than it appears. It is a common mistake to believe that being an expert in CBT automatically confers an expertise in PST. Providers who have a background in CBT do have an easier time acquiring the therapeutic skills in conducting PST (Hegel et al., 2004), but it is not a foregone conclusion that a CBT expert can automatically do PST. Fortunately, and under the generous auspices of the Hartford Foundation, Dartmouth University, and the University of California at San Francisco, training in PST is easily accessible to health and mental health professionals. All that is required is a 1-day workshop in PST and applying the technique to two to three training cases under telephone supervision by one of the many network experts in PST. After certification in PST, monthly, toll-free telephone supervision is available as needed. For more information, visit www.impact.ucla.edu and www.coped.ucsf.edu. To view sample PST sessions, visit www.impact.ucla.edu and click on the IMPACT resources tab.

REFERENCES

Alexopoulos, G. S., Katz, I. R., Reynolds, C. F., III, & Ross, R. W. (2001). Depression in older adults. *Journal of Psychiatric Practice, 7*(6), 441–446.

Alexopoulos, G. S., Kiosses, D. N., Heo, M., Murphy, C. F., Shanmugham, B., & Gunning-Dixon, F. (2005). Executive dysfunction and the course of geriatric depression. *Biological Psychiatry, 58*(3), 204–210.

Alexopoulos, G. S., Raue, P., & Areán, P. (2003). Problem-solving therapy versus supportive therapy in geriatric major depression with executive dysfunction. *American Journal of Geriatric Psychiatry, 11*(1), 46–52.

Areán, P. A., Gum, A., Bolstrom, A., McCulloch, C., Gallagher-Thompson, D. E., & Thompson, L. (2005). Treating depression in low-income elderly. *Psychology and Aging, 20*(4), 601–609.

Areán, P. A., Hegel, M. T., Vannoy, S., Unutzer, J., & Fan, M. Y. (2006). *PST compared to community psychotherapy for depression in older medical patients.* Manuscript submitted for publication.

Areán, P. A., Perri, M. G., Nezu, A. M., Schein, R. L., Christopher, F., & Joseph, T. (1993). Comparative effectiveness of social problem-solving therapy and reminiscence therapy as treatment for depression in older adults. *Journal of Consulting and Clinical Psychology, 61*(6), 1003–1010.

Buckner, R. L. (2004). Memory and executive function in aging and AD: Multiple factors that cause decline and reserve factors that compensate. *Neuron, 44*(1), 195–208.

Chao, L. L., & Knight, R. T. (1997). Prefrontal deficits in attention and inhibitory control with aging. *Cerebral Cortex, 7*(1), 63–69.

D'Zurilla, T. J., & Nezu, A. M. (1999). *Problem-solving therapy: A social competence approach to clinical intervention.* New York: Springer.

Hartman, M., Nielsen, C., & Stratton, B. (2004). The contributions of attention and working memory to age differences in concept identification. *Journal of Clinical and Experimental Neuropsychology, 26*(2), 227–245.

Hegel, M. T., & Areán, P. A. (2003). *Problem-Solving Therapy for Primary Care: A treatment manual for Project IMPACT.* Dartmouth University. www.impact.ucla.edu.

Hegel, M. T., Dietrich, A. J., Seville, J. L., & Jordan, C. B. (2004), Training residents in Problem-Solving Therapy: A pilot feasibility and impact study. *Family Medicine, 36*(3), 204–208.

Hussain, R. A., & Lawrence, P. S. (1981). Social reinforcement of activity and problem solving training in the treatment of depressed institutionalized elderly patients. *Cognitive Therapy and Research, 5*(1), 57–69.

Lyketsos, C. G., Toone, L., Tschanz, J., Rabins, P. V., Steinberg, M., Onyike, C. U., et al. (2005). Population-based study of medical comorbidity in early dementia and "cognitive impairment, no dementia (CIND)": Association with functional and cognitive impairment—The Cache County Study. *American Journal of Geriatric Psychiatry, 13*(8), 656–664.

Mackin, R. S., & Areán, P. A. (2005). Evidence-based psychotherapeutic interventions for geriatric depression. *Psychiatric Clinics of North America, 28*(4), 805–820.

Mynors-Wallis, L. (1996). Problem-solving treatment: Evidence for effectiveness and feasibility in primary care. *International Journal of Psychiatry in Medicine, 26*(3), 249–262.

Mynors-Wallis, L., Davies, I., Gray, A., & Barbour, F. (1997). A randomized controlled trial and cost analysis of problem-solving treatment for emotional disorders given by community nurses in primary care. *British Journal of Psychiatry, 170*(2), 113–119.

Mynors-Wallis, L. M., Gath, D. H., Day, A., & Baker, F. (2000). Randomized controlled trial of problem-solving treatment, antidepressant medication and combined treatment for major depression in primary care. *British Medical Journal, 320*(7226), 26–30.

Nezu, A. M. (1986). Efficacy of social problem-solving therapy approach for unipolar depression. *Journal of Consulting and Clinical Psychology, 54*(2), 196–202.

Nezu, A. M., & Perri, M. G. (1989). Social problem-solving therapy for unipolar depression: An initial dismantling investigation. *Journal of Consulting and Clinical Psychology, 57*(3), 408–413.

Ridderinkhof, K. R., Span, M. M., & van der Molen, M. W. (2002). Perseverative behavior and adaptive control in older adults: Performance monitoring, rule induction, and set shifting. *Brain and Cognition, 49*(3), 382–401.

Rovner, B. (submitted). Improving function in age-related macular degeneration. Unpublished manuscript.

Schulz, R., & Martire, L. M. (2004). Family caregiving of persons with dementia: Prevalence, health effects, and support strategies. *American Journal of Geriatric Psychiatry, 12*(3), 240–249.

Teri, L., Logsdon, R. G., Uomoto, J., & McCurry, S. M. (1997). Behavioral treatment of depression in dementia patients: A controlled clinical trial. *Journals of Gerontology: Series B, Psychological Sciences and Social Sciences, 52*(4), P159–P166.

Thompson, L. W. (1996). Cognitive-behavioral therapy and treatment for late-life depression. *Journal of Clinical Psychiatry, 57*(Suppl. 5), 29–37.

Afterword

BOB G. KNIGHT

The therapy systems described in Chapters 4 through 6 led to distinct approaches to Helen in several ways, perhaps most notably in how her problems were conceptualized and what additional information the authors sought out in order to work with her. Although each author focused on Helen's caregiving issues as a primary concern, problem-solving therapy (PST) led to a focus on how she approached caring for her parents and gathered information that identified flaws in her attempts to resolve the dilemmas that she faced. Problem-solving therapy also turned quickly to referrals for case management assistance. The cognitive-behavioral therapy (CBT) approach guided a focus on how she thought about her current problems and how her behavior maintained depression, with particular attention to self-nurturing and increasing pleasant activities in her life. Interpersonal psychotherapy (IPT) focused on current and past relationship history to identify aspects that led to her depression and emphasized increasing current social support as a way to alleviate depression.

Each approach then described its intervention plan differently. Cognitive behavioral therapy used the language of thoughts and behaviors, PST the language of problem-solving exercises, and IPT the language of relationships and patterns of relating to others. It is interesting to speculate how different the actual therapies would look. Early in my clinical experience, I had many opportunities to do cotherapy, often with very little notice or preparation. It always struck me how easily the other therapist and I could work together, even when we were from different disciplines and different theoretical perspectives. When I mentioned this to a frequent partner in these cotherapies (a clinical social worker who was quite psychodynamic), his response was that our written notes would look entirely different. As you compare these systems and think about your own clinical work with older adults, I urge you to consider whether the systems really lead to different interventions. For example, it struck me that all three mentioned increasing Helen's engagement in pleasant activities, an intervention most obviously grounded in Peter Lewinsohn's pleasant events theory for depression, a behavioral approach. To varying degrees, all three also suggested finding additional community resources to relieve her of some of the work of caregiving.

Each author took a somewhat different stance on the rationale for thinking about differences in work with older adults. Areán and Huh primarily expected older adults to need more support as they engaged in PST due to declines in executive function, a construct and an observation with roots in neuropsychology. They also discussed changes related to social class and environmental issues. Hinrichsen used my own contextual, cohort-based maturity/specific challenge (CCMSC) model to discuss an overview of potential changes, although he argued that IPT needs very little change for use with older adults as long as their problems fit the IPT model. Laidlaw used a model with some similarities to CCMSC but with a greater focus on role transitions and physical illness, and he brought the components of that model into the conceptualization of Helen's case, finding some differences but little need to modify techniques.

The authors' concepts of the limits of each system also differed. Problem-solving therapy can work with a variety of clients, with modifications to fit their individual needs, but would eventually be unusable as cognitive ability declines with dementia. Interpersonal psychotherapy is intrinsically limited to the set of problems leading to depression that it is designed to address and is described as not fitting anxiety disorders well. Cognitive behavioral therapy is modifiable and broad in its application; however, Laidlaw suggested that a client like Helen may want to follow up with a psychodynamic approach to deal with past history issues.

It is also of interest to consider what the authors did not address. Only Laidlaw discussed Helen's potential for suicide. Only Hinrichsen engaged specifically with the nature of her prior relationship with her parents. None of the three specifically addressed the history of hypo-manic episodes.

It intrigued me that all three viewed Helen as primarily a care-giver. The case example is adapted from the history of a client whom I saw many years ago (Knight, 1992). I have worked a great deal with caregivers, and I never categorized Helen as a caregiver in my thinking about her. Her severe depression, her history of cycling moods, and her suicide risk have always been much more salient in my thinking than her caring for her parents. In part, this difference was due to the clear history of recurrent depression prior to moving in with her parents.

To be fair to the authors, they were dealing with a case vignette and I recall the actual person. One could speculate, though, that we are all somewhat vulnerable to seeing older clients through age-related stereo-types, with caregiving as an example of an age-related schema for viewing older clients.

I also wonder whether the shared concern with getting Helen more active is more grounded in the activity theory of aging, a classic geron-tological theory that is part of the conventional wisdom about older adults: that older people need to be more active and more socially en-gaged to feel good. The activity theory has a lot of intuitive appeal, but research suggests a much more nuanced view. The person's individual history of engagement in activity and socializing must be considered, and the type of activity matters. For social involvement, it appears that informal contact (especially with a confidant) and quality of support are more beneficial than a simple increase in quantity of contact. Carstensen's socioemotional selectivity theory suggests patterns of de-creasing numbers of social contacts and maintenance of life satisfac-tion, again a more nuanced view than activity or disengagement.

The different approaches to this case example clearly illustrate the ways that theory guides us in thinking about working with older adults. The differences also seem to point to ways that we differ in our work with clients that are not guided by theory but by more personal styles of perceiving clients. Hopefully, the examples and these observations can evoke a similar reflection on your own approach to working with older clients.

In the following chapter, Scogin and Yon close this section by describing the research evidence base supporting these therapy systems as well as others that have been shown effective in working with older adult clients.

REFERENCE

Knight, B. (1992). *Older adults in psychotherapy: Case histories.* Newbury Park, CA: Sage.

Evidence-Based Psychological Treatment with Older Adults

FORREST SCOGIN AND ADRIANA YON

E vidence-based practice (EBP) has become a topic of increased emphasis across health care disciplines, including psychology (American
Psychological Association [APA], 2005). A fundamental aspect of EBP is
the use of well-researched, evidence-based treatments (EBTs). This chapter reviews several approaches to identifying EBTs for the psychological
treatment of geriatric depression. The earlier chapters in this section provide details about many of the EBTs highlighted in this chapter.

Efforts to identify psychological treatments with strong evidentiary
foundations have been under way for many years with increasing consensus on methods for defining standards of evidence and analysis of that evidence. As research on psychological treatments with older adults was
moving forward in the 1980s and 1990s, two complementary approaches
to summarizing literature were gaining popularity: meta-analysis, the
quantitative aggregation of studies on a given topic, and the categorical
approach to classifying treatments based on the extent of supporting research. The goal of such reviews is to lead practitioners to use evidence-
based approaches, provide consumers with information on treatment
choices, and direct investigators to areas with promise.

With the older adult population growing so rapidly, clinicians and researchers realized that they could not assume that older adults responded

to psychological treatment as favorably as did younger individuals. However, controlled research on the process and outcome of psychotherapy
with older adults, and therefore researchers' ability to quantify strength of
treatment, has had a fairly brief history. The first studies (with adequate
methodology) to display the efficacy of psychotherapeutic treatment for
older adults were conducted in the 1980s (Gallagher & Thompson, 1982;
Steuer et al., 1984). These studies had, as a primary goal, to establish that
elders would respond favorably to psychological interventions for depression, and the results were very promising. The quantity and quality of psychotherapy research with older adults continues to increase; however, it is
still not bountiful, and many important questions are unanswered. As a
consequence, evidence-based practice guidelines have come later to the
field of geropsychology because the number of studies needed to summarize areas was lacking.

In this chapter, we review the results of the two primary approaches to
summarizing the evidence base with respect to psychological treatments
for geriatric depression. We also present in greater detail what we consider
to be exemplary studies addressing depression in older adults and conclude
with some ideas about research, training, and policy issues worthy of further consideration.

THE EVIDENCE-BASED PRACTICE MOVEMENT

Many of the ideas infusing psychology's effort to advance EBP come
from parallel work being done in medicine, often called evidence-based
medicine (EBM), that arose in the United Kingdom, as exemplified by
the *Cochrane Reviews*. Few would argue with the general principle that
health care providers should be informed by current scientific information. However, some in psychology believe that such a focus could lead to
limits being placed by third-party payers on clinician choice in treatment delivery, such that only certain favored treatments would be allowed. Additional concerns frequently voiced were that reviews of the
evidence base relied too heavily on randomized controlled trials and a
feature of these trials, the manualized intervention. Partially in response
to these concerns, and with an effort to engage in self-determination,

the American Psychological Association established a policy defining EBP in psychology.

The approach taken by psychologists to EBP (APA, 2005) is based on three elements: the best available research evidence, clinician expertise, and an appreciation of patient characteristics, values, and context. The optimal outcome of this policy would be an integration and application of the scientific literature by a skilled provider mindful of what the patient wants and needs. The present chapter focuses on the first part of these three elements, the best available research evidence on the efficacy of psychological treatments for older adults.

META-ANALYSES WITH OLDER ADULTS

One approach to summarizing a field is meta-analysis. Smith, Glass, and Miller (1980) conducted the pioneering meta-analysis in the field of psychotherapy. They were able to conclude that the converging evidence was that psychotherapy in many forms had significant effects. Hundreds of other meta-analyses with similar results have followed (Lipsey & Wilson, 1993).

Effect sizes are presented in various summary statistics and have evolved over the years. This evolution makes comparison of effect sizes from different reviews somewhat complicated, but generally (and simply) speaking, the effect size is an effort to express the difference between a treatment and a control (or comparison treatment) in a standardized fashion. This often means expressing the difference in standard deviation units, such that an effect size of .75 suggests that the mean score of the treatment condition is ¾s of a standard deviation better off than the control condition mean. Such standardization allows studies with different measures to be aggregated and expressed as a summary statistic that is relatively easy to understand.

Reviewers of geriatric mental health treatments awaited the accumulation of a suitable number of studies before attempting to answer questions about the efficacy of psychotherapy conducted with older adults. One of the first attempts was in response to a conclusion by a 1991 National Institutes of Health Consensus Conference on Late-Life

Depression that was interpreted as downplaying the role of psychologically based treatments. The consensus document concluded that psychological treatments for older adults were "moderately effective" and were listed third as a treatment with pharmacotherapy and electroconvulsive therapy (National Institutes of Health, 1991). Scogin and McElreath (1994) used meta-analytic techniques to conclude that, regardless of the orientation, the effect size (d) for psychological treatment (versus no treatment or placebo) was .78 for depressive symptoms. Seventeen studies were included in this review, and cognitive-behavioral therapy (CBT) and reminiscence therapy (RT) fared especially well. This meta-analytic review came at a particularly opportune time and has been widely cited, partially as evidence contrasting the lukewarm summary of the 1991 consensus statement.

Several other meta-analyses of the older adult literature have followed, with results generally in accord with the 1994 review. These reviews have also explored more specific questions. For instance, Engels and Varney (1997) suggested that individual treatments for geriatric depression were more effective than group interventions ($d = .63$). Another review found that outreach programs offering treatment to depressed elders yielded an effect ($d = .77$) comparable to that observed with younger adult participants (Cuijpers, 1998). Pinquart and Sörensen (2001) found clinician-rated depression effects substantially larger than self-reported depression effects (1.03 vs. .43) and longer interventions (> 9 sessions) more effective than shorter.

These quantitative reviews suggest that the effects of psychotherapies for geriatric depression tend to be robust. The literature is relatively small in terms of number of investigations but marked by fairly strong methodology and resultant internal validity. However, many interesting practical and scientific questions are untapped in these reviews. For example, to what extent do cognitive limitations and physical frailty moderate effects? Can they be diminished through compensatory efforts such as making the delivery and implementation of treatments as simple as possible? What is the role of specialized training in the delivery of services to depressed older adults? How can effective treatments be made accessible to older adults?

CATEGORICAL REVIEWS WITH OLDER ADULTS

Another approach to identifying evidence-based treatments is less quantitative than the aforementioned meta-analytic approach. In this approach, treatments are categorized as evidence-based if a threshold of scientific support exists for their efficacy. Several acronyms have been used to identify this approach: empirically validated treatments (EVTs), empirically supported treatments (ESTs), and, more recently, evidence-based treatments (EBTs). According to the APA policy, EBTs are one of the elements of evidence-based practice, to be considered in concert with clinician expertise and client characteristics, values, and preferences. The identification of EBTs is based on the following premises: (a) Care can be enhanced by up-to-date empirical knowledge; (b) it is difficult for clinicians to keep up with newly emerging information; (c) if clinicians do not stay current, their performance will deteriorate; (d) clinicians need summaries of the expert reviews and the means to readily access this information; and (e) consumers need up-to-date information to aide in treatment selection (Chambless & Ollendick, 2001). These assertions seem logical and intuitive, but in the spirit of this chapter, it must be noted that they are not evidence-based.

Psychology's efforts to identify psychological EBTs were first undertaken by a committee convened by APA's Division 12 (Clinical Psychology). The Taskforce on Promotion and Dissemination of Psychological Procedures created criteria by which nominated treatments were judged to be sufficiently supported for endorsement as an EST. The criteria used are not reviewed here because they overlap substantially with those used by the older adult coding teamwork presented in some detail later in the chapter. Twenty-five treatments were identified (Chambless et al., 1996). The work of this initial task force did not focus on particular populations, such as children and older adults.

The first efforts to identify psychological EBTs in older adults made use of criteria developed by the Division 12 task force. Gatz and colleagues (1998) identified empirically validated treatments for depression, anxiety, sleep disorders, alcohol abuse, life review and reminiscence therapy, caregiver interventions, and behavioral problems in dementia. The criteria that Gatz et al. used allowed them to label treatments as "well-established" or "probably efficacious." Relevant to the present chapter, Gatz et al. found sufficient support for the following treatments: cognitive, behavioral, psychodynamic, and life review. Because these treatments also appear in the updated EBT list, we do not review them in detail here.

The Committee on Science and Practice of the Society for Clinical Psychology (also known as Division 12 of the APA) updated the criteria and procedures used by the original task force and created a 34-page coding manual for categorizing EBTs (Hawley & Weisz, 2001). The two-tiered system of "well-established" and "probably efficacious" was changed to a single category "evidence-based" to create a simpler system of communication and avoid largely unproductive discussions about whether a treatment was at one or the other level. The manual also attempted to avoid criticisms of the previous efforts by providing specific criteria with clear indicant definitions that must be met before labeling a treatment evidence-based. The criteria are specific; thus, results obtained from current reviews using the updated coding manual should be replicable by other groups using the coding procedures.

The current committee and subsequent review of the older adult literature was organized by the first author of this chapter and was formally sanctioned by Section 2 (Clinical Geropsychology) of the Society of Clinical Psychology. This committee was composed of review teams that addressed some of the most relevant areas in mental health and aging: anxiety, sleep, depression, memory and cognitive training, behavioral disturbance in dementia, and caregiver distress. The results of the depression review have been published (Scogin, Welsh, Hanson, Stump, & Coates, 2005) and are summarized here. The findings of the other review teams are slated for publication in 2006.

What follows is a brief overview of the procedures used by the depression review team in determining the evidence-based status of treatments. First, the review team became familiar with the Hawley and Weisz (2001) coding manual, after which they reviewed a series of "practice" articles. These articles were reviewed by all six teams to ensure that individuals in the teams and across the committee would obtain similar results if coding the same article.

Once reliability of the coding system was established, the next step was to identify relevant literature. Articles must have gone through the peer review process; therefore, the majority of the literature was found in professional journals. The team endeavored to identify articles reporting both evidence for and against treatments in question.

Several hundred studies were initially identified. From this large set, 116 were identified as potential evidence for psychological treatment, and after reviewing the abstracts a further 81 were eliminated because they were found to be epidemiological studies or reviews of the literature.

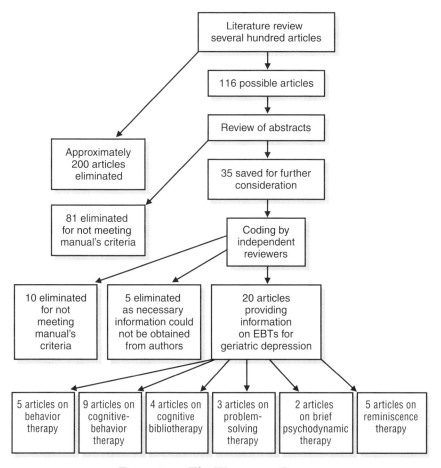

Figure 7.1   The Winnowing Process

The remaining 35 articles were further examined. This winnowing process is illustrated in Figure 7.1.

Reviewers coded each article based on the criteria outlined in the coding manual. Besides being peer-reviewed, several key points must have been met (Table 7.1). Both between-group (with prospective designs and random sampling) and within-group (or single-case designs) were acceptable, but a minimum of 30 participants having a mean age of 60 or over across studies (at least two studies) must have received the treatment in question. The treatment must have also been applied to individuals with the same target problem, in this case, depression; a target problem was not restricted to clinical diagnoses, so studies including participants with depressive symptoms were also included. The treatment must have been the same across studies, with "sameness" defined in the coding manual if the same treatment manual or protocol was used, or the authors reported it as being the same as that used in a separate treatment outcome study. If there was a question as to whether the treatment was the same, the reviewers were expected to review treatment manuals and/or contact the authors to determine the exact protocol followed. A summary of findings

Table 7.1   Criteria for Evidence-Based Treatments

1. At least two peer-reviewed between-group, within-group, single-case design studies (or a combination) with:
   a. Minimum of 30 subjects across studies
   b. Same age group
   c. Same treatment
   d. Same target problem
   e. Prospective design
   f. Random assignment
2. Treatment must be:
   a. Better than control or comparison condition
   b. Equivalent to an already established EBT
3. The majority of applicable studies must support the treatment.
4. The treatment procedures must show acceptable adherence to the treatment manual or drug protocol.

about procedures used was then presented to the entire review team, who voted on whether the treatments were the "same."

Results must also indicate that the treatment is either better than a control condition or comparable to an already established EBT. The coding manual explains that a treatment is considered better than a control condition when at least 50% of the outcome measures assessing the target problem display significant between-group treatment effects. Further, the majority (at least 51%) of the applicable studies must have supported the treatment, and those testing the treatment must have shown acceptable adherence to a clearly defined treatment manual or protocol. However, the treatment in question may be found comparable to an already established EBT if the comparison treatment is an EBT and the scores on 50% of the target problem outcome measures were found to have been non-significantly different from or better than the scores obtained by the comparison treatment group. More detail on the coding procedure is available in Scogin et al. (2005).

The 35 remaining articles identified by the depression review team were rated by at least two independent reviewers. Each reviewer decided whether the studies met criteria for being an EBT based on the manual. During this stage of the review, 10 of the 35 remaining articles were dismissed because one or more criteria were not met (e.g., no treatment protocol, nonrandom assignment). Five more studies were eliminated because necessary information critical to the coding decisions could not be obtained from study authors. Twenty articles remained to be fully coded and considered for evidence on various treatments.

The independent raters of the depression review team were found to be highly reliable. Most coding discrepancies were easily settled after a vote from at least 75% of the review team. For instance, the team was forced to decide whether to include in their review combination treatments containing both psychological and pharmacological components. Many well-known studies have investigated the effects of combination treatments for both acute (Beutler et al., 1987; Thompson, Coon, Gallagher-Thompson, Sommer, & Koin, 2001) and maintenance (Reynolds et al., 1999) effects. The team decided to exclude these due to the fact that the inclusion of pharmacological treatment components would make it difficult to determine the independent efficacy of the psychological treatment in question. Also, few of these studies use the same combination of psychological and pharmacological treatment, and so based on the coding manual could not be considered the "same treatment."

Results of our review suggest that there is a breadth of empirically supported treatment options for geriatric depression. The team was able to identify six different treatments meeting EBT criteria, though some clearly had more support than others. We provide some further information on these EBTs in the sections that follow.

Behavioral Therapy

Most behavioral therapy manuals were adapted from the work of Peter Lewinsohn and colleagues (Lewinsohn, 1974; Lewinsohn, Antonuccio, Breckenridge, & Teri, 1984). Behavioral theory holds that depression is a direct result of an imbalance of unpleasant and pleasant events in one's life. Therefore, participants completing a course of behavioral therapy for depression are asked to focus on the relationship between their mood and behavior. This is accomplished by participants monitoring both their pleasant and unpleasant activities and corresponding moods. Therapists serve as a coach and supporter as they aid the participants to identify, plan, and increase pleasant events as well as note fluctuations in mood.

Five studies were found to support behavioral therapy (Gallagher & Thompson, 1982; Lichtenberg, Kimbarow, Morris, & Vangel, 1996; Rokke, Tomhave, & Jocic, 1999; Teri, Logsdon, Uomoto, & McCurry, 1997; Thompson, Gallagher, & Breckenridge, 1987). Across studies, behavioral therapy was found to be superior to a control condition or as efficacious as another EBT (brief psychodynamic therapy and cognitive behavior therapy). There were no studies unsupportive of behavioral therapy as a treatment for geriatric depression.

Cognitive-Behavioral Therapy

Treatments in this well-researched area were primarily derived from the work of Beck and colleagues (Beck, Rush, Shaw, & Emery, 1979) and often used the treatment manual modified by Thompson, Gallagher-

Thompson, and Dick (1995) for use with older adults. The major premise of this approach is that thinking and cognitive activity influence emotions and that by identifying and altering maladaptive thinking patterns clients can experience depressive symptom reduction. Therapists use behavioral experiments and thought-monitoring techniques to help clients appreciate the links between cognition and emotion.

Seven studies were found supportive of CBT (Campbell, 1992; Floyd, Scogin, McKendree-Smith, Floyd, & Rokke, 2004; Fry, 1984; Gallagher & Thompson, 1982; Gallagher-Thompson & Steffen, 1994; Rokke et al., 1999; Thompson et al., 1987), with one study nonsupportive (DeBerry, Davis, & Reinhard, 1989). Cognitive-behavioral therapy was found to produce significantly greater effects than control conditions and was nonsignificantly different in effectiveness from other EBTs.

Cognitive Bibliotherapy

Cognitive bibliotherapy is self-administered CBT. All investigations coded used the self-help book *Feeling Good* (Burns, 1980) as the primary intervention, with minimal contact from a therapist or research assistant. The treatment was designed to be 4 weeks in duration and was self-paced.

Four studies were found supportive of cognitive bibliotherapy in comparison to control conditions (Floyd et al., 2004; Landreville & Bissonnette, 1997; Scogin, Hamblin, & Beutler, 1987; Scogin, Jamison, & Gochneaur, 1989). No studies were found nonsupportive of cognitive bibliotherapy.

Problem-Solving Therapy

Problem-solving therapy (PST) is based on the idea that clients can learn a problem-solving approach as an active, adaptive coping strategy. Clients apply this approach to problems they identify as contributing to their difficulties. The treatment manual most associated with this approach is that developed by Nezu and colleagues (Nezu, Nezu, & Perri, 1989).

Three studies were found supportive of PST (Alexopoulos, Raue, & Areán, 2003; Areán et al., 1993; Hussain & Lawrence, 1981). No studies were nonsupportive.

Brief Psychodynamic Therapy

Brief psychodynamic therapy (BPT) focuses on identifying conflicts and unresolved issues around dependence and independence, exploration of the therapeutic relationship, and facilitation of client insight. Studies investigating BPT used Horowitz and Kaltreider (1979) and Rose and DelMaestro (1990) to guide the intervention.

Two studies (Gallagher-Thompson & Steffen, 1994; Thompson et al., 1987) were found supportive of BPT. No studies were found nonsupportive.

Reminiscence Therapy

In RT, participants are asked to review their life histories and focus on the significant aspects of positive and negative life events. This review is designed to aid participants in gaining a better sense of perspective and accept both the successes and failures of their lives. Birren and Deutchman (1991) is an example of one of the RT manuals used.

Four studies provided support for RT (Areán et al., 1993; Goldwasser, Auerbach, & Harkins, 1987; Serrano, Latorre, Gatz, & Montanes, 2004; Watt & Cappeliez, 2000). One study (Klausner et al., 1998) was located that did not provide support for RT.

Conclusion

Thus, after reviewing the literature, using the criteria established by the Committee on Science and Practice, six psychological treatments for geriatric depression were found to be EBTs. In previous presentations of these data questions were raised as to whether there should really be six; specifically, the question has been raised as to whether cognitive bibliotherapy should be counted as separate from CBT and whether brief psychodynamic treatment has sufficient support given that only one investigative team has done both supporting studies. Regardless of these questions, the fact that there are several viable treatment options is encouraging and suggests that dissemination of this information to health care providers, consumers, and policy makers should be a high priority.

Persons familiar with the depression treatment literature may be surprised that interpersonal psychotherapy (IPT) was not included in the list of EBTs. Interpersonal psychotherapy has received empirical support as maintenance treatment for geriatric depression, that is, as an intervention to prevent relapse or recurrence of depressive episodes (Reynolds et al., 1999). But it has not received sufficient support as an isolated psychological treatment for acute depression to meet the criteria used in the Hawley and Weisz (2001) manual.

IDENTIFYING EVIDENCE-BASED TREATMENTS

There have been few recent topics in clinical and counseling psychology that have created greater controversy than the identification of EBTs. We alluded to a few of the concerns in the introductory paragraphs of the chapter, but here we broach additional concerns against the backdrop of the EBTs just listed. In our estimation, a very legitimate criticism is that EBTs give undue weight to brand names and do not address active ingredients. Put differently, what is it about CBT, for example, that leads to reductions in depressive symptoms? Some would argue that it is the common factors, or those elements shared by all psychological treatments, that carry the preponderance of the effects (Garfield, 1973). Nonetheless, having several treatments with an evidentiary foundation provides choices for providers and consumers in terms of preferences even though in an overall sense the treatments may be more alike than different in terms of process and outcome. Other task force efforts have examined evidence-based change principles and evidence-based relationship factors and found that the literature on aging is not sufficiently rich for these important questions. Further discussion of issues related to the development and future of psychotherapy for older adults is contained in Norcross and Knight (2000) and Knight (2004).

A corollary to the brand name concern is that identified EBTs will assume such favored status that development of innovative approaches might be discouraged—an unfortunate by-product of this effort.

EXEMPLARY STUDIES OF
GERIATRIC DEPRESSION

Meta-analytic and categorical reviews are popular methods for summarizing the status of a field. A complementary method is to review in more detail studies that represent some of the best work done in the field. In this section, we present overviews of three studies we consider exemplary.

Thompson et al. (2001)

This investigation tested the scientifically and practically important question of whether combining a psychological intervention (CBT) and a pharmacological intervention (desipramine) yielded better outcomes than the treatments provided singly. Intuitively, combining two efficacious treatments should produce superior outcomes. Thompson et al. (2001) enrolled 102 older adults meeting criteria for major depression into one of the three treatments. The CBT was delivered based on the manual developed by this research group that has become a standard in the field. All treatment conditions resulted in significant and substantial improvement in depressive symptoms. For most of the analyses, the combined treatment produced greater improvement than desipramine alone. The CBT alone and combined treatment produced similar improvements, but the CBT alone was equivalent to and on some occasions superior to desipramine alone. Of particular importance, the combined treatment was most effective with more severely depressed older adults. These data make a powerful case for the inclusion of a psychologically based EBT in the treatment of geriatric depression.

Unutzer et al. (2002)

This study represents probably the strongest test of the collaborative care model of geriatric depression treatment. Collaborative care is based on a multidisciplinary approach provided in primary care settings. In this instance, primary care physicians, psychiatrists, and a depression care manager formed the collaboration team. A total of 1,801 older adult participants were randomized to collaborative care or to usual care across 18 primary care clinics. Those receiving collaborative care (known by the acronym IMPACT) were offered the choice of either antidepressant medication or problem-solving treatment in primary care (PST-PC), a 6- to 8-week-session version of PST, delivered by the depression care specialist. Fifty-one percent of the patients expressed an initial preference for the psychological intervention.

IMPACT followed a stepped care model whereby patients received augmented or alternative treatments if sufficient response was not achieved by the existing intervention. Results suggested that collaborative care resulted in decreased depression severity scores and decreased depression diagnoses compared to the usual care control condition. This study has significant implications for geriatric depression treatment as it suggests that an interdisciplinary approach may be optimal and that many older adults are favorably disposed toward psychological interventions.

Ciechanowski et al. (2004)

Another recent investigation of geriatric depression treatment examined the efficacy of a home-based intervention program (Ciechanowski et al., 2004). The core treatment was an eclectic blend of problem-solving therapy, social and physical activation, and recommendations for antidepressant medication where indicated. This program was compared to usual care in a randomized trial method. The participants were experiencing minor depression or dysthymia and evidenced significant medical comorbidity. Participants receiving the enhanced care were significantly more likely to experience substantial reductions in depressive symptoms and to report improved quality of life and emotional well-being. This integrated program, like the IMPACT intervention, suggests the utility of combined intervention approaches for geriatric depression.

CONCLUSION

Our review of the literature leads us to the conclusion that there is a fairly broad but not deep evidence base for psychological interventions for depressed elders. By this we mean there are a number of approaches that appear to have sufficient support for evidence-based status but few that have the kind of replication that marks the maturity of a field. Also, the studies that have been conducted to date have primarily occurred in academic settings with higher resource participants. We do not know how well many of these interventions would fare with those with low literacy, cognitive limitations, and physical frailty, who represent the most challenging candidates for psychologically based geriatric depression treatments. Nonetheless, the results of our review (and those conducted by others) encourage us to inform stakeholders (consumers, providers, and payers) that there are some effective and attractive mental health options for depressed older adults. This statement could not have been made 15 years ago as at that time there were not a sufficient number of studies available to make this assertion. There are still those who would contend that extant studies of psychological treatments have such methodological flaws (e.g., lack of comparison to double-blind pharmacotherapy conditions) that solid conclusions as to efficacy cannot be reached, but these criticisms seem to have diminished in recent years as more, otherwise well-controlled studies have accrued.

Identifying EBTs in the field of psychology becomes imperative as the American Psychological Association continues to encourage efforts to include evidence-based treatments in practice. The belief is that if psychology as a discipline does not identify such treatments, someone else will. Identifying treatments with empirical support is the first step in providing evidence-based care. Not only must the treatment's merit be considered, but clinicians' expertise and clients' values and preferences should be taken into account as well. Identifying such treatments can propel future research and education. And, once educated about such treatments, practitioners will have a wide variety of solid treatments to offer their clients, so patient choice can be taken into account.

In the movement toward evidence-based practices, further research must be conducted. For instance, a more thorough look at client variables (e.g., medical comorbidity, cognitive functioning, resource level) would aid in determining which treatments work for particular groups. Just as it is unsafe to assume that older adults respond similarly to psychological treatments as younger adults, it is unsafe to assume that all older adult clients will respond in the same way. As we noted earlier, the evidence base is broad but not deep, thus studies that extend EBTs to different populations and settings will enrich the efficacy profile.

REFERENCES

Alexopoulos, G., Raue, P., & Areán, P. (2003). Problem solving therapy versus supportive therapy in geriatric major depression with executive dysfunction. *American Journal of Geriatric Psychiatry, 11,* 46–52.

American Psychological Association. (2005). *Report of the 2005 Presidential Task Force on Evidence-Based Practice*. Retrieved July 14, 2006, from http://www.apa.org/practice/ebpstatement.pdf.

Areán, P. A., Perri, M. G., Nezu, A. M., Schein, R. L., Christopher, F., & Joseph, T. X. (1993). Comparative effectiveness of social problem-solving therapy and reminiscence therapy as treatments for depression in older adults. *Journal of Consulting and Clinical Psychology, 61*, 1003–1010.

Beck, A. T., Rush, J., Shaw, B., & Emery, G. (1979). *Cognitive therapy of depression*. New York: Guilford Press.

Beutler, L., Scogin, F., Kirkish, P., Schretlen, D., Corbishley, A., Hamblin, D., et al. (1987). Group cognitive therapy and alprazolam in the treatment of depression in older adults. *Journal of Consulting and Clinical Psychology, 55*, 550–556.

Birren, J. E., & Deutchman, D. E. (1991). *Guiding autobiography groups for older adults*. Baltimore: Johns Hopkins University Press.

Burns, D. (1980). *Feeling good*. New York: Signet.

Campbell, J. M. (1992). Treating depression in well older adults: Use of diaries in cognitive therapy. *Issues in Mental Health Nursing, 13*, 19–29.

Chambless, D. L., & Ollendick, T. H. (2001). Empirically supported psychological interventions: Controversies and evidence. *Annual Review of Psychology, 52*, 685–716.

Chambless, D. L., Sanderson, W. C., Shoham, V., Bennett Johnson, S., Pope, K. S., Crits-Cristoph, P., et al. (1996). An update on empirically validated therapies. *Clinical Psychologist, 49*, 5–18.

Ciechanowski, P., Wagner, E., Schmaling, K., Schwartz, S., Williams, B., Diehr, P., et al. (2004). Community-integrated home-based depression treatment in older adults. *Journal of the American Medical Association, 291*, 1626–1628.

Cuijpers, P. (1998). Psychological outreach programmes for the depressed elderly: A meta-analysis of effects and dropouts. *International Journal of Geriatric Psychiatry, 13*, 41–48.

DeBerry, S., Davis, S., & Reinhard, K. E. (1989). A comparison of meditation-relaxation and cognitive behavioral techniques for reducing anxiety and depression in a geriatric population. *Journal of Geriatric Psychiatry, 22*, 231–247.

Engels, G. I., & Varney, M. (1997). Efficacy of non-medical treatments of depression in elders: A quantitative analysis. *Journal of Clinical Geropsychology, 3*, 17–35.

Floyd, M., Scogin, F., McKendree-Smith, N. L., Floyd, D. L., & Rokke, P. D. (2004). Cognitive therapy for depression: A comparison of individual psychotherapy and bibliotherapy for depressed older adults. *Behavior Modification, 28,* 297–318.

Fry, P. S. (1984). Cognitive training and cognitive-behavioral variables in the treatment of depression in the elderly. *Clinical Gerontologist, 3,* 25–45.

Gallagher, D. E., & Thompson, L. W. (1982). Treatment of major depressive disorder in older adult outpatients with brief psychotherapies. *Psychotherapy: Theory, Research, and Practice, 19,* 482–489.

Gallagher-Thompson, D. E., & Steffen, A. M. (1994). Comparative effects of cognitive-behavioral and brief psychodynamic psychotherapies for depressed family caregivers. *Journal of Consulting and Clinical Psychology, 62,* 543–549.

Garfield, S. L. (1973). Basic ingredients or common factors in psychotherapy? *Journal of Consulting and Clinical Psychology, 41,* 9–12.

Gatz, M., Fiske, A., Fox, L. S., Kaskie, B., Kasl-Godley, J. E., McCallum, T. J., et al. (1998). Empirically validated psychological treatments for older adults. *Journal of Mental Health and Aging, 4,* 9–46.

Goldwasser, A. N., Auerbach, S. M., & Harkins, S. W. (1987). Cognitive, affective, and behavioral effects of reminiscence group therapy on demented elderly. *International Journal on Aging and Human Development, 25,* 209–222.

Hawley, K. M., & Weisz, J. R. (2001). *Procedural and coding manual for identification of evidence-based treatments.* Unpublished manual, University of California at Los Angeles.

Horowitz, M., & Kaltreider, N. (1979). Brief therapy of the stress response syndrome. *Psychiatric Clinics of North America, 2,* 365–377.

Hussain, R. A., & Lawrence, P. S. (1981). Social reinforcement of activity and problem-solving training in the treatment of depressed institutionalized elderly patients. *Cognitive Therapy and Research, 5,* 57–69.

Klausner, E. J., Clarkin, J. F., Spielman, L., Pupo, C., Abrams, R., & Alexopoulos, A. (1998). Late-life depression and functional disability: The role of goal-focused group psychotherapy. *International Journal of Geriatric Psychiatry, 13,* 707–716.

Knight, B. G. (2004). *Psychotherapy with older adults* (3rd ed.). Thousand Oaks, CA: Sage.

Landreville, P., & Bissonnette, L. (1997). Effects of cognitive bibliotherapy for depressed older adults with a disability. *Clinical Gerontologist, 17,* 35–55.

Lewinsohn, P. (1974). A behavioral approach to depression. In R. Friedman & M. Katz (Eds.), *The psychology of depression: Contemporary theory and research* (pp. 157–176). New York: Wiley.

Lewinsohn, P. M., Antonuccio, D. C., Breckenridge, J. S., & Teri, L. (1984). *The coping with depression course.* Eugene, OR: Castalia.

Lichtenberg, P. A., Kimbarow, M. L., Morris, P., & Vangel, S. J. (1996). Behavioral treatment of depression in predominately African-American medical patients. *Clinical Gerontologist, 17,* 15–33.

Lipsey, M. W., & Wilson, D. B. (1993). The efficacy of psychological, educational, and behavioral treatment: Confirmation from meta-analysis. *American Psychologist, 48,* 1181–1209.

National Institutes of Health. (1991). *Diagnosis and treatment of depression in late life* (Vol. 9, No. 3). Bethesda, MD: National Library of Medicine.

Nezu, A. M., Nezu, C. M., & Perri, M. G. (1989). *Problem solving therapy for depression: Theory, research, and clinical guidelines.* Chichester, West Sussex, England: Wiley.

Norcross, J. G., & Knight, B. G. (2000). Psychotherapy and aging in the 21st century: Integrative themes. In S. H. Qualls & N. Abeles (Eds.), *Psychology and the aging revolution* (pp. 259–286). Washington, DC: American Psychological Association.

Pinquart, M., & Sörensen, S. (2001). How effective are psychotherapeutic and other psychosocial interventions with older adults? A meta-analysis. *Journal of Mental Health and Aging, 7,* 207–243.

Reynolds, C. F., Frank, E., Perel, J. M., Imber, S. D., Cornes, C., Miller, M. D., et al. (1999). Nortriptyline and interpersonal psychotherapy as maintenance therapies for recurrent major depression: A randomized controlled trial in patients older than 59 years. *Journal of the American Medical Association, 281,* 39–45.

Rokke, P. D., Tomhave, J. A., & Jocic, Z. (1999). The role of client choice and target selection in self-management therapy for depression in older adults. *Psychology and Aging, 14,* 155–169.

Rose, J., & DelMaestro, S. (1990). Separation-individuation conflict as a model for understanding distressed caregivers: Psychodynamic and cognitive case studies. *Gerontologist, 30,* 693–697.

Scogin, F., Hamblin, D., & Beutler, L. (1987). Bibliotherapy for depressed older adults: A self-help alternative. *Gerontologist, 27,* 383–387.

Scogin, F., Jamison, C., & Gochneaur, K. (1989). Comparative efficacy of cognitive and behavioral bibliotherapy for mildly and moderately depressed older adults. *Journal of Consulting and Clinical Psychology, 57,* 403–407.

Scogin, F., & McElreath, L. (1994). Efficacy of psychosocial treatments for geriatric depression: A quantitative review. *Journal of Consulting and Clinical Psychology, 62,* 69–74.

Scogin, F., Welsh, D., Hanson, A., Stump, J., & Coates, A. (2005). Evidence-based psychotherapies for depression in older adults. *Clinical Psychology: Science and Practice, 12,* 222–237.

Serrano, J. P., Latorre, J. M., Gatz, M., & Montanes, J. (2004). Life review therapy using autobiographical retrieval practice for older adults with depressive symptomatology. *Psychology and Aging, 19,* 272–277.

Smith, M. L., Glass, G. V., & Miller, T. I. (1980). *The benefits of psychotherapy.* Baltimore: Johns Hopkins University Press.

Steuer, J. L., Mintz, J., Hammen, C. L., Hill, M. A., Jarvik, L. F., McCarley, T., et al. (1984). Cognitive-behavioral and psychodynamic group psychotherapy in treatment of geriatric depression. *Journal of Consulting and Clinical Psychology, 52,* 180–189.

Teri, L., Logsdon, R., Uomoto, J., & McCurry, S. (1997). Behavioral treatment of depression in dementia parents: A controlled clinical trial. *Journal of Gerontology: Series B, Psychological Sciences and Social Sciences, 52,* P159–P166.

Thompson, L. W., Coon, D. W., Gallagher-Thompson, D., Sommer, B. R., & Koin, D. (2001). Comparison of desipramine and cognitive/behavioral therapy in the treatment of elderly outpatients with mild-to-moderate depression. *American Journal of Geriatric Psychiatry, 9,* 225–240.

Thompson, L. W., Gallagher, D., & Breckenridge, J. S. (1987). Comparative effectiveness of psychotherapies for depressed elders. *Journal of Consulting and Clinical Psychology, 55,* 385–390.

Thompson, L. W., Gallagher-Thompson, D., & Dick, L. P. (1995). *Cognitive-behavioral therapy for late life depression: A therapist manual.* Palo Alto, CA: Older Adult and Family Center, Veterans Affairs Palo Alto Health Care System.

Unutzer, J., Katon, W., Callahan, C. M., Williams, J. W., Hunkeler, E., Harpole, L., et al. (2002). Collaborative care management of late-life depression in the primary care setting: A randomized controlled trial. *Journal of the American Medical Association, 288,* 2836–2845.

Watt, L. M., & Cappeliez, P. (2000). Integrative and instrumental reminiscence therapies for depression in older adults: Intervention strategies and treatment effectiveness. *Aging and Mental Health, 4,* 166–177.

PART

III

⟹∙◆∙⟸

The Contexts of Geropsychology Practice

SARA H. QUALLS

The theme of this part of the book is practical application of psychotherapy for depressed older adults. Therapists new to work with older adults are often most daunted by assessing and treating depression. What do you need to know to make a geropsychology practice work in the real world? The authors in this section were asked to address particular contexts of practice for clinicians new to working with aging clients. Three key themes we wanted to address are the effects of cultural diversity on psychotherapy for depression, specific issues that arise in residential long-term care settings, and the business contexts of practice.

Variations in depression treatment for diverse cultural groups are reviewed by Crowther, Robinson Shurgot, Perkins, and Rodriguez in Chapter 8. Initially, they challenge the reader about existing definitions of race and culture. The limitations of existing categories affect our efforts to apply research to practice and can confuse therapists about discrepancies between the categories they use for clients and the clients' self-defined cultural identities. This chapter reviews the literature on how different cultural groups conceptualize depression and psychotherapy, as well as variations in structures for social relationships in later life. In line with the focus of this book on practical suggestions for therapists, the authors apply this knowledge to practical guidance for psychotherapists.

Among the distinctive aspects of work with older populations, probably none is as daunting to practitioners as work in residential long-term care environments. In her chapter, Frazer walks the reader through the distinctions among residential environments, with practical guidance for adapting psychotherapy to each setting. She applies an ecological framework to depression in particular residential environments. This chapter analyzes the ways regulatory policies in particular long-term care settings impact psychological services. This chapter is a must reading for any therapist beginning work in assisted living or nursing homes.

Hartman-Stein describes the business and organizational aspects of psychotherapy practice with older adults by offering the reader detailed guidance for doing business with Medicare. Practitioners often project their worst fears about legal and financial disasters onto the Medicare system. In her chapter, Hartman-Stein provides clear information on operating a practice with older adults that complies with the regulatory and ethical demands of Medicare policy. Assuming you can stay safe within Medicare policy, how do you actually build your aging client base? Again, Hartman-Stein offers practical information and guidance about positioning your practice to grow based on service access patterns and attitudes of the current cohort of older adults.

The old adage "the devil is in the details" can be as true with psychotherapy practice with older adults as with any other professional pursuit. The chapters in this section propel you toward clarity about which details warrant your focus, and offer some highly useful strategies to succeed in managing details in this highly complex area of practice.

8

The Social and Cultural Context of Psychotherapy with Older Adults

MARTHA R. CROWTHER, GIA ROBINSON SHURGOT,
MARTINIQUE PERKINS, AND RACHEL RODRIGUEZ

The population of the United States is growing older and becoming more ethnically diverse. According to Census Bureau projections, the number of persons age 65 and older will increase from 35 million in the year 2000, to 66 million by 2030, and to 82 million by 2050, a figure accounting for 20.3% of the entire population (U.S. Bureau of the Census, 2000). This "gerontological explosion" will also occur across groups of minority elders, whose respective population sizes will nearly double by 2050 (U.S. Bureau of the Census, 2000). These two demographic trends highlight the increasing diversity of our aging population, a group that defies simple characterization by encompassing divergent historical, social, and cultural experiences.

Several recent reports also denote the importance of race, ethnicity, and culture in mental health research and practice, including *Mental Health: Culture, Race, and Ethnicity—A Supplement to Mental Health: A Report of the Surgeon General* (U.S. Department of Health and Human Services, 2001), the American Psychological Association's (APA, 2004) "Guidelines for Psychological Practice with Older Adults," and APA's

(2003) "Guidelines on Multicultural Education, Training, Research, Practice, and Organizational Change for Psychologists." Hence, the challenge for geropsychologists lies in exploring and considering the diverse sociocultural context of older adults in their clinical work, which includes issues of ethnicity, culture, gender, income/education, rural settings, sexual orientation, and disability.

This chapter provides an overview of the diverse sociocultural context of psychotherapy with older adults, some general considerations when conducting clinical work with diverse elders, and recommendations for future readings. Given the need to cover such a broad array of sociocultural topics, we have divided the chapter into two sections. The first section focuses on ethnic minority elders and the second addresses other populations that should be considered when addressing the social and cultural context of psychotherapy with older adults.

DEFINING RACE, ETHNICITY, CULTURE, AND MINORITY STATUS

Prior to describing issues concerning ethnicity, race, culture, and minority status, we define these terms because they are often, and erroneously, used interchangeably. *Race* is generally defined in terms of biological and genetically transmitted physical characteristics of individuals; for others, it is a social construct that denotes particular experiences shared by many individuals who belong to a category called race (Gould, 1997). Racial categories in the United States include White (people of European, Arab, and Central Asian origin), Black (people of African origin), Native American (people of American Indian, Eskimo, and Aleut origin), Asian (people of East Asia and Pacific Islander origin), and Hispanic (people of South and Central American origin). Although these racial categories are often used, distinctions among races are arbitrary and dubious at best (Zuckerman, 1990). Furthermore, racial groupings do not provide information about the specific factors accounting for psychological differences observed between groups (Zuckerman, 1990). Hence, race alone is of little value in clinical practice and research.

Ethnicity, another term often used loosely with race and culture, describes groups of individuals who share a common nationality, geographic origin, culture, or language (Betancourt & Lopez, 1993). Ethnic categories include Caucasian, African American, Asian and Pacific Islander, Latino, and Native American. As with race, ethnicity is used to categorize individuals into homogeneous groups and to attribute psychological differences to culture based on group membership. But without identifying and assessing cultural factors, ethnicity has limited utility in explaining psychological differences between groups (Betancourt & Lopez, 1993). As an example, the term Native American includes individuals from 300 different tribes and languages; this term might be helpful in lumping individuals into one homogeneous group but does little to explain the cultural heterogeneity found within a specific ethnic group. Hence, as with race, the term ethnicity alone has limited practical utility.

Culture is often used in conjunction with race and ethnicity due in part to the lack of a universal definition of culture. Generally, culture is considered a dynamic system of rules (explicit and implicit) that is established by groups to ensure their survival. It involves attitudes, values, beliefs, norms, and behaviors that are shared by a group of people and that are communicated across generations (Matsumoto & Juang, 2004). Culture comprises what individuals have learned from experiences in the environment, interactions with other individuals, and the impact of those experiences (Morales, 1999). Mental health is shaped by culture. Specifically, culture impacts the manner in which individuals communicate and report their symptoms, the meanings they attribute to their symptoms, how they cope with their symptoms, whether they seek mental health care, what type of care they seek, and how they go about seeking care (U.S. Department of Health and Human Services, 2001). Hence, culture helps explain psychological differences among ethnic groups and is a more useful term in clinical practice.

Another term often used interchangeably with race, ethnicity, and culture is *minority status*. Minority status refers to groups that share a history of being denied access to resources and privileges in terms of economic opportunity, communicative self-representation (the right to self-identify or to refer to oneself in self-chosen or preferred terms), or preferred cultural lifestyle (Foucault, 1986; Habermas, 1987). For instance, Jim Crow laws denied African Americans the right to vote, get an education, and advance economically and forced them to live in segregated areas. African Americans were also denied communicative self-representation by being called names like "Negro" and "boy" until the civil rights movement and legislation of the 1960s (Mpofu & Conyers, 2004). Native American children were forced to attend boarding schools created by the government and religious groups with the goal of replacing the practice of Native American language, dress, beliefs, and religions with the lifestyle of White civilization and assimilation into the majority culture (Morales, 1999). Latino children were punished for using Spanish in public schools in order to force them to learn English (Sowell, 1981). Japanese Americans were placed in internment camps during World War II. This history of being denied access to resources and privileges has shaped the life experiences and beliefs of ethnically diverse older adults and explains differences among ethnic minority elders in their use of ethnic labels to describe themselves (i.e., identifying as Black as opposed to African American). The history of racism and discrimination also accounts for the mistrust of government, medical, and social service institutions among ethnic minorities, which in turn is a major barrier to receiving mental health treatment (U.S. Department of Health and Human Services, 2001). Consequently, in addition to culture, minority status is an important issue to explore in clinical practice with diverse elderly.

THE ROLE OF CULTURE

Now that the definitions and relevance of race, ethnicity, culture, and minority status have been described, we turn to a discussion of the role of culture because it is a key concept that shapes the mental health of individuals and explains psychological differences among ethnic groups. Several publications have described cultural issues to consider and adapt in the psychological assessment and treatment of ethnic minority adult populations (Council of National Psychological Associations for the Advancement of Ethnic Minority Interests, 2003; Herring, 1999; Paniagua, 1998; Sue & Sue, 1999). However, culturally diverse older adults differ from younger adults as a result of greater institutional policies of racism and discrimination experienced in their lifetime; elders rely to a greater extent on their minority segregated communities, their cultural values, their traditional language, and their kinship systems than do younger adults (Morales, 1999). In this section, we describe how culture influences psychotherapy generally and pinpoint some cultural issues more relevant to older adults.

Shared Cultural Values among Ethnic Minorities

In addition to family and extended kinship networks, African, Latino, Asian, and Native Americans share similar cultural values, such as familism, a concept of time, and time needed to establish trust with the psychotherapist. Familism refers to strong feelings of loyalty, reciprocity, and solidarity among members of the same family (Sabogal, Marin, Otero-Sabogal, Marin, & Perez-Stable, 1987). Familism values are higher among ethnic minority family caregivers compared to Whites (Knight et al., 2002). Familism values imply that emotional problems should be handled within the family, and the elder's care should remain with the family. Familism values may also explain why there is reluctance to seek services outside the family and the community, as well as why fewer ethnic minority elders are placed in nursing homes compared to Whites.

For many ethnic minorities, time is conceptualized as fluid and flexible. Hence, the idea of having a set 45-minute session, having time-limited treatment, and jumping straight into psychotherapy work at the beginning of a session is foreign and in sharp contrast to this notion of time as fluid and flexible. Explaining the psychotherapy process to ethnic minorities and allowing time to exchange pleasantries is helpful. However, flexibility on the part of the psychotherapist is also necessary to schedule longer appointments during nonbusiness hours and frequently to reschedule appointments, as older adults spend a considerable amount of time visiting doctors. Related to this issue of time, suggesting that ethnic elders write down their appointments on a calendar might be considered offensive when these elders have never used a calendar in their lives; a business card with the appointment reminder or a reminder phone call on the day of the appointment might be more culturally appropriate.

Allowing time to establish trust with the psychotherapist is also important as some ethnic minorities distrust professionals associated with formal agencies due to the history of racism and discrimination in the United States. Providing a description of one's professional training and education, as well as one's background that led to speaking their cultural language, is helpful in establishing trust. This process might entail providing more personal information than psychotherapists are accustomed to with other clients; however, it is a crucial aspect in developing trust with ethnic minorities. Among some ethnic minorities, it is often a family member who will seek services for the older adult; in these cases, it may be important to first establish trust with that family member.

Respect for elders is another common cultural value among ethnic minorities. Addressing elders as Mr. and Mrs., followed by their last names, ascribes the respect that these elders have gained in their communities as they aged. Within certain cultural groups, other ways of being addressed might be favored; for instance, among Latinos being referred to as Don or Doña, followed by their first names, might be more appropriate. Still other seniors might prefer to be called by their first names. Given that there are always individual differences in elders' preferences, we suggest asking older adults how they would like to be addressed. Discussing these issues early in psychotherapy allows for clarification of individual preferences, but also enables ethnic elders to choose their own communicative self-representation, a right that has been denied to them in the course of American history more so than for younger generations.

Related to this issue of respect, it has been our experience that some ethnic elders spend a considerable amount of time in psychotherapy describing their family networks, their family's accomplishments, and their family's immigration or migration experiences to and in the United States. These disclosures serve to portray ethnic elders' status and role in the family, the respect ascribed to them as they aged, as well as the adversities they experienced and overcame while immigrating or migrating. By discussing these life experiences, psychotherapists can obtain a better understanding of the psychological meaning of familism values among ethnic elders and how their immigration and migration stories shaped them.

In addition to describing their families in the United States, some ethnic elders talk about family members who were left behind in their country of origin, including those with whom they do not necessarily have frequent contact. Similarly, geographically dispersed family members may be described in detail. These disclosures serve to relay the losses encountered when immigrating and the loneliness and isolation experienced when growing old in a country in which frequent family interactions are limited by the geographic dispersion of family members and economic demands (e.g., adult children working during the day). These disclosures might also reveal ethnic elders' feelings and thoughts related to identifying with two cultures and experiencing split loyalty. This geographic dispersion is not commonly encountered in ethnic elders' countries of origin because family members tend to live close to each other and daily interactions with extended families are common. Language barriers also contribute to this loneliness and isolation by restricting social contact outside the home. The scarcity of culturally sensitive day care centers and limited transportation services are other barriers to reducing the loneliness and isolation experienced by ethnic elders.

Another common cultural value among ethnic minorities is the use of religion to frame and cope with their mental health problems. Ethnic minorities commonly describe the importance of prayer, attendance of religious services, and personal relationship with God to address their suffering and problems in life. Ethnic minorities might relate that they talk to God or feel that God talks to them; this is not necessarily indicative of delusional thinking or schizophrenia, in the absence of other symptoms. Consequently, psychotherapists need to determine how religious coping fits or complements the psychological treatment that they are providing to ethnic minorities.

Many ethnic minority elders have migrated to the United States from other countries. When conceptualizing a case and planning treatment, mental health professionals working with this group of ethnic minority elders should consider the length of time the elder has been in the United States and the person's level of acculturation. The mental health practitioner also needs to know what brought the older adult and/or his or her family to the United States and the subsequent culture change.

For example, recent research has found that Mexican-born Mexican Americans had significantly lower prevalence rates across a wide range of mental health disorders then did U.S.-born Mexican Americans (Hansen, Pepitone-Arreola-Rockwell, & Green, 2000).

Divergent Cultural Values among Ethnic Minorities

In this subsection, we discuss cultural values specific to a racial/ethnic group; we initially focus on a cultural value found among younger and older members of that group and then address how the cultural value may apply specifically to older adults in psychotherapy. As stated earlier, ethnic elders share some common cultural values; however, there are differences in beliefs among cultural groups. Among Latinos, salient cultural values include *marianismo, fatalismo,* and *personalismo*. Marianism comprises specific sex-role expectations: Women are expected to be submissive, to take care of children at home, and to devote their time to activities for the benefit of their children and husband, and men are expected to be dominant, strong, and the financial providers (Paniagua, 1994). Marianism might be evident when Latinas describe their roles raising their children and grandchildren or express reluctance in obtaining help from other family members with caregiving tasks or daily activities because it is their duty to provide these to the family. For Latinos, marianism might be noticeable when they are reluctant to describe their feelings in psychotherapy because doing so might be interpreted as a sign of weakness. The use of analogies and having a male therapist might facilitate the psychotherapy process for Latinos because "entre hombres se bromea y se aclaran los problemas" (among men, jokes can be said and problems can be resolved).

Another common cultural value, fatalism, is the belief that individuals cannot control or prevent adverse events if they are the will of God or powerful external agents (Rothman, Gant, & Hnat, 1985). In psychotherapy, fatalism might be evident when Latina/o elders express hopelessness about their problems. Psychotherapists need to offer hope by teaching techniques that can help clients address their problems and by motivating clients to change their behaviors, thoughts, and feelings.

Personalism indicates an orientation toward people rather than toward impersonal (institutional) relationships (Paniagua, 1994). Personalism may explain pathways to service or selection of a therapist or other types of assistance (Cuellar, Arnold, & Gonzalez, 1995). Personalism may also account for Latinos/as asking personal questions of their psychotherapists; this might be part of the process to establish a more personal relationship, not necessarily to break client-therapist boundaries. Once trust has been established, it is also not uncommon for some Latinos/as and other ethnic minority groups such as Native Americans to view psychotherapists as part of their extended family. Consequently, in some cases, termination of therapy might be considered as devastating as the loss of a family member.

Among Asian Americans, filial piety is an important cultural value that might arise in psychotherapy discussions. Filial piety refers to a set of moral principles taught at a very young age and reinforced throughout one's life; essential elements include duty, obligation, importance of the family name, service, and self-sacrifice to one's elders (Wong, 1988). Although related to familism values, filial piety differs in that it derives from Confucian principles. Filial piety might explain Asian American elders' expectations of assistance from their children and their disappointment or emotional distress when children do not come through.

Among Native Americans, interdependence and nonverbal communication are salient cultural values that might be evident in psychotherapy work. Interdependence describes the process by which all members of the Native American family contribute economically and to child-rearing activities, as well as the roles enacted within the family context (John, 1988). As a result of interdependence and a strong sense of tribalism, solutions to problems, material goods, and time are shared among Native Americans (Morales, 1999). Consequently, psychotherapists are rarely accepted into the Native American community without consultation with and permission from the tribal council (Morales, 1999). In addition, certain tribes (e.g., the Navajo) learn to communicate without the use of language; hence, elders do not feel they should have to ask for assistance but that family members, tribal officials, and service agencies should be able to sense their needs and respond to them (John, 1988).

This poses obvious difficulties when reaching out and providing psychotherapy services to Native American elders.

Family and Extended Kinship Networks

For African, Latino, Asian, and Native American older adults, family and extended kinship networks are important because they provide instrumental and emotional support. The role of keeper of cultural traditions becomes more respected with increasing age (Morales, 1999). Family and extended kinship networks influence how ethnically diverse adults seek and obtain mental health treatment. Our clinical experience indicates that adult children often act as gatekeepers to accessing ethnic elders in the family, as well as navigators of the medical and mental health system. Factors that contribute to this include adult children wanting to protect their elders from possible harm, language barriers that impede elders seeking direct care, and lack of knowledge about services available. Consequently, adult children and other family members may need to be involved in the decision process to seek and participate in psychotherapy services. Furthermore, adult children and other family members may need to be present in the beginning of psychotherapy treatment until trust has been established with the older adult and the family. Similarly, depending on the elder's case, family involvement in psychotherapy sessions may be necessary to help alleviate psychological distress in the older adult. This might be particularly important for families who infantilize the older adult in spite of remaining physical abilities.

We have found it helpful to do outreach with adult children as well as community leaders who have close ties to ethnic elders and establish a trusting relationship with these individuals first to access elders and be able to provide them psychotherapy services. Outreach can include providing presentations on psychoeducational topics, such as coping with the blues, memory loss, and caregiving, and demystifying the psychotherapy process at health fairs, senior and medical centers, and churches in the community. Outreach can also entail working closely with case managers or church leaders who already have a trusting and close relationship with ethnic elders and their families and holding a joint meeting with the case managers or church leaders to introduce the psychotherapist and explain how psychotherapy would benefit the older adult.

ADAPTING PSYCHOTHERAPY TO WORK WITH OLDER ETHNIC MINORITIES

In addition to considering the cultural context of ethnic elders in psychotherapy by paying close attention to shared and divergent cultural values, adaptations to psychotherapy may also be needed. Taking notes should be minimized during sessions to reduce suspicion and mistrust of professionals and service agencies, which are a legacy of racism and discrimination in the United States. Ethnic elders can also benefit from being socialized into psychotherapy by explaining that psychotherapy will focus on their current problems (as opposed to their childhood), teaching them skills to deal with their problems, and providing homework assignments to facilitate the acquisition and application of new techniques. Furthermore, it is helpful to clarify that obtaining psychotherapy services does not mean they are crazy; stigma associated with mental health problems is a predominant concern among ethnic minority elders. Offering education about the various services available to ethnic minority elders is also helpful; acting as a case manager or professional linking them to services facilitates the navigation of the complex medical and social system.

Older adults are the most diverse group in American society because of varied physiological changes, mental and physical health status, lifestyle behaviors, life events, income and education levels, and ethnic minority status. Given the amount of heterogeneity within the older adult cohort, diversity issues should be incorporated into psychotherapy. Earlier we addressed issues to consider when working with ethnic minority elders in psychotherapy. We now discuss how gender, income, and education may impact psychotherapy with older adults.

Gender

According to the 2000 U.S. Census, there were 35 million adults over the age of 65, with 59% of the population female and 41% male (Gist &

Hetzel, 2004). The average life expectancy past 65 is 18 years for women and 15 years for men (Federal Interagency Forum on Aging Related Statistics, 2004). In 2004, 3% of women and 2% of men age 65 and older had a serious mental illness, with 18% of women and 11% of men having clinically relevant depressive symptoms (Federal Interagency Forum on Aging Related Statistics, 2004). These statistics suggest that, compared to men, women are living longer and with more tendencies to have a mental illness.

A limited amount of research is available on gender differences in psychotherapy with older clients. Lagana (1995) examined predictors of expectations about mental health counseling in a sample of 57 (34 men and 23 women) retired professors and found no gender differences. However, differences were identified regarding stressors and comfort with psychotherapy. The women in the sample were more exposed to greater psychological stressors, for instance, widowhood. They also indicated that they were more comfortable discussing feelings in a therapy session than the men in the sample. However, the results do not generalize to other older adults given that the sample comprised only college professors.

Pilisuk and colleagues (Pilisuk, Montgomery, Parks, & Acredolo, 1993) examined how stress, social support, and locus of control affected measures of health among older men and women from two senior centers. The results showed that stronger influences of social support and sense of control increased capability to cope with stressors and sickness, but only for the male subjects. Pilisuk et al. considered the implications of the results because having an internal locus of control could make men deny the importance of symptoms and continually rate health favorably. These men would also be less likely to seek help, a factor that could affect not only general medical attention but also psychotherapy usage.

Given the projected growth in the older adult population, more emphasis will need to be placed on creating psychotherapeutic environments that facilitate the therapy process for both older men and older women. For example, there may be gender differences in the expression of emotion. We have found that showing men faces that display different emotions has been helpful in getting them to label what they are feeling. Additional considerations include gender differences in comfort level with psychotherapy and amount of therapy required.

Income and Education

As with any form of health care, the client's income and level of education often impact mental health service utilization. Successive cohorts of older persons have higher levels of education and a greater acceptance of psychology. In 2003, 72% of individuals age 65 and older had at least a high school diploma; of that percentage, 17% had a bachelor's or advanced degree (Federal Interagency Forum on Aging Related Statistics, 2004). By 2030, it is expected that 83% of older adults will have a high school diploma and at least 24% will have a bachelor's degree (Abeles et al., 1998). Income level has also risen for older adults, yet with Social Security benefits being the primary source of income for the majority of older adults, the future economic outlook may not be promising. In 2002, Social Security provided 39%, personal earnings 25%, pensions 19%, and assets 14% of the total income for individuals age 65 and older (Federal Interagency Forum on Aging Related Statistics, 2004). At the same time, 10% of older adults were below the poverty level; 24% were African American, 21% were Hispanic, and 12% were over 75 years of age. The average income for older males was $15,276 and for older females was $8,579 (Federal Interagency Forum on Aging Related Statistics, 2004). Factors such as poverty, poor quality of education, unemployment, inadequate health care, and limited health insurance coverage all contribute to poor mental health (Abeles et al., 1998) and a decrease in mental health usage (Wei, Sambamoorth, Olfson, Walkup, & Crystal, 2005).

Wei et al. (2005) examined factors surrounding the use of psychotherapy for depression in older adults. Their sample consisted of community-dwelling Medicare beneficiaries, age 65 and older, who had at least one claim of depression. The data obtained from the Medicare Current Beneficiary Survey showed a significant difference in rates of psychotherapy usage by education and income. Beneficiaries with a college education versus a noncollege education were twice as likely to use psychotherapy. A higher proportion of psychotherapy use was also found for higher-income than lower-income beneficiaries; however, the effect of income was insignificant when education level was factored into the analysis.

Walker and Clarke (2001) compared mental health service for younger and older adults in terms of referrals, attendance rates, outcomes, and length of time in therapy. Although the income and educational levels of the subjects were not indicated, older adults spent the same amount of time in therapy as the younger adults, with the treatment being effective for both groups. The older adults, however, missed fewer sessions, causing the overall duration required for therapy to be shorter. Walker and Clarke attributed the attendance rate of the elderly to the fact that they appreciated the free service more, a valid observation that needs to be considered for future mental health treatments for older adults.

Often we ignore the intersection of race, culture, and socioeconomic status. Race and culture have become the primary variables we examine when we are considering diversity among older adults. However, income should also be considered given that income may impact access and utilization of mental health services for many older adults. This is particularly true when we consider older adults living in rural areas. Twenty-seven percent of persons 65 and older live in rural areas (U.S. Bureau of the Census, 1994). Older adults who live in rural areas typically have fewer resources and poorer mental and physical health status than do their urban counterparts (Guralnick, Kemele, Stamm, & Greving, 2003). In many communities there are no psychosocial services available to meet the needs of the rural elderly. Mental health researchers have found that community-dwelling elderly persons with significant symptoms of depression use more general medical services and incur higher health care costs than elders who do not show such symptoms (Ganguli, Fox, Gilby, & Seeberg, 1995; Unutzer et al., 1997). Where specialized services do exist, they tend to be concentrated in more densely populated cities and suburban areas. Obtaining mental health services for older people is most problematic in rural areas of the country where there is a general overall scarcity of such services for all age groups and a lack of specialized expertise in diagnosis and treating the mental health needs of the elderly (Buckwalter, Smith, Zevenbergen, & Russell, 1991; McCulloch & Lynch, 1993).

Rural Poverty: Special Concerns for Providing Services for Rural Elders

Rural elders are at great risk for experiencing mental health problems; mental health practitioners need to consider therapy with this subgroup of elders. Although it is not clear exactly what characteristics of poverty contribute to psychotherapy outcomes, several explanations have been suggested, including neighborhood or residential stability and its isolating effects, lack of community resources and mental health services, and stress. As the first set of baby boomers reach the age of 65 in the next few years, the impact of income and education will grow in importance as we devise strategies to address the psychotherapy needs and challenges of this next cohort of older adults.

Additional special populations within the older adult cohort that should be considered in psychotherapy include gays and lesbians, disabled seniors, and older adults who are the primary caregivers for their adult children and/or grandchildren. In the recommendations for future reading, we have included articles applicable to these populations.

CONCLUSION

Members of ethnic minority groups are less likely to seek treatment for mental health concerns (Wyckle & Musil, 1993), and older ethnic minorities require special attention in terms of assessment and treatment. There has been progress in developing diagnostic measures that are culturally valid and reliable (Iwamasa & Hilliard, 1999), but continued efforts are needed in this area.

Ethnic minority status may play a role in determining the manifestation of mental disorders (e.g., Shadlen & Larson, 1999), so the incorporation of specific cultural beliefs and behaviors into standard clinical treatments is greatly needed (Shiang, Kjellander, Huang, & Bogumill, 1998). For example, Hilliard and Iwamasa (2001) found that Japanese American older adults conceptualized anxiety differently from the traditional psychiatric conceptualization of anxiety. As a possible explanation, they suggest that somatic symptomatology may be perceived as encompassing particular forms of mental distress in the Asian culture. The fourth edition of the *Diagnostic and Statistical Manual of Mental Disorders* (APA, 1994) addresses ethnic and cultural issues, including the role of culture in the expression and evaluation of symptoms, as well as the impact of culture on the therapeutic relationship, but the information included is based on insufficient research and is not widely used.

Ethnic minority groups differ in general status, acculturation level, language, religion/spiritual beliefs, cultural traditions and values, and gender roles. Based on the heterogeneity that exists both between and within each ethnic minority group, it is important to consider not only the racial designation of the individual but his or her specific ethnic identification. Additionally, individual differences become a crucial part of the mental health profile (Whitfield & Baker-Thomas, 1999). Examining older adults from an individual perspective does not shift the focus away from their ethnic identification. On the contrary, it allows the mental health practitioner to understand the traits and qualities that exist within a culture and how those traits and qualities are manifested in an individual by examining the interactions among cultural, social, biological, environmental, and psychological factors.

There is a dearth of culturally competent mental health professionals. This is a major problem because the literature suggests that therapist-client match in language and ethnicity is related to the success of the treatment. The increasing diversity of the older adult population requires that we train a cadre of mental health professionals sensitive to the impact of ethnic minority status and age on case conceptualization, diagnosis, and treatment.

This chapter was not meant to be a comprehensive review of the field of cultural competency and aging. Rather, our overview was intended to stimulate interest in issues that affect older people, their families, and the mental health professionals with whom they interact.

RECOMMENDED READING

To learn more about specific social and cultural issues of psychotherapy with older adults, see the following resources.

Coon, D. W., & Zeiss, L. M. (2003). The families we choose: Intervention issues with LBT caregivers. In D. W. Coon, D. Gallagher-Thompson, & L. Thompson (Eds.), *Innovative interventions to reduce dementia caregiver distress: A clinical guide* (pp. 267–295). New York: Springer.

Eggebeen, D. J., & Wilhelm, M. O. (1995). Patterns of support given by older Americans to their children. In S. A. Bass (Ed.), *Older and active: How Americans over 55 are contributing to society* (pp. 122–168). New Haven, CT: Yale University Press.

Guralnick, S., Kemele, K., Stamm, B. H., & Greving, A. M. (2003). Rural geriatrics and gerontology. In B. H. Stamm (Ed.), *Rural behavioral health care: An interdisciplinary guide* (pp. 193–202). Washington, DC: American Psychological Association.

Hilliard, K. M., & Iwamasa, G. Y. (2001). The conceptualization of anxiety: An exploratory study of Japanese American older adults. *Journal of Clinical Geropsychology, 7*(1), 53–65.

Iwamasa, G. Y., & Sorocco, K. H. (2002). Aging and Asian Americans: Developing culturally appropriate research methodology. In G. N. Hall & S. Okazaki (Eds.), *Asian American psychology: The science of lives in context* (pp. 105–130). Washington, DC: American Psychological Association.

Matthews, A. K., & Peterman, A. H. (1998). Improving provision of effective treatment for racial and cultural minorities. *Psychotherapy: Theory, Research, Practice, Training, 35*(3), 291–305.

Morales, P. (1999). The impact of cultural differences in psychotherapy with older clients: Sensitive issues and strategies. In M. Duffy (Ed.), *Handbook of counseling and psychotherapy with older adults* (pp. 132–153). New York: Wiley.

National Research Council. (2004). *Understanding racial and ethnic differences in health in late life: A research agenda.* Washington, DC: National Academies Press (Panel on Race, Ethnicity, and Health in Late Life, R. A. Bulatao & N. B. Anderson, Eds., Committee on Population, Division of Behavioral and Social Sciences and Education).

Tully, C. T. (2000). Empowerment and older lesbians and gays. In C. T. Tully (Ed.), *Lesbians, gays, and the empowerment perspective* (pp. 195–229). New York: Columbia University Press.

REFERENCES

Abeles, N., Cooley, S., Deitch, I., Harper, M., Hinrichsen, G., Lopez, M., et al. (1998). What practitioners should know about working with older adults.

Professional Psychology: Research and Practice, 29, 413–427 (Brochure for APA, revised and reprinted).

American Psychiatric Association (Ed.). (1994). *Diagnostic and statistical manual of mental disorders* (4th ed.). Washington, DC: Author.

American Psychological Association. (2003). Guidelines on multicultural education, training, research, practice, and organizational change for psychologists. *American Psychologist, 58*, 377–402.

American Psychological Association. (2004). Guidelines for psychological practice with older adults. *American Psychologist, 59*, 236–260.

Betancourt, H., & Lopez, S. R. (1993). The study of culture, ethnicity, and race in American psychology. *American Psychologist, 48*, 629–637.

Buckwalter, K. C., Smith, M., Zevenbergen, P., & Russell, D. (1991). Mental health services of the Rural Elderly Outreach Program. *Gerontologist, 31*, 408–412.

Council of National Psychological Associations for the Advancement of Ethnic Minority Interests. (2003). *Psychological treatment of ethnic minority populations.* Washington, DC: Association of Black Psychologists.

Cuellar, I., Arnold, B., & Gonzalez, G. (1995). Cognitive referents of acculturation: Assessment of cultural constructs in Mexican Americans. *Journal of Community Psychology, 23*, 339–356.

Federal Interagency Forum on Aging Related Statistics. (2004). *Older Americans 2004: Key indication of well being.* Washington, DC: U.S. Government Printing Office.

Foucault, M. (1986). *The history of sexuality: Vol. 3. The care of the self.* New York: Vintage Books.

Ganguli, M., Fox, A., Gilby, J., Seeberg, E., & Belle, S. (1995). Depressive symptoms and associated factors in a rural elderly populations: The MoVIES project. *American Journal of Geriatric Psychiatry, 3*, 144–160.

Gist, Y., & Hetzel, L. (2004). *We the people: Aging in the United States* (Census 2000 Special Reports). Washington, DC: U.S. Department of Commerce.

Gould, S. J. (1997). This view of life: Unusual unity. *Natural History, 106*, 20–23, 69–71.

Guralnick, S., Kemele, K., Stamm, B. H., & Greving, A. M. (2003). *Rural geriatrics and gerontology.* In B. H. Stamm (Ed.), *Rural behavioral health care: An interdisciplinary guide* (pp. 193–202). Washington, DC: American Psychological Association.

Habermas, J. (1987). *The theory of communicative action: Vol. 1. Life-world and systems: A critique of functionalist reason* (T. McCarthy, Trans.). Boston: Beacon Press.

Hansen, N. D., Pepitone-Arreola-Rockwell, F., & Greene, A. F. (2000). Multicultural competence: Criteria and case examples. *Professional Psychology: Research and Practice, 31*(6), 652–660.

Herring, R. D. (1999). *Counseling with Native American Indians and Alaska Natives: Strategies for helping professionals.* Thousand Oaks, CA: Sage.

Hilliard, K. M., & Iwamasa, G. Y. (2001). Japanese American older adults' conceptualization of anxiety. *Journal of Clinical Gerontology, 7,* 53–65.

Iwamasa, G. Y., & Hilliard, K. M. (1999). Depression and anxiety among Asian American elders: A review of the literature. *Clinical Psychology Review, 19*(3), 343–357.

John, R. (1988). The Native American family. In C. H. Mindel, R. W. Habenstein, & R. Wright (Eds.), *Ethnic families in America: Patterns and variations* (3rd ed., pp. 325–363). New York: Elsevier.

Knight, B. G., Robinson, G. S., Longmire, C. V. F., Chun, M., Nakao, K., & Kim, J. H. (2002). Cross cultural issues in caregiving for persons with dementia: Do familism values reduce burden and distress? *Ageing International, 27,* 70–94.

Lagana, L. (1995). Older adults' expectations about mental health counseling: A multivariate and discriminant analysis. *International Journal of Aging and Human Development, 40*(4), 297–316.

Matsumoto, D., & Juang, L. (2004). An introduction to the study of culture and psychology. In D. Matsumoto & L. Juang (Eds.), *Culture and psychology* (3rd ed., pp. 1–28). Belmont, CA: Wadsworth/Thomson Learning.

McCullogh, J. B., & Lynch, M. S. (1993). Barriers to solutions: Service delivery and public policy in rural areas. *Journal of Applied Gerontology, 12,* 388–403.

Morales, P. (1999). The impact of cultural differences in psychotherapy with older clients: Sensitive issues and strategies. In M. Duffy (Ed.), *Handbook of counseling and psychotherapy with older adults* (pp. 132–153). New York: Wiley.

Mpofu, E., & Conyers, L. M. (2004). A representational theory perspective of minority status and people with disabilities: Implications for rehabilitation education and practice. *Rehabilitation Counseling Bulletin, 47*(3), 142–151.

Paniagua, F. A. (1994). *Assessing and treating culturally diverse clients: A practical guide.* Thousand Oaks, CA: Sage.

Paniagua, F. A. (1998). *Assessing and treating culturally diverse clients* (2nd ed.). Thousand Oaks, CA: Sage.

Pilisuk, M., Montgomery, M., Parks, S., & Acredolo, C. (1993). Locus of control, life stress, and social networks: Gender differences in the health status of the elderly. *Sex Roles, 28*(3/4), 147–166.

Rothman, J., Gant, L. M., & Hnat, S. A. (1985). Mexican-American family culture. *Social Service Review, 59*, 197–215.

Sabogal, F., Marin, G., Otero-Sabogal, R., Marin, B. V., & Perez-Stable, E. J. (1987). Latino familism and acculturation: What changes and what doesn't? *Hispanic Journal of Behavioral Sciences, 9*, 397–412.

Shadlen, M. F., & Larson, E. B. (1999). What's new in Alzheimer's disease in a primary care setting. *American Journal of Geriatric Psychiatry, 6*, S34–S40.

Shiang, J., Kjellander, C., Huang, K., & Bogumill, S. (1998). Developing cultural competency in clinical practice: Treatment considerations for Chinese cultural groups in the United States. *Clinical Psychology: Science and Practice, 5*, 182–210.

Sowell, T. (1981). *Ethnic America: A History.* New York: Basic Books.

Sue, D. W., & Sue, D. (1999). *Counseling the culturally different: Theory and practice* (3rd ed.). New York: Wiley.

Unutzer, J., Patrick, D. L., Simon, G., Grembowski, D., Walker, E., Rutter, C., et al. (1997). Depressive symptoms and the cost of health services in HMO patients aged 65 years and older: A 4-year prospective study. *Journal of the American Medical Association, 277*, 1618–1623.

U.S. Bureau of the Census. (1994). *Population profile of the United States: 1993.* Washington, DC: U.S. Government Printing Office.

U.S. Bureau of the Census. (2000). *Projections of the total resident population by 5-year age groups, race, and Hispanic origin with special age categories: Middle series, 1999–2000 and 2050–2070.* Retrieved September 23, 2005, from www.census.gov/population/projections/nation/summary/np-t4.a-g.txt.

U.S. Department of Health and Human Services. (2001). *Mental health: Culture, race, and ethnicity—A supplement to mental health: A report of the surgeon general.* Rockville, MD: U.S. Department of Health and Human Services, Substance Abuse and Mental Health Services Administration, Center for Mental Health Services.

Waidmann, T. A., & Liu, K. (2000). Disability trends among elderly persons and implications for the future. *Journal of Gerontology: Social Sciences, 55B*, S298–S307.

Walker, D., & Clarke, M. (2001). Cognitive behavioural psychotherapy: A comparison between younger and older adults in two inner city mental health teams. *Aging and Mental Health, 5*(2), 197–199.

Wei, W., Sambamoorth, U., Olfson, M., Walkup, J., & Crystal, S. (2005). Use of psychotherapy for depression in older adults. *American Journal of Psychiatry, 162*(4), 711–717.

Whitfield, K., & Baker-Thomas, T. (1999). Individual differences in aging among African-Americans. *International Journal of Aging and Human Development, 48*(1), 73–79.

Wong, M. G. (1988). The Chinese American family. In C. H. Mindel, R. W. Habenstein, & R. Wright (Eds.), *Ethnic families in America: Patterns and variations* (3rd ed., pp. 230–257). New York: Elsevier.

Wyckle, M. L., & Musil, C. M. (1993). Mental health of older persons: Social and cultural factors. *Generations, 17*(1), 7–12.

Zuckerman, M. (1990). Some dubious premises in research and theory on racial differences: Scientific, social, and ethical issues. *American Psychologist, 45*, 1297–1303.

Psychotherapy in the Context of Long-Term Care

DEBORAH W. FRAZER

The therapist-patient relationship is embedded in a complex context that can be conceptualized as an ecology, replete with relationships, structures, interdependencies, policies, and physical characteristics. An array of possible participants in this ecology include family and friends; a set of health care or service personnel; religious, educational, leisure, and other community resources; and a residence. The ecological context impacts how the therapist conducts psychotherapy: what challenges may exist, what resources may be available, what rules and regulations must be followed, what outcome measures are appropriate, and what ethical issues may be prominent. This chapter looks at how three types of older adult residential settings—independent, assisted living, and nursing home—impact the psychotherapeutic process and provides guidance on how therapists can maximize effectiveness in each setting.

GENERAL PRINCIPLES ACROSS ALL RESIDENTIAL SETTINGS

First, therapists need to be familiar with the range of residential options available to older adults in their community. People often move between or among residential and medical settings. For example, someone may be hospitalized from a private home for a hip fracture, be discharged to a nursing home for rehab, then to an assisted living facility for a longer recuperation, and finally return home to independent living. A sadder trajectory is the move from independent living to increasingly higher levels of care as a dementing illness progresses.

Second, therapists can help older individuals to understand and accept the *ecological context* that will best reduce distress and improve well-being. Changing the environment or changing the level of services in an environment can reduce distress. Lawton and Nahemow's (1973) ecological theory of adaptation and aging provides guidance for this therapeutic formulation. The theory describes the interaction between an older person's *competence level* and the *environmental press* (or demands) of the environment in which she or he is living. To summarize, an individual is at the *adaptation level* when there is a good fit between the overall competence of a person and the demands of the setting. When the fit is poor, the individual experiences distress. If the environment is too demanding, the individual can become overwhelmed. If the environment does not have enough stimulation, the individual can become bored, apathetic, or lonely. Changes in environmental demands have a more pronounced effect as an individual loses competence. From this model, the therapist could help the patient consider shoring up or compensating for declining competence level (e.g., staying in the private home with more help) or changing the environmental demands (moving to assisted living).

Third, therapists should become knowledgeable about the written or unwritten discharge criteria for any residential setting in which they are working. When will the family or a landlord say "Enough!" in a private home or apartment: A burned pot? A fire? An episode of getting lost or wandering? What are the state regulations about discharge from assisted living: A Stage II wound? Inability to safely evacuate in case of fire? What are the facility's or company's policies about discharge from assisted living: Repeated falls? An episode of getting lost or wandering? What are the nursing home's policies about discharge: "Unmanageable" behavioral disturbance? Surfacing these implicit rules can alleviate patient and family anxiety, as well as identify critical therapeutic issues.

Fourth, therapists should understand that the residential options from independent through assisted living to nursing home care do not necessarily constitute a *continuum of care*, with the highest acuity in the nursing home. For example, very high acuity care can be provided at home with 24/7 private duty nursing or hospice services. However, the range of options does represent a continuum of *social press*, from very private in a home to the intensely social or congregate setting of a nursing home (typically with a roommate and group dining). Matching a patient to the right environment is partially a matter of need for care and partially a preference for level of social press.

For the therapist, the continuum represents a significant difference in practice. For example, in in-home therapy, the therapist must construct a *virtual team*, perhaps consisting of family members, neighbors, clergy, physicians, visiting nurse, and physical therapist. In the complex, highly differentiated nursing home setting, the therapist must establish a working relationship with all the personnel relevant to the patient. This might include the certified nursing assistant, unit director, housekeeper, social worker, activities therapist, physician, and physical therapist. These contacts are generally brief hallway exchanges, not requiring the planned phone calls typical of in-home care. With few colleagues in the independent setting, the therapist will need to become more knowledgeable about community resources (unless, of course, there is a highly skilled family member or geriatric care manager). In the nursing home setting, specific personnel are assigned to specific resources, so the therapist need only discover who provides access to which resources at that particular facility. All nursing homes are required to conduct care conferences for each resident, generally every 3 months, and generally including a social worker, nurse, and activities professional. However, influence on decision making is better achieved informally at the nurses' station, through trusting relationships.

CHARACTERISTICS OF RESIDENTS IN RESIDENTIAL SETTINGS

Table 9.1 displays the demographic information on residents in assisted living and nursing home settings. Assisted living residents are significantly

Table 9.1 Demographics of Nursing Home and Assisted Living Facility Residents

Demographics	Nursing Homes (%)	Assisted Living Facilities (%)
Age		
65–74	13.6	14.0
75–84	34.3	35.6
85 and older	52.1	50.4
Race		
White	86.1	96.2[a]
Non-White	19.9	3.8
Sex		
Male	26.7	22.8
Female	73.3	77.2[a]
Marital Status		
Married	17.6	16.6
Widowed/divorced/separated	73.2	71.5
Never married	8.6	11.9
Unknown	0.7	0
Income		
Less than $10,000	54.4	47.5[a]
$10,000–$20,000	26.4	27.1
More than $20,000	19.2	25.5[a]
Functional Status[b]		
No ADL/IADL	2.2	3.8
1–2 ADLs	19.9	32.5[a]
3 or more ADLs	74.4	52.1[a]
IADL only	2.9	11.1[a]
Some ADL or IADL	0	0
Unknown	0.7	0.4
General Health		
Excellent or very good	5.1	11.5[a]
Good	26.2	3.9
Fair or poor	66.9	49.6[a]
Unknown	1.8	1.0

Table 9.1   *(Continued)*

Demographics	Nursing Homes (%)	Assisted Living Facilities (%)
Percent with Specific Condition		
Alzheimer's disease/dementia	46.1	35.3[a]
Diabetes	19.7	14.9[a]
Hip fracture	5.4	6.8
Emphysema/asthma/COPD	9.6	8.5
Mental disorder	28.9	25.2
Stroke	21.5	14.9[a]

Source: Trends in Residential Long-Term Care: Use of Nursing Homes and Assisted Living and Characteristics of Facilities and Residents (Report), by B. C. Sillman, K. Liu, and C. McGilliard, 2002, Washington, DC: Urban Institute.

[a] Assisted living estimate is significantly different from the nursing home estimate.

[b] Functional status refers to ability to do daily activities; ADL = Activities of daily living; IADL = Instrumental activities of daily living.

more likely to have higher income and be White and female than nursing home residents. As expected, they are significantly less impaired functionally and medically. These, of course, represent only averages; the therapist may encounter quite a bit of variability of patients within and among settings.

Independent Residential Settings

The broad category of independent living covers a wide range of living options. It might be a single-family house, apartment, or condo where the patient has lived for many years, or it could be an apartment in a building that houses primarily older adults (a "naturally occurring retirement community" or NORC). It could mean subsidized senior housing or one of the new, privately owned active adult communities for those 55 and older. Finally, it could be the independent section of a continuing care retirement community (CCRC), which contains all three levels of care within one organization, building, or campus. All of these independent living situations assume that the patient is safely managing the tasks of daily living by himself or herself or with assistance provided by others (not the housing provider).

Regulations

Other than the discharge criteria mentioned earlier, the main regulations that apply in independent living are the patient's health insurance regulations and the therapist's obligation to confer with the primary care physician. If providing in-home care, the therapist will need to check on the facility's (e.g., apartment house) security regulations (signing in/out, being announced, providing identification).

Promoting Well-Being

Some independent settings (CCRCs, most subsidized senior housing, and some co-op apartment buildings) have social workers available to the residents. Many independent seniors have family members who are knowledgeable and actively engaged. In these circumstances, the family or social workers may take on the primary tasks of promoting well-being in the biological, psychological, social, and spiritual realms. Family members or social workers can help with health monitoring (including changes in cognitive status), arranging for health care appointments and transportation, and ensuring appropriate diet, exercise, socialization, spiritual engagement, and mental stimulation. To promote autonomy and security, family members can encourage financial and legal planning. However, if such persons are not available, it behooves the therapist to become familiar with a wide array of community services and products that may be available. Begin with the Area Agency on Aging (AAA or Triple A) and, through it, learn about the wide array of services that are oriented to seniors. As examples, psychotherapists need to know about senior centers, transportation for seniors/handicapped persons, in-home companion and home health services, care management services, elder care lawyers, financial planners, long-term care insurance options, senior moving companies, senior-oriented real estate agents, geriatricians and geropsychiatrists, adult day care programs, geropsychiatric inpatient and partial hospital programs, driving assessment programs (usually found in rehab settings), and community-based recreational, educational, and religious activities.

Therapists should learn (through books, workshops, or working with colleagues) the basics of home safety (e.g., no throw rugs, use of bathroom grab bars, use of stair lifts) and also know where to get expert advice (e.g., through AAA or an occupational therapist). As always, the final decision on home safety issues is with the elder if he or she is decisionally capable, and if not, the decision rests with the designated decision maker (usually a family member). An occupational therapist may see a dangerous throw rug where the elder sees a treasured memory. Therapists can try to negotiate a compromise in such a situation (e.g., use the rug as a wall hanging) or remind everyone involved of the elder's decision-making capacity. Older homes can be notoriously risky, but decisionally capable elders have the right to assume those risks.

The longer you practice in a geographic area, the broader your network and the deeper your resource knowledge become. Attend local conferences, network through the AAA and the Alzheimer's Association, offer to speak at senior centers, and get to know local academics who are interested in aging. And, of course, you're always learning from your patients and their families!

Treatment Approaches

The number of people involved in an independent elder's care can range from a single therapist to a full array of family members and professionals. For a completely capable, independent senior, the treatment approach is similar to that for a younger individual, and may be straightforward, one-on-one care. With increasing medical, social, or psychological complexity, it may be necessary to construct (with the patient's permission) a virtual team, consisting of the primary care physician, geropsychiatrist, one or more family members, visiting nurses, and physical therapists. Although phone consultation with these team members is not reimbursed, the additional communication is invaluable in developing coordinated, focused treatment. Explicit conversations with the patient must be held to establish the boundaries and limits of confidentiality with team members and should be documented in progress notes.

It is important to establish that the therapist's role is psychotherapy, not care management. Ideally, the patient, a family member, or other designee will do ongoing care management; if not, the therapist may need to take initiative in selectively communicating with other parties. If no designee is available or acceptable to the elder, the therapist can offer to contact a private geriatric care manager (for those who can afford the services) or the AAA (for those who can use public services). If the elder refuses service but is in imminent physical or financial danger, the therapist can contact Adult Protective Services. Occasionally, therapists will have to tolerate the discomfort of working with a decisionally capable elder who chooses to live in a vulnerable situation. In that case, the therapist's role will involve close monitoring and developing an emergency plan should the situation deteriorate.

In resource-rich independent environments (especially CCRCs), the therapist should investigate how and when resources are available. For example, what can the social worker provide? How, when, and who should the patient or therapist call for help? If the patient is undergoing an especially stressful period, psychologically and/or medically, does the CCRC permit temporary assisted or skilled care? Indeed, even for those residing in home or apartment settings, local assisted living providers may offer short-term respite stays. An assisted living respite stay can, in some circumstances, prevent a psychiatric inpatient stay. Mastering this knowledge gives the therapist a wide array of treatment options, up to and including a temporary change of housing or care.

Measurement of Outcomes

When seeing a patient in an independent setting (whether in-home or office), outcome measurement is similar to that for an office practice. The most individualized process is to set objective, measurable goals and document their attainment or lack thereof. In addition, scales can be useful. For depression, the short-form Geriatric Depression Scale serves well. For anxiety, depression, and/or pain, a simple weekly self-rating on a 1 to 10 scale yields an ongoing measurement. Some managed care insurers require a measurement on the Global Assessment of Functioning from the *DSM-IV* for every set of sessions that are authorized. For a fuller discussion of outcome measures, see Frazer (1998).

Assisted Living Settings

As with independent residential settings, this category covers a wide array of options. The one feature common to all varieties of assisted living is that the residents have access to personal care and other support-ive services for the activities of daily living (ADLs) and instrumental ac-tivities of daily living (IADLs). The latter include complex activities such as housekeeping, cooking meals, managing medication, and arrang-ing for transportation; the former include basic activities such as bathing, dressing, and grooming. Assisted living settings are known by many different terms, including group homes, adult homes, personal care homes, retirement homes, and assisted living communities. They can range from small private homes with government-subsidized care for as few as four persons to large resort-like communities operated by hotel chains. They may or may not have a range of activities and licensed nurs-ing staff or consultants.

Assisted living facilities (ALFs) pride themselves on promoting auton-omy, choice, and independence. They have rapidly developed in the past 15 years as an alternative to nursing home care for those who do not need daily skilled care. Families often seek out ALFs to avoid the elder's charge that they are "putting me away" in a nursing home. The concept is still evolving, with some debate about whether ALFs can promote a *social model* of aging (compared to a *medical model*), and whether and for how long a person can *age in place* in the ALF setting. Generally, they require private payment, al-though some states are experimenting with subsidizing ALFs to decrease the pressure on, and cost of, nursing homes. Assisted living facilities some-times have a *memory neighborhood* (a secured or locked unit for individuals with dementia and/or behavioral problems). Some ALFs are entirely dedi-cated to dementia care, and the entire facility is secured. At their best, ALFs promote a more dignified life for elders than highly institutionalized nurs-ing homes. At their worst, they accept or retain elders for whom they can-not provide safe care. The choice about moving from ALF to nursing home is often determined by the family's ability and willingness to pay large sums for additional care in the ALF. This choice can be confusing and highly emotional for the elder and the family.

Regulations

In contrast to nursing facilities, which are federally regulated, assisted living facilities are regulated at the state level. There is little consistency among states in how they regulate, or don't regulate, this type of residential service. If a therapist provides service on site in assisted living, it is important to know the state regulations and the provider policies on documentation of psychological services. In addition, Medicare carriers differ on coding location for assisted living; therapists should check with their carrier about coding for location, whether written physician orders are necessary, and whether documentation in the patient's chart (sometimes called "resident file") is required.

Staff

In larger ALFs, the staff will typically include an executive director and a wellness coordinator. The wellness coordinator supervises direct care staff and may or may not be an LPN or RN. In addition, there may be an admissions/marketing director and an activities director. The direct care staff members typically have minimal training and may be known as personal care assistants. Because of ALFs' commitment to autonomy and choice, residents can choose to stay with their community physician and pharmacy. There is rarely a medical director, although there may be a consulting physician who sees a majority of the residents. The facility may or may not offer physical and occupational therapy, home health agencies, hospice, or volunteers. Dietary, housekeeping, and laundry tasks may be done by the personal care assistants (in the "universal worker" model), or there may be separate departments.

Promoting Well-Being

Assisted living facilities have a strong orientation toward customer satisfaction. They need a high census and relatively low costs to stay in business, and they must work to attract private pay dollars. They especially appeal to families who have promised "I will never put you in a nursing home," yet who are unable to care for a family member at home. Therefore, ALFs tend to work hard to appear attractive and provide a respectful atmosphere and stimulating activities. However, to keep costs down, staffing is often quite low. Therefore, the therapist is often a welcome addition, providing another set of professional eyes and ears to spot residents' problems. At times, the presence of on-site psychological services provides a marketing edge. Activities staff are usually pleased to work with the therapist and resident on specific activity-oriented goals.

Treatment Approaches

Larger ALFs provide private rooms; some provide private suites. In these cases, when providing therapy in the room, privacy is maintained. However, if the therapist is on-site frequently and sees a number of people, privacy can be threatened in the communal spaces (dining room, living room, community/rec room). Patients will frequently self-identify, calling out a greeting to the therapist. Investigating alternative building entrances and exits to minimize public exposure should be explored.

Frequent themes that are specific to ALF residents include disagreements with family about frequency of visits and feeling like a "prisoner" or "inmate." These issues are especially acute when a parent has been moved from his or her own hometown to that of the daughter or son. There are many complaints about the food and the activities. Residents with specific disabilities, especially hearing, vision, memory, and mobility problems (and combinations of these disabilities), are at risk for depression. Recent estimates of moderate to severe dementia rates in ALFs are 23% to 42% (Zimmerman, Sloane, Heck, Maslow, & Schulz, 2003). Helping residents to feel respected, loved, and cared for, as well as feeling that they are living a life of meaning and purpose, is a challenge.

Several therapeutic approaches are especially conducive to the assisted living setting. One approach is to identify compensatory strategies for disabilities (e.g., books on tape, voice amplifiers, tape recording for combination memory/vision problems). Another approach is to hold one or more family meetings when families disagree about visiting schedules. The therapist plays an invaluable role in validating each family member's needs and desires and helping everyone to reach consensus about a practical, if not ideal, visiting schedule. A third approach addresses the residents' needs for time away from the facility to decrease the sense of confinement (being "inmates"). Problem solving about trips to a church, synagogue, or mosque, a senior center, restaurants, and artistic performances or exhibits are excellent opportunities for larger discussions about life goals. Finally, a critical but difficult therapeutic approach engages the residents' need to feel useful and even to give to others. Because so much of daily life is done *for* ALF residents (such as cleaning, cooking, shopping), they easily feel bored, useless, and depressed. Finding an opportunity for ALF residents to be givers rather than receivers, creators rather than consumers, enhances their sense of meaning and purpose and decreases depressive symptoms. Residents' children or activities staff may need to be prodded to help provide these meaningful opportunities.

Involvement of Staff

Communication with the assisted living staff is essential for the therapist's ongoing assessment of the patient. Quick questions to the personal care assistants about maintenance of daily living skills, eating, sleeping, and activity patterns, and amount of visiting by family members are invaluable confirmations of the patient's self-report. Generally, the personal care staff are delighted to be consulted and will begin to voluntarily offer observations to the therapist. Likewise, the assistants are usually pleased to be part of the team for implementing behavioral plans. However, they are not likely to be oriented toward documentation—either reading it or writing it. A simple plan, described verbally and requiring only a verbal response, works best. Unlike nursing assistants in the nursing home, personal care assistants are generally not taught, or expected, to document much.

The wellness coordinator and executive director are generally open to suggestions for the elder's care, especially if it will please the resident and the family and not place undue financial or time burdens on anyone. Again, verbal suggestions are preferable to written, as the charts and files in ALFs are not used much as a central communication device.

Measurement of Outcomes

In addition to the outcomes mentioned for patients residing in independent settings, several measures can be added for ALF residents. The wellness coordinator and/or personal care assistants can report on compliance with personal care, with physical and occupational therapy, and appetite and weight recommendations. The activities director can report on participation in activities and ability to establish and sustain relationships with others. All can report on public episodes of tearfulness or verbal or physical aggression.

Nursing Homes

The number of nursing homes rapidly increased in the 1960s, when the newly formed medical assistance program (Medicaid) began to pay for the care of institutionalized elders whose personal funds had been depleted. Federal and state governments jointly fund Medicaid. With government funding assured, many for-profit homes were developed, providing care along with the older homes for the aged sponsored by religious institutions. The ownership of the newer homes ranged from mom and pop small operations to large corporate chains.

Although initially envisioned as a medical insurance program for the poor, Medicaid has been overwhelmed by meeting the demands of the nursing home entitlement. The government funding, though assured, is very low and inadequate for high quality of care. In the 1980s, concerns about poor quality of care came into focus with the publication of the Institute on Medicine's (1986) report. As a follow-up to that report, Congress began the Nursing Home Reform process with the passage of OBRA '87 (Omnibus Budget Reconciliation Act, 1987; P.L. 100-203), followed by OBRA '89 (P.L. 101-239). These documents set in motion a series of extensive regulations for nursing homes and systems for monitoring compliance with those regulations.

The Minimum Data Set (MDS) is at the core of nursing home reform. Now in its second revision (with the release of the third version expected soon), the MDS is an extensive assessment tool that aspires to objectively measure a wide range of functional, biological, and psychosocial facets of each individual residing in the country's nursing homes. The data are used at an individual level for care planning and can be aggregated to profile the residents of a facility, a state, or the nation. Items can be aggregated for a facility and then combined to identify "quality indicators." Surveyors can use the data to identify areas where a given facility deviates significantly from other facilities, suggesting areas of deficiency. Facilities can use the data to target and monitor areas for quality improvement. Families can view the quality indicators on the Medicare web site under "Nursing Home Compare" (www.medicare.gov).

Concerns about quality have been accompanied by concerns about cost. Just as the funding for the nation's hospitals was changed from a daily rate to diagnosis-related groups in the 1980s, the funding for nursing homes was changed from a daily rate to a prospective payment system in the 1990s. These two systems attempt to reward efficiency of care and to provide additional resources for care of individuals with the highest need or acuity level. States can use the MDS to calculate a facility's case mix index (CMI), or acuity level (the average care needs of the residents). This CMI becomes a basis for funding, with higher CMI facilities receiving higher payments. Because of this funding bias, nursing homes today have moved toward a bimodal population: A large percentage are still individuals who require a traditional long-term stay, perhaps until death, but a growing percentage are individuals who require an intensive short-term stay, primarily for rehabilitation. These are often people who were residing at home or in an assisted living facility; they may have broken a hip, had a knee replaced, or had a stroke, and expect to return home following intensive nursing-home-based rehabilitation. These funding patterns favor the growth of the high-acuity, high-need population in nursing homes, encouraging service to those with lesser care needs through assisted living or home care.

Regulations

Nursing homes are one of the most highly regulated industries in the country. State surveyors regularly check on every aspect of the environment and care, ranging from the temperature of the refrigerator to the shoe style of the nursing assistants. Nursing home administrators and directors of nursing are masters of regulatory detail and are held highly accountable. Therapists should meet with the administration to decide on how and where documentation will appear in the chart and who will place it there (therapist or unit clerk?—filing your own is more time-consuming, but more reliable). If the facility has a documentation consultant, it may be wise to meet with that person as well. The following is an example of recent advice from a consultant: If a single page contains multiple progress notes (a facility preference to keep the overall chart size down), then each note must be initialed, but a full signature must appear at the bottom of the page. Another area of disagreement may be whether the therapist should write only in the therapy section, or whether the therapist should also put a brief alert in the physician's progress notes that the patient was seen. The therapist must be extremely careful to comply with all documentation regulations to avoid causing survey problems for the facility.

Nursing homes are complex organizations, with broad and deep divisions of labor. The patient-therapist relationship exists within a complex web of interrelationships (see Figure 9.1). The primary departments are administration (with the nursing home administrator as executive), and nursing (with the director of nursing at the helm). Each of these has layers of supporting personnel, including nurses, certified nursing assistants

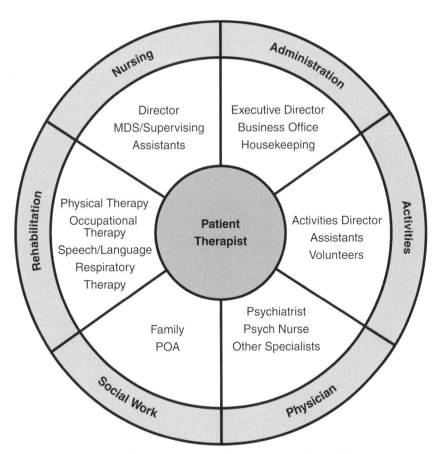

Figure 9.1   The Therapeutic Context in Residential Settings

and dietary, housekeeping, business office, admissions, and maintenance staff. In addition, there are typically departments for activities and social service (which may include chaplains and volunteers) and either rehab staff or consultants (including occupational therapy, physical therapy, speech and language therapy, and respiratory therapy). There is a designated medical director, consulting physicians, consulting pharmacists, psychiatrists and psychiatric nurses, hearing, vision, and dental specialists, podiatrists, and consulting hospice staff. Finally, there usually is an on-site beautician and periodically a visiting apparel store. Any or all of these people may, at one time or another, be helpful as therapeutic partners or part of a therapeutic team. As therapists feel increasingly part of the total nursing home community, they can convey that sense of a caring community to the patients.

Promoting Well-Being

Unlike the relatively low staffing in ALFs, staff-resident ratios are higher in nursing homes (although many would argue that they are not high enough). Unfortunately, most of the staff have specific tasks that must be performed for a large number of residents (e.g., cleaning the rooms, delivering and retrieving the food trays, doing morning and evening care, showering, feeding, delivering medications). The best staff people are able to accomplish their tasks while simultaneously engaging in a respectful, gentle, and loving interaction with the residents. These individuals, working with the residents on a daily basis, are truly therapeutic agents. At the other extreme are staff who are brusque, rough, impatient, or disinterested. Therapists working with these staff to develop a more caring approach can dramatically improve a patient's sense of well-being. Activities and social work staff are typically easy allies. The therapist will usually develop more in-depth knowledge of the patient over time and can therefore make suggestions to the social worker about specific unmet needs (e.g., new glasses) or ideas for activity pursuits.

Therapeutic Approaches

Aside from the general therapeutic team approach already mentioned, the therapist may want to specifically adapt the usual therapeutic assessments and modalities to the nursing home MDS-based environment. The current MDS version 2.0 can be viewed online at www.cms.hhs.gov /quality/mds20/mdsallforms.pdf. The user's manual, which includes information about the instrument's development, use, and statistical characteristics, can be viewed at www.cms.hh.gov/quality/mds20. At the end of the user's manual are the resident assessment protocols (RAPs), which give instructions for a much more detailed assessment of specific triggered conditions (i.e., conditions that were identified by particular combinations of answers on the MDS). A preliminary 3.0 version is available for viewing at www.cms.hhs.gov/quality/mds30.

Therapists working in nursing homes should ally themselves with the home to capture the most accurate and consistent picture of the resident on the MDS. By making this commitment, the therapist becomes an asset to the home, as well as to the resident. The therapist should understand the nursing home's specific process for completing the MDS. Because of the critical importance of coding the MDS correctly for care planning and reimbursement, most nursing homes have one or more RNs assigned to that task. The RN may be known as the MDS nurse or, more formally, as an RNAC (RN assessment coordinator). Therapists should meet with these nurses and determine the best methods of communication and mutual support.

In MDS 2.0, the most relevant sections for therapists are Sections B (Cognitive Patterns), C (Communication Patterns), E (Mood and Behavior Patterns), F (Psychosocial Well-Being), N (Activity Pursuit Patterns), and P (Special Treatments and Procedures). Therapists should check the most recent MDS as part of their evaluations. If there is a discrepancy between the therapist's and the MDS coordinator's evaluations, the therapist should bring it to the attention of the RNAC. For example, Item 2 of Section B (Cognitive Patterns) is "Short-term memory okay—seems/appears to recall after 5 minutes." Most nurses do not complete a Mini-Mental State Exam (MMSE; Folstein, Folstein, & McHugh, 1975) before filling out that item. If the score for short-term recall on the MMSE is 0 for 3 but is 0 (memory okay) on the MDS, the therapist should advise the assessment nurse to change the MDS rating based on the therapist's data. The quantitative measure produces a more accurate picture of the resident and may produce different triggers for resident nursing care.

Section E (Mood and Behavior Patterns) is often the most relevant section for therapists. Item 1 (Indicators of depression, anxiety, sad mood) includes verbal expressions of distress; sleep-cycle issues; sad, apathetic, anxious appearance; and loss of interest. Items 2 and 3 rate mood persistence and change. Item 4 (Behavioral Symptoms) rates the frequency and alterability of five categories of behavior: wandering, verbally abusive behavioral symptoms, physically abusive behavioral symptoms, socially inappropriate/disruptive behavioral symptoms, and resists care. Resident assessment protocol 8 covers Mood States and RAP 9 covers Behavioral Symptoms.

Nursing homes differ in how they use therapists for mood and behavior issues. Many homes will refer verbally and cognitively capable depressed residents for both antidepressant therapy and psychotherapy, but refer behavioral issues for pharmacological intervention only. Some homes try to use therapists for behavior management strategies but are unable to commit the staff time or effort to implement a detailed plan. The greatest danger for a home is when a therapist develops a complex behavioral plan and documents it in the chart but the staff do not carry out the plan. That discrepancy is easily picked up and cited as a deficiency by surveyors. Therapists should never make behavioral recommendations in the written chart without prior verbal discussion with the nurse to ensure feasibility of the program. When mood and/or behavior improve, be sure to alert the MDS nurse. Worsening of depressed mood and increasing percentages of depressed residents are used as quality measures.

Involvement of Staff

As mentioned earlier, any member of the nursing home community may be useful as a therapeutic partner at various times. Most frequently, however, the nurses and nursing assistants will serve as the strongest therapeutic agents. Figures 9.2 and 9.3 provide examples of an MDS-based version of cognitive-behavioral therapy, using supervisory nurses for assessment, referral, care planning, supervision, and documentation and certified nursing assistants as therapeutic agents. The supervisory

Step One: Distinguish between Probable Mood Disorder, Distressed Mood (sadness or anxiety), and No Distress.

Actions:
- *Review the scores on MDS Section E1.*
- *Probable* Mood Disorder suggested by a score of 1 or 2 on any of the following items: a (negative statements); d (angry with self or others); f (unrealistic fears); h (health complaints); i (anxious complaints); l (sad, pained, worried look); m (crying).
- *Distressed Mood* suggested by a score of 0 on above 7 items, but a score of 1 or 2 on any other item in Section E1. If resident capable, administer Geriatric Depression Scale. If score ≥ 5 *refer* as per Step Three and *document* in chart.
- *No apparent distress* if resident receives a score of 0 on all items in Section E1. *Implement usual care; do not proceed.*

Step Two: Assess for danger to self or others.

Action:
- *Inquire about suicidal/dangerous thoughts or actions* as per RAP Module 8.
- If suicidal risk or danger to others indicated, *follow emergency procedures.*
- *Document findings and actions taken in progress notes.*

Step Three: Refer residents with probable Mood Disorder to appropriate professionals.

Action:
- *Refer* to physician, mental health professional, and/or consulting pharmacist for further evaluation and treatment. *Request* Geriatric Depression Scale be administered (as part of evaluation) and that results be documented in chart.
- *Document* Section E scores and referrals made in progress notes.

Step Four: Care plan and implement CNA Distressed Mood Program for customers with probable Mood Disorder or Distressed Mood.

Care plan statement:
- Participate in Distressed Mood Program _____ times per _____ (day, week) for _____ (weeks) with _____ (assigned CNA).
- See attached for CNA instructions.

Step Five: Care plan and implement additional measures to improve mood.

Care plan suggestions:
- Increase family visits to _____ times per _____ by _____ .
- Increase activity participation to _____ per _____ by _____ .
- Increase social interaction to _____ interactions per _____ by _____ .
- Increase customer-staff conversations to _____ per _____ by (*staff person*) actively listening to customer _____ times per _____ .

Figure 9.2 Distressed Mood Program Performed by Nurse Supervisor

Step Six: Supervise care plan implementation.	Action: • *Assign* CNA to implement Distressed Mood Program. • *Teach* CNA how to implement Distressed Mood Program. • *Document* name of responsible CNA and care plan initiation/progress in progress notes. • *Document* additional care provided by other team members (social service, activities).
Step Seven: Monitor results and revise care plan as appropriate.	Action: • *Readminister* MDS; *document* scores in progress notes. If Distressed Mood persists or worsens in spite of intervention (MDS Section E2), refer for professional consultation. • If Distressed Mood improves, *document* improvement in progress notes, and revise care plan as necessary. • If Distressed Mood resolves (no symptoms checked in MDS Section E), document improvement in progress notes, eliminate from care plan, and institute usual care.

Figure 9.2   *(Continued)*

nurse uses the MDS Section E, Item 1 to distinguish between a "probable mood disorder," a "distressed mood," and "no apparent distress." He or she then assesses for suicidality and takes action as per RAP 8. For those with "probable mood disorder," the nurse refers to appropriate professionals. For both "probable mood disorder" and "distressed mood," the nurse engages the nursing assistant in a "distressed mood program."

The nursing assistant's distressed mood program uses a basic strategy of increasing pleasurable events and decreasing unpleasurable events (Teri & Logsdon, 1991; Teri, Logsdon, Uomoto, & McCurry, 1997). It is summarized in a simple, one-page instruction sheet, complete with MDS Section E, Item 1 outcome measures. Although many nursing assistants are shy about working with written materials and record keeping, some enjoy being engaged in this type of endeavor. Another alternative is to have the therapist read the written program to the nursing assistant and keep the written records, while eliciting ideas and verbal reports of outcomes from the assistant. This works especially well when the nursing assistant is not fully comfortable with written English. This type of program can be used with the therapist guiding the overall

Step One: You and resident together choose a pleasant activity that the resident enjoys.

Other Pleasant Events

☐ Hand massage with lotion   _____
☐ Back rub   _____
☐ Singing or humming   _____
☐ Listening to music   _____
☐ Looking at magazines   _____
☐ Talking about the "old days"   _____
☐ Sweet treats   _____
☐ Getting a manicure   _____
☐ Reading the Bible   _____
☐ Rolling yarn   _____
☐ Sewing a sew card   _____
☐ Talking about pets   _____
☐ Looking at photos   _____
☐ Taking a little walk   _____

Step Two: Do this enjoyable activity together one time each day for one week.

Add this pleasant event every day:

_____
_____

Step Three: You and resident together choose one unpleasant thing that the resident *does not* enjoy.

Other Unpleasant Events

☐ Too much noise   _____
☐ Feeling rushed   _____
☐ Not enough privacy   _____
☐ Feeling cold   _____
☐ Feeling exposed   _____
☐ Hair washed in shower   _____
☐ Getting into arguments   _____
☐ Uncomfortable clothes   _____
☐ Feeling lonely   _____
☐ Feeling afraid   _____

Step Four: Remove one unpleasant thing each day for one week.

Remove this unpleasant event every day:

_____
_____

Step Five: Report what you observe back to the nurse supervisor after one week.

Resident:

	more	less
Makes negative statements	____ more	____ less
Asks repetitive questions	____ more	____ less
Makes repetitive verbalizations	____ more	____ less
Makes angry statements	____ more	____ less
Negative about him or herself	____ more	____ less
Makes fearful statements	____ more	____ less
Worried about health	____ more	____ less
Seeks attention or reassurance	____ more	____ less
Unpleasant in morning	____ more	____ less
Unable to sleep	____ more	____ less
Sad or worried	____ more	____ less
Crying or tearful	____ more	____ less
Pacing, restless	____ more	____ less
Withdrawn from activities	____ more	____less
Withdrawn from other people	____ more	____ less
Unwilling to try ADLs	____ more	____ less

Figure 9.3   Distressed Mood Program Performed by Certified Nursing Assistants. Adapted from "Cognitive Behavioral Interventions for Treatment of Depression," by L. Teri and D. Gallagher, 1991, *Gerontologist, 31*, pp. 413–416.

effort of both nurse and nursing assistant, or it could be used as a stand-alone by the nursing department, with only periodic consultation by a therapist.

Other such MDS-based versions of psychotherapeutic modalities could easily be developed for other triggered conditions. For example, Section F (Psychosocial Well-Being), Item 2 (Unsettled Relationships) would be a natural fit for an MDS version of interpersonal therapy (Hinrichsen & Clougherty, 2006).

Measurement of Outcomes

The nursing home setting offers the richest opportunity for outcome measures, compared to independent or assisted living. Therapists can use their own office practice psychological measures and scales, but in addition, they can use the extensive documentation from many of the disciplines required by nursing homes. The therapist can always find monthly, if not weekly weights, records of physical and occupational therapy attendance, records of activity attendance, social work records of family contact, and dietary records. Furthermore, when a resident is on an antipsychotic medication, he or she is supposed to have specific behaviors recorded on a per-shift basis. Unfortunately, these behavior-monitoring records are often not very accurate. By negotiating for a specific patient for a specific period of time, the therapist can usually get more accurate recordings. All of these sources of data are very helpful in documenting progress toward specific, objective, attainable goals.

ETHICAL ISSUES IN RESIDENTIAL SETTINGS

All therapists are required to uphold the general ethical standards of their profession. However, geriatric patients in residential settings pose particularly knotty ethical dilemmas on a regular basis (Duffy, 2002; Kane & Caplan, 1990; Moye & Zehr, 2000; Zehr, 2003). Frequently, a therapist's training in ethics can provide a clear voice of reason in otherwise tumultuous ethical situations. This section focuses on three critical areas of ethical practice in residential settings.

Decision-Making Capacity

This determination is most frequently at the core of every ethical dilemma. Should the feeding tube be inserted or removed? Should the couple be permitted or enabled to have sexual activity? Should she be hospitalized? Should he be given more morphine? Should she receive psychotherapy?

Staff, family, residents, and their lawyers often think these are separate questions, to be decided in team meetings, in ethics committees, or, in the worst-case scenario, in court. However, in every one of these situations, the underlying issue is a relatively simple one: Who is the decision maker? We can invoke the 80/20 rule: In 80% of the cases, it is clear that either the resident or the person with power of attorney is the decision maker; in 20% of the cases, it is unclear whether the resident has decision-making capacity, or who actually *is* the decision maker, and what *are* the resident's preferences.

The therapist has a unique role to play in helping to resolve these dilemmas. One should be familiar with formal assessment of decision-making capacity (American Bar Association Commission on Law and Aging & American Psychological Association, 2005). In addition, it is often critical to teach the other residential team members about the concept of decision-making capacity and the ethical dilemmas involved therein. Assisted living facilities are often quick to please families (the payers) and therefore to assign them decision-making authority. Nursing facilities may be more inclined to go with professional medical judgment, with less attention to patient preference. Therapists can use sessions to gently elicit patient preferences about care, as well as to assess and monitor decision-making capability. Document and verbally share (with permission) information about patient care preferences with staff and family. Help staff and family anticipate difficult care decisions and reach consensus beforehand. Help everyone understand that the emergency bias is always toward more intervention; if less intervention is desired, it needs to be assertively documented and enforced.

Here is a cautionary word about powers of attorney: Those appointed often feel that they have sole decision-making authority. Worse, they rarely understand the concept of "substitute judgment," that is, that they are to make decisions *as the resident would*, not based on their own beliefs, values, or preferences. Educating those with power of attorney about substitute judgment and the need to continue to include the nondecisionally capable resident as much as possible in discussions is a very important therapeutic and advocacy role.

Decision-making capacity is required to give informed consent for psychological treatment. The therapist should explain the proposed treatment and the resident's right to accept or decline treatment and, if at all possible, obtain written consent. If the resident has another person take care of financial matters (so that the Medicare Explanation of Benefit form will go to that person), it is wise to obtain verbal consent from the resident to contact the financial party and explain the treatment, costs, and benefits to that party as well as to the resident.

Privacy and Confidentiality

All long-term care settings, whether in the home, ALF, or nursing home, can pose privacy dilemmas. Spouses, children, or hired caregivers can violate privacy at home. Personal care assistants can walk in on sessions in ALF rooms or suites. The most difficult privacy situations occur in nursing homes, where having a roommate is the norm and staff often walk in and out of rooms. The goal becomes to provide care with the maximum possible privacy, if complete privacy is not possible. Creative solutions may include finding more private spaces that are available for the session time (e.g., an empty dining room); changing the session time to fit a roommate's scheduled time out of the room; using an amplifier to allow the therapist to speak very softly; and sitting very close to the resident.

Confidentiality is the protection of patient information, limiting access to those who need to know. HIPAA regulations have mandated special confidentiality precautions for psychotherapy notes. However, in nursing homes and many ALFs, documentation in the medical chart or resident file is required. In addition, insurers require documentation of services. Because of the potentially wide exposure of patient information, chart information should be limited to the minimum required, including date, beginning and end time of session, diagnosis, long- and short-term goals, type of intervention, progress toward goals, and expected time frame. Details of the session's content or patient's psychodynamics should be omitted.

When reviewing the HIPAA guidelines with patients (and obtaining their signature indicating that they received the Notice of Privacy Practices), therapists should be sure to explain the limitations of confidentiality, especially the "danger to self or others" concept. In long-term care, the far more prevalent concern is suicide. Patients generally seem accepting of the idea that if they express to the therapist an intention to commit suicide, the therapist will need to discuss it with their physician.

Conflict of Interest

A therapist operating in a long-term care institutional setting faces an inherent potential conflict of interest: a primary commitment to the best interests of the patient versus a need to work for the benefit of the host institution (ALF or nursing home). Whether an employee or consultant, the therapist must be viewed as part of the team to be permitted to operate in a facility. When a patient's best interests and institutional needs collide, the therapist suffers a conflict of interest. Patients who are aggressively (and at times, correctly) critical of institutional policies or personnel create such dilemmas. Such a dilemma is created when ALF residents require a higher level of care, but the facility wants to hold them for census reasons. Staff who are disrespectful to a resident in front of a therapist create such dilemmas. Administrators who side with a (paying) family member against a patient's wishes create such dilemmas.

These conflicts of interest cannot be avoided. The most successful way to operate requires a realization that what is in the best interest of the patient is ultimately in the best interest of the institution, and vice versa. The therapist should adopt a problem-solving, consensus-building strategy rather than allow adversarial positions to develop. Unfortunately, the therapist needs to spend nonreimbursable time educating and persuading institutional staff and family members that consensus decisions are stronger decisions. Ultimately, if a particular institution cannot align its institutional goals with the patient's best interests, it may require that the resident leave that facility.

Therapists who are new to institutional work may need to give themselves a year or two of observation and learning before becoming a vocal member of the care team. They need to establish credibility, read the politics and power lines, figure out how to get things accomplished without ruffling feathers, and develop personal efficiencies of documentation, billing, and communication. With these efficiencies, therapists in long-term care can be successful financially. However, to achieve excellence, the therapist will always have to temper financial success with significant nonreimbursable time to staff and families. This work is not for the faint-hearted, nor for those who wish only for financial success. It is a calling, as well as a profession.

CONCLUSION

Working in a long-term care setting is complex and challenging, yet ultimately rewarding. The therapist is called on to have empathy and compassion for the patient, but also for staff, family members, and even the institutions themselves. How can we reduce depression and increase well-being among older adults? At least part of the answer lies in bringing to bear all of the positive resources inherent in patients' living environments and eliminating or reducing the environmental press or demand that has negative consequences for patients. This requires us to look beyond the intimate therapeutic encounter to the surrounding environment of care for creative avenues to successful therapeutic intervention.

RECOMMENDED READING

American Psychological Association. (2006). *Psychological services for long-term care: Resource guide.* APA Committee on Aging web site (apa.org/pi/aging/longterm.html).

Frazer, D. W., & Jongsma, A. E. (1999). *The older adult psychotherapy treatment planner.* New York: Wiley.

Lichtenberg, P. A., Crose, R., Frazer, D., Smith, M., Kramer, N., Rosowsky, E., et al. (1998). Standards for psychological services in long-term care facilities. *Gerontologist, 38,* 122–127.

Molinari, V. (Ed.). (2000). *Professional psychology in long term care*. New York: Hatherleigh Press.

REFERENCES

American Bar Association Commission on Law and Aging & American Psychological Association. (2005). *Assessment of older adults with diminished capacity: A handbook for lawyers.* Washington, DC: American Bar Association and American Psychological Association.

Duffy, M. (2002). Confidentiality and informed consent versus collaboration: Challenges in psychotherapy ethics in nursing homes. *Clinical Gerontologist, 25*(3/4), 277–292.

Folstein, M. F., Folstein, S. E., & McHugh, P. R. (1975). "Mini-Mental State": A practical method for grading the cognitive state of patients for the clinician. *Journal of Psychiatric Research, 12,* 189–198.

Frazer, D. W. (1998). Quality psychotherapy: Measures for tracking change. In P. E. Hartman-Stein (Ed.), *Innovative behavioral healthcare for older adults: A guidebook for changing times* (pp. 57–77). San Francisco: Jossey-Bass.

Hinrichsen, G., & Clougherty, K. F. (2006). *Interpersonal therapy for depressed older adults.* Washington, DC: American Psychological Association.

Institute of Medicine. (1986). *Improving the quality of care in nursing homes.* Washington, DC: National Academy Press.

Kane, R. A., & Caplan, A. L. (Eds.). (1990). *Everyday ethics: Resolving dilemmas in nursing home life.* New York: Springer.

Lawton, M. P., & Nahemow, L. (1973). Ecology and the aging process. In C. Eisdorfer & M. P. Lawton (Eds.), *The psychology of adult development and aging* (pp. 619–674). Washington, DC: American Psychological Association.

Moye, J., & Zehr, M. (2000). Resolving ethical challenges for psychological practice in long-term care. *Clinical Psychology: Science and Practice, 7,* 337–344.

Teri, L., & Logsdon, R. G. (1991). Identifying pleasant activities for individuals with Alzheimer's disease: The Pleasant Events Schedule-AD. *Gerontologist, 31,* 124–127.

Teri, L., Logsdon, R. G., Uomoto, J., & McCurry, S. M. (1997). Behavioral treatment of depression in dementia patients: A controlled clinical trial. *Journal of Gerontology: Series B, Psychological Sciences and Social Sciences, 52*(4), 159–166.

Zehr, M. (2003). Ethical issues. In E. Rosowsky & J. M. Casciani (Eds.), *Long-term care professional educational program manual* (pp. 115–132). Macomb, IL: WIU Curriculum Publications Clearinghouse.

Zimmerman, S., Sloane, P. D., Heck, E., Maslow, K., & Schulz, R. (2005). Introduction: Dementia care and quality of life in assisted living and nursing homes [Special issue]. *Gerontologist, 45*(1), 5–7.

The Basics of Building and Managing a Geropsychology Practice

Paula E. Hartman-Stein

Information about the business aspects of managing a geriatric mental health care practice is largely absent from graduate school curricula and pre- and postdoctoral training programs and found rarely even in continuing education course offerings. The practice of psychotherapy was once a cottage industry that did not require a great deal of business acumen to ensure success, but with the advent of managed care and other changes due to the industrialization of the health care industry, mental health practitioners in private practice require business savvy. With information and suggestions specific to building and maintaining a niche practice in geriatric mental health, this chapter highlights three commandments of effective business: Know thy business, Know thy market, and Know thy customer.

Many of the ideas in this chapter originate from interviews conducted while writing articles for the *National Psychologist* as well as lessons learned from my own consulting and clinical psychology practice devoted to older adults and their families. The information covered is not all-inclusive of necessary knowledge for running a successful practice. One valuable resource book, *How to Survive and Thrive as a Therapist* (Pope &

Vasquez, 2005), provides general ideas and resources for psychologists in private practice. An excellent guide that covers generic principles for business management, marketing, and publicity is *The Martha Rules: 10 Essentials for Achieving Success as You Start, Build, or Manage a Business* (Stewart, 2005). Related to her recent legal problems, Stewart describes coping strategies that promote resilience and hopefulness when experiencing business setbacks. Many of her recommendations, such as the importance of giving information away, viewing media sources as customers, and investing in your reputation, to name a few, have practical implications related to economic survival in geriatric behavioral health care.

KNOW THY BUSINESS

Keeping up with guidelines, regulations, and practice trends is essential for competence in any area of behavioral health practice. Avoiding professional isolation is another key ingredient to ensure competence.

Recommended Reading

Clinicians who are considering providing behavioral health care services to older adults should begin by carefully studying three articles: the *APA Guidelines for Psychological Practice with Older Adults* (American Psychological Association, 2004), *What Practitioners Should Know about Working with Older Adults* (Abeles et al., 1998), and *Standards for Psychological Services in Long-Term Care Facilities* (Lichtenberg et al., 1998). Part of a solid foundation of knowledge, these articles describe unique aspects of clinical work with the geriatric population and highlight areas that need to be mastered to gain competence in the field.

Other sources of practical information include the APA practice web site, www.apapractice.org, APA Division 12-2's web site, www.geropsych.org, and www.centerforhealthyaging.com, where articles published in the *National Psychologist* since 1993 about Medicare and other practice issues can be easily accessed.

If, after studying these resources, you feel motivated to learn more, then this is an area worth pursuing. To be successful in any new business or area of professional development, the work involved in learning it must be inherently interesting because much investment of time and energy lies ahead (Stewart, 2005).

Attend Continuing Education Programs in Geropsychology Topics

The graying of the American population has made it more likely that the generalist-trained psychologist will see older clientele, ready or not. As a result, more continuing education (CE) programs offering content in clinical geropsychology are popping up. This book is a result of the first annual series of weekend CE programs offered through the University of Colorado, Colorado Springs, that focused on the basics of psychotherapy with depressed older adults as well as business issues impacting geriatric mental health practice. Check out this annual series each year as well as the APA convention offerings from Division 12, Section 2 (Clinical Geropsychology) and Division 20 (Adult Development and Aging). State psychological associations offer increasing numbers of programs with geropsychology content.

Become an Apprentice and Seek Consultation

When entering a new field of clinical practice, obtaining consultation about clinical cases and business development is well worth the time, effort, and expense. One source to locate consultants is the Division 12, Section 2 web site (www.geropsych.org), which lists geropsychologists who are willing to provide advice and consultation to practitioners.

To expand networking and mentorship opportunities, consider joining organizations such as APA's Division 12, Section 2 (Clinical Geropsychology) Division 20 (www.apadiv20.phhp.ufl.edu), the American Society of Aging (www.asaging.org), or Psychologists in Long-Term Care (www.wvu.edu/~pltc/PLTChome.html). To learn from clinicians and researchers who are experts in the field peruse professional journals such as *Generations, Gerontologist, Clinical Gerontologist,* and the Fall 2005 issue of *Clinical Psychology: Science and Practice,* which is devoted to assessment and treatment of depression in older adults. While attending CE seminars and workshops, make it a point to meet the speakers whom you admire. They often appreciate meeting attentive members of the audience and sharing business cards for later contact. At regional and state associations there are opportunities to meet local experts. National or state listservs also are valuable resources. Consider organizing a coalition or group of local geriatric mental health professionals to meet regularly to discuss business problems and provide clinical and collegial support.

For assistance in developing a business plan, one valuable and free resource is the small business development center found in most regions of the country, an organization funded with federal dollars to help small businesses thrive. Contact your local Chamber of Commerce to learn more about this free service, one of the best-kept business secrets.

Basics of Medicare Regulations for Psychology

The single most important business aspect of geriatric behavioral health is to learn the rules of billing and coding of the Medicare system. The federal system remains the primary source of payment for the majority of older adults' health care costs. There are senior managed care insurance products, but the numbers of beneficiaries enrolled in these systems are relatively small compared to those using the national Medicare system.

The process of becoming a Medicare provider is relatively painless. Go to the web site (www.CMS.gov) and click on the Center for Medicare and Medicaid (CMS) forms page, scrolling down to CMS 855 to download and print the application form. Any licensed provider recognized by CMS can apply, and after a relatively straightforward credentialing process, the regional Medicare carrier, also known as the fiscal intermediary, assigns the applicant a provider number. Unlike managed care panels, there is no obligatory number of years of practice following licensure that are required before becoming a provider. Because of this relatively open door policy, traditional fee-for-service Medicare is the final frontier of independent practice in the United States (Hartman-Stein, 1998b).

After applying to become a Medicare provider, the clinician must sign an agreement to follow the regulations of the Medicare system. The potential ramifications of ignorance about the regulations are sobering and serious. Audits that uncover incorrect diagnostic and procedural coding with accompanying poor clinical documentation can result in demands for back payment for completed professional work, monetary penalties of $12,500 per claim, plus triple damages, potential loss of Medicare provider status, the closing of nonprofit clinics and private practices, and criminal prosecution. According to James Georgoulakis, PhD, the APA representative to the American Medical Association's Relative Update Committee, in 2005 about 170 psychologists received jail time for fraudulent billing under Federal Sentencing Guidelines (J. Georgoulakis, personal communication, January 3, 2006).

To work ethically and professionally with older adults, a basic working knowledge of Medicare regulations is as essential as knowledge of how to assess for cognitive deficits or provide psychotherapy with the older depressed patient. Unfortunately, unless they have personally experienced a Medicare audit, many psychologists either ignore or simply do not attend to new regulations and information provided by regional Medicare insurance carriers and the federal government.

Keeping up with coding or regulatory changes is imperative. Reading the Medicare carrier's newsletters, checking the CMS web site, and attending available seminars are the usual ways to keep yourself current. Information spread through professional association listservs can also be helpful, but keep in mind that insurance carrier rules vary greatly by region.

The *National Psychologist*, an independent newspaper, is another source of pertinent information for clinicians. Mark Regna, CEO of a behavioral health practice, criticized the APA several years ago for lack of emphasis in educating its members about Medicare issues such as billing code changes: "Psychologists need to worry less about where to set up the chairs in their office and more about the meat and potatoes of business, that is, how to bill properly" (Hartman-Stein, 2002, p. 8).

Before describing some basics about the federal regulations, the debunking of the commonly held myth of the Medicare conspiracy theory against mental health is in order. I have met colleagues who strictly adhere to evidence-based clinical practice spout the opinion that CMS simply does not like psychology and mental health care and that "the feds are out to get us." Knowledge of the facts quickly dispels the notion that the feds examine mental health claims without basis. The following are some sample findings of pertinent investigations:

- An audit from the Office of Inspector General (OIG) in 1998 showed psychologists and psychiatrists to be the second greatest offenders in erroneous billing, behind only podiatrists (Hartman-Stein, 1998a).
- In January 2001 the OIG reported that an inspection of 450 psychiatric services in nursing homes found that 39% of psychological testing services were unnecessary, and 27% of all mental health services in the nursing homes were medically unnecessary.
- In May 2001 an OIG report revealed that Medicare allowed $185 million in 1998 for inappropriate mental health services.

The defensive stance is that these reports reflect poor documentation rather than deliberate fraudulent practice. This is true in some cases, but in an interview in *Psychotherapy Finances* (Klein, 2003), James Georgoulakis stated that about 90% of the cases that go to the Department of Justice wind up with the providers owing money—reimbursement of fees plus fines.

Effective October 1, 2005, CMS has begun a demonstration project covering California, New York, and Florida with the purpose of monitoring the individuals who monitor the audits. According to Georgoulakis, "We are going to have increased audits, there is no question about that. For every dollar Congress puts into monitoring, they get four dollars in return" (Hartman-Stein, 2005a, p. 20). Check out the web site (www.CERTprovider.org) for information on the new program, Comprehensive Error Rate Testing Program.

Mental health practitioners clearly are not the only professionals under scrutiny. Kevin Gerold, acting deputy director of program integrity at CMS, explained, "We are instructing contractors to permit their nurse reviewers, when looking at medical records, to interpret that record in the context of the care provided. But in no way will we overlook poor documentation. People who document poorly will continue to have problems" (Hartman-Stein, 2002, p. 8). According to Gerold, the scrutiny makes a difference. He reported that Operation Restore Trust, a federal program to decrease fraud, found that a 15% overall error rate for claims for all medical providers dropped to 6% after the program was instituted. In December 2004, CMS announced it was taking steps to cut Medicare fraud and payment errors in half over the next 4 years (Heavey, 2004).

In the event of heightened anxiety and regrets of choosing to provide mental health services for older adults, be assured that regulations are far from impossible to comprehend and follow. A responsible, careful clinician can learn and keep up with the basic rules. But keeping up with changes takes time and diligence.

Some clinicians believe that there is a way around studying Medicare regulations by joining a large group practice or working in an institution such as a hospital. Think again. A major caveat is that there is no true layer of protection from the rules. Ignorance of them is not an excuse in an audit. To expect that the administration of a facility or private practice will take the hit and protect the individual psychologist is naive at best. The reputation of the individual clinician and his or her license to practice psychology or medicine are ultimately at stake.

Audit triggers include the following: use of a code that provides a higher reimbursement rate when documentation supports a lower level of code, showing a high percentage of the same code (e.g., billing only for initial interviews), excessive visits to nursing home patients, and excessive testing hours for a single day (Hartman-Stein, 1999). An individual provider's profile of claims can also trigger an audit. For example, if a clinician has a procedure profile of billing a code well over the average of his or her peers, that clinician's work will be audited (J. Georgoulakis, personal communication, January 3, 2006).

Although there are volumes of Medicare regulations, the following tenets constitute a practical foundation for clinicians:

Tenet 1: *Regional insurance carriers have the power to interpret CMS directives.* No uniform national policy exists for all aspects of Medicare regulations governing payment for clinical services. The federal system allows the insurance companies that have contracts with CMS to have differing interpretations of federal guidelines, explaining why Medicare policies vary in some respects by region. For example, some Medicare carriers require treatment plan updates every 90 days for patients seen in nursing home settings and 6-month updates required for out-patients. It takes some searching through regulations posted on the Web to find these idiosyncratic rules because these are not across the board standards.

CMS requires Medicare carriers to publish new policies on their web site and have a time open for comment by individual clinicians or groups. Unlikely as it may sound, individuals can make a difference by fighting for clinically relevant changes. For example, Joe Casciani, PhD, from San Diego advocated for a change in the policy of National Heritage Insurance Company that initially restricted health and behavior interventions to 2 hours of treatment *per year* for any medical condition. Largely as a result of his efforts, the carrier agreed to reimburse the health and behavior interventions for its California beneficiaries for 1 hour of assessment and up to 12 hours or 48 units of treatment sessions per year (Hartman-Stein, 2005c). Although the number of allowed treatment units is not extensive, Casciani's efforts and support from his state psychological association resulted in a significant policy change.

Despite the general rule that there are regional variations allowed in the interpretations of regulations, there are general principles that clinicians need to know.

Tenet 2: *Medical necessity is imperative to justify reimbursement of a claim.* One of the core tenets determining whether a claim for a clinical service payment is legitimate and acceptable is whether it meets the criteria for medical necessity. The purpose of the clinical service must be the alleviation or mitigation of a medical condition. When clinicians think in terms of those basic parameters, there is less mystery behind the concept. For example, if the service is primarily for personal growth or prevention, such as a cognitive fitness program, or for socialization purposes, such as a support group for new residents in an assisted living setting, or to answer a legal question, it is not medically necessary and therefore not a Medicare-covered service. The patient must also be able to participate appropriately in the service, such as psychotherapy in which communication is an essential component of the treatment. If a patient has language deficits, the clinician must be able to document how the patient and therapist communicate with one another.

Tenet 3: *No fishing expeditions are allowed.* Screening services for mental health problems are not reimbursable under Medicare. Observable symptoms or problem behaviors must be noted in the clinical record when explaining the reason for the clinical intervention. For example, if an administrator of a long-term care facility requests cognitive screenings for every newly admitted patient into a nursing home or assisted living setting, do not agree to provide these services. Medicare coverage does not pay for automatic screening for cognitive deficits or depression. Some facilities will pay for such clinical services for their prospective patients in order to lessen the chance of inappropriate placement of a resident, but it is "erroneous billing" to make a claim for clinical evaluations of every admission under Medicare Part B, the section on coverage of mental health services. Documented symptoms or signs of mood or cognitive deficits must be available to meet medical necessity requirements.

Tenet 4: *The federal government and private payers use the National Correct Coding Initiative* (NCCI) *in determining edits.* There are numerous specific rules about coding that require some diligent searching. Information on NCCI edits can be found at http://www.cms.hhs.gov/physicians /cciedits; for example, the current procedural terminology (CPT) code for psychotherapy services cannot be paid on the same date of service as the initial psychiatric interview (90801). Another edit is that the health and behavior code, 96155, family intervention without the patient present, is no longer reimbursable by the Medicare carriers.

Tenet 5: *Psychologists have a limited number of clinical procedural codes available to them.* The following procedures have codes: initial clinical interview, psychological assessment services, psychotherapy services, and health and behavior assessments and interventions. The procedural codes for psychological testing were completely changed and revamped for 2006, differentiating when the psychologist is working with the patient, when a technician is working with the patient, and when the patient works with the computer (Hartman-Stein, 2005a). To stay informed about the definitions of codes, clinicians need to invest in or at least have ready access to the most current CPT code manual.

Tenet 6: *Thorough documentation of a clinical service is required for every claim, and each chart note should be able to stand on its own merit.* The following are recommendations for the charting of every treatment session:

- Type your notes whenever feasible because legibility of chart notes is one of the most critical elements in the event of a Medicare audit. "The easier the record is to audit, the less likely it will be audited in great detail," according to Jim Georgoulakis, PhD, consultant to APA, during an interview for the *National Psychologist* (Hartman-Stein, 2004b, p. 11).
- Match the date of service in the clinical record to the date on the claim form. Mistakes in this detail can easily occur, so check dates carefully.
- Track and record the number of treatment sessions, for example, session number 4 for this episode of treatment.
- Document start and stop times of the treatment session.
- Include the diagnosis code number as well as descriptor. Check that the diagnosis on the claim form matches the diagnosis on the chart note. Some computer billing software has the original diagnosis recorded as the default diagnosis. Billing personnel must check that the diagnosis the clinician charted in case progress notes matches the diagnosis on the claim form.
- Use the diagnostic code numbers from the 2006 *International Classification of Diseases,* ninth revision (*ICD-9-CM;* World Health Organization, 2005). According to J. Georgoulakis (personal communication, October 28, 2005), "The cross walk from the *ICD-9-CM* to the *DSM-IV* is fairly consistent but is not a straight one-to-one. All psychologists would be better off in submitting claims if they utilized the *ICD-9-CM* for all diagnoses; for example, using the mental disorder section codes for psychotherapy and the physical disorders with the Health and Behavior codes." A general rule is that when coding the diagnosis for neuropsychological

testing procedures, use diagnostic codes from the nervous system section of the *ICD-9-CM*.

- Record the Global Assessment of Functioning (GAF) score from the *Diagnostic and Statistical Manual of Mental Disorders,* fourth edition, text revision (*DSM-IV-TR*) for both psychiatric and health and behavior interventions.
- On chart notes and assessment reports, use only abbreviations that are commonly recognized. Nursing home and hospital billing departments are good sources for lists of acceptable medical abbreviations.
- Include a description of treatment, operationalizing treatment in behavioral terms.
- Document medications reported by the patient.
- Record outcome measures, prognosis, and homework assignments.
- To authenticate the record, include a signature, title, and date on every chart note.
- Chart notes need to be individualized, clinically rich descriptions of the patient and the treatment provided. Auditors generally frown on canned, cookie-cutter notes.

Appendix A at the end of this chapter illustrates a sample form for case progress notes useful for both psychotherapy and health and behavior interventions.

Tenet 7: *Develop a Medicare compliance plan for your practice.* Although having a compliance manual for your practice is technically voluntary, a viable, active compliance plan is considered to be the best single insurance in the event of an adverse audit (J. Georgoulakis, personal communication, July 2, 2005; Hartman-Stein, 2000). To begin developing a compliance plan, obtain a copy of the guidelines published in the *Federal Register* (www.oig.hhs.gov/authorities/docs.physician.pdf) and place it in a three-ring binder. Read through the elements required in the manual, as outlined here, and designate a section of the binder for each of the component parts. Compliance manuals are to reflect the uniqueness of an organization, describing the services the practice offers as well as what risks these services may entail. The content in the manual should contain evidence that chart entries and claims are checked periodically, including documentation of phone conversations and written correspondence with insurance company personnel. The manual should contain documentation of any questions, problems, or actions that result from the monitoring process. Georgoulakis recommends conducting an internal audit of charts monthly or at least every quarter and hiring an external reviewer to examine approximately 30 charts per year for each clinician in the practice for proper documentation and coding (Hartman-Stein, 2000). Remember to review the OIG web site annually.

The Office of Inspector General's "Compliance Program Guidance for Individual and Small Group Physician Practices," published in the *Federal Register* (2000), includes the following components of an effective compliance program:

- Internal monitoring and auditing, including what is being monitored, how it is done, and who is doing the monitoring.
- Implementing compliance and written practice standards.
- Designating a compliance officer (e.g., the owner of the practice or the office manager). Include a typed page indicating who the compliance officer is and under whose authority the person was appointed.
- Conducting training and education of all staff in the practice, both professional and clerical. The training can be an in-service or a continuing education program.
- Responding appropriately to detected offenses and developing corrective action. For example, include a statement in the manual that a monthly staff meeting will occur to discuss any changes in coding, problems with billing, or any newly published regulations.
- Ensuring that open communication is the standard in the practice; that is, the director or owner of the practice supports discussion and disclosure of any compliance problems without any fear of retribution.
- Enforcing disciplinary standards through well-publicized guidelines for employees to follow so they take seriously their compliance responsibilities. For example, include in the compliance

manual a letter to each employee stating that the practice is committed to exceptional patient care and adherence to policies that govern that care.

KNOW THY MARKET AND THY CUSTOMER

Let's assume you have gotten over your fear of Medicare regulations, and you are serious about developing a niche practice in geropsychology. The next step is to figure out how to obtain patient referrals, that is, how to market your practice. In some psychology circles, the very term "marketing" connotes activities that are unbecoming, unprofessional, or beneath what a psychologist should have to do. What naive, if not arrogant thinking! Unless employed by a Veteran's Administration, large community hospital, or health maintenance organization that has a ready supply of patients, clinicians must develop, maintain, and constantly add to their referral network. This aspect of business lacks the serious tone of federal regulations, but the ramifications are significant. Without ongoing effective strategies to generate referrals, the practice will not be solvent.

The following are core basic tenets about work settings, strategies of marketing and publicity, and serving the customer.

Tenet 1: *When beginning a geropsychology practice, consider joining an established group practice. Better yet, colocate with a group of primary care physicians.* Newly licensed psychologists, those who are new to a community, or clinicians just beginning to work with older adults will build up clientele and their reputation over time. To ensure a base of steady work, join an established group or attempt to obtain an exclusive service contract with a long-term care facility. But be advised: In urban or suburban regions of the country, nursing homes without contracts with psychology or psychiatric groups are rare. In rural settings, the long-term care facilities may be clamoring for geriatric behavioral health consultants. Pros and cons exist for working for a nursing home as a lone wolf independent contractor versus being part of a group that does such work. The major pro is that the money earned does not need to be shared.

After psychologists were designated independent providers in the Medicare system in the early 1990s, entrepreneurial psychologists formed companies that obtained exclusive nursing home contracts. These companies often need newly licensed psychologists to fill their contractual agreements. The companies vary in their pay structure, benefits, and training opportunities. Especially for those starting out in this area of psychology, they offer a ready source of work.

If a psychologist has credentials from a postdoctoral fellowship in geropsychology or other postdoctoral training, he or she may be able to join an established mental health private practice and become the resident expert in older adult care. Such credentials are attractive to community mental health centers that historically have not designated geriatric mental health a priority area because there is community pressure to develop programs for the coming elder boom.

An alternative to the traditional model of providing specialized mental health services is the collaborative care approach of the behavioral health care consultant within a primary care setting (Gray, Brody, & Johnson, 2005; Haley, 2005). Areán and Ayalon (2005) assert that geropsychologists have skills to become depression care managers for older adults within primary care practices, but such a narrow role may be impractical except in a research context. Although there are complexities in figuring out the reimbursement strategies that work in such a setting, colocating within a primary care practice is an ideal and perhaps preferable situation for geropsychologists. In the context of primary care, the psychologist has ready access to older adult patients having difficulties managing their chronic illnesses as well as to the older adults with depression, anxiety, and memory impairment. To work effectively in this setting, the psychologist must have a background in health psychology interventions as well as knowledge of how to code properly using the health and behavior CPT codes. Behavioral health care consulting within primary care is an evolving and promising role for the geropsychologist of the future.

Tenet 2: *Never keep all of your referral eggs in one basket.* When working in private practice, dependence on referrals from a small number of referral sources is a mistake, regardless of the briskness of current business. For example, when I served as psychological consultant to a hospital-based geriatric assessment center, there was a high and steady volume of referrals for several years, until the retirement of the chief of service, who was a psychology-friendly geriatrician. The new chair of geriatrics reduced my referrals of new patients dramatically within weeks of taking over the position. There were no apologies and no explanations, only one phone call from her staff nurse announcing that the orders for cognitive testing for the previously referred patients who were scheduled but not yet evaluated were withdrawn. This change of personnel resulted in layoffs, reducing the personnel in my practice. That once full basket of referrals emptied very suddenly and without warning, requiring me to scramble for new referral sources.

The key to business success is to have a variety of referral sources at all times and to constantly look for new ones. It helps to track monthly the number of referrals received and their sources. There are many rewards to having one's own independent practice, but there is no income security as a freelancer.

Tenet 3: *Primary care physicians and adult children of older adults are the most likely sources of referrals for an outpatient specialty geropsychology practice.* Although there are growing numbers of older adults, they typically do not readily seek out psychological or behavioral health care. Older adults are most likely to seek treatment when their primary care physician encourages them to do so. Therefore, psychologists who do not work in a primary care setting need to cultivate primary care physicians as customers to help them with diagnosis and treatment of their older adult patients. A recent analysis in my outpatient practice revealed that 90% of new older adult patient referrals came from primary care physicians. Developing collegial relationships with adult internal medicine and family practice physicians is imperative to success in geriatric behavioral health care.

Maintaining the referral sources is another skill that takes time and effort. Once the physician's office makes a referral, promptly write a letter thanking the physician for allowing you to share in the treatment of his or her patient and communicating your diagnostic impressions and the basics of the treatment plan, the same protocol that subspecialty physicians follow when they are referred a patient by a primary care physician. Kirk Strosahl, PhD, a proponent of an integrated behavioral health care approach, described the traditional mental health system in the United States as "a complete flop." In an interview for the *National Psychologist,* he said, "There is no other specialty that is so secretive. The primary care physicians often see mental health services as a big black box" (Hartman-Stein, 2001, p. 16). Strosahl said that primary care physicians complain about receiving no feedback from clinicians in the traditional model of mental health care. Under the new privacy rules that began in April 2003, members of the health care team are encouraged to share information about treatment of the patient. Communicating with the physician at the start of treatment and whenever there is a significant change in the patient's condition is a good strategy. Physicians have little time for phone calls except in patient emergencies, but in my experience they appreciate letters and progress notes about their patients.

After physician referrals, the second most fruitful source of referral is the adult child of the older adult. Becoming known to this audience occurs through typical marketing methods, such as community talks and seminars, many of which are pro bono, for organizations such as the Alzheimer's Association, women's groups, churches, and service-oriented or civic groups (e.g., Lion's Club, Chamber of Commerce, hospital-sponsored seminars; Hartman-Stein & Ergun, 1998). Adult children will search for a clinician on the Internet, making an informative personal web site a source of potential referral.

Developing a reputation for high-quality service and responsiveness to referral sources takes time, often years. The benefits will accrue with persistent effort.

Tenet 4: *Do not expect older adults to pay more than nominal out-of-pocket fees for services offered by clinicians, even nontraditional, personal growth programs.* Knowledge of customers includes awareness of how and for what they will spend their money (Stewart, 2005). Before offering a new service, such as a memory enhancement program, check out what other groups charge for similar programs. In my experience, relatively small numbers of older adults, including those who have accrued considerable wealth during their working years, are willing to pay more than a nominal fee for programs such as those promoting cognitive fitness, memory enhancement, or personal coaching. Physical fitness trainers are more widely accepted, but cognitive coaches are perhaps too new a commodity to have widespread acceptance. Hospitals and other nonprofit organizations offer free seminars on health and wellness topics, and colleges and universities offer free courses to seniors. It is tough to beat against free offerings, no matter how fascinating your program may sound. A more financially fruitful endeavor is to link up with retirement communities, community mental health centers, or assisted living centers that have a marketing budget that will pay for speakers or programs on topics that interest both older adults and their adult children.

Tenet 5: *Grants are a potential source of revenue for business and research-minded geropsychologists.* Applying for Small Business Innovation Research grants, which are federal grants meant to stimulate technological innovation and increase private sector commercialization, is one avenue to explore for the savvy researcher-entrepreneur (Hartman-Stein, 2004a). Also look for opportunities to serve as a paid consultant for grants on older adult care that are sponsored through hospitals, mental health centers, and other nonprofits.

Tenet 6: *There are numerous consulting opportunities within the geropsychology field, but all take sweat equity to develop (Hartman-Stein, 2005b). Remain patient, persistent, and creative.* Retirement communities offer opportunities for developing group programs for new residents, such as adjustment and socialization groups. (Be aware: These are not reimbursable through Medicare, but some progressive facilities will pay for such programs through their marketing budgets.) Be creative and team up with other organizations. For example, I introduced the concept of holding a senior spelling bee in northeastern Ohio by meeting with several agencies before finding a sponsor for the community-based cognitive activity. The second organization I asked was willing to underwrite this venture, hiring me to be the coordinator and emcee for the bee. The event was a success in the community, bringing excellent publicity for the sponsoring agency. As a result, the senior spelling bee is now an annual event in our area (Hartman-Stein & McClure, 2006).

Legal consultation and conducting capacity evaluations are potentially financially sound endeavors, as are consulting with agencies involved with elder abuse prevention (American Bar Association, 2005; Hellman, 2005; Moye, 2005).

Trust departments of banks are another potential source for training opportunities for trust officers in recognizing dementia and problems in decision-making capacity of older adult clients.

Tenet 7: *Utilize health and behavior interventions with older adults.* Consider offering group programs on topics such as coping with Alzheimer's disease or mild cognitive impairment, diabetes, emphysema, cardiac disease, chronic pain, renal disease, arthritis, osteoporosis, and macular degeneration, to name a few. Designing and implementing disease management programs is an effective way to integrate medical care and behavioral health care (O'Donohue, Naylor, & Cummings, 2005). Geropsychologists with background and training in health psychology are ideal providers to organize and lead such programs. With the advent of the health and behavior codes, payment for such programs is feasible.

CONCLUSION

Psychologists have been independent providers under the Medicare system in the United States only since the early 1990s. Largely as a result of this historic medical-economic change, the field of clinical geropsychology was created, a relatively young area of specialty within psychology. A successful niche outpatient practice in geriatric behavioral health care can be successful only with close ties to primary care physicians, ideally in colocation with family practitioners or internal medicine physicians to provide integrated health care delivery. In the less than ideal world, frequent and close contact with a variety of primary care physicians is essential for business survival. Niche practices concentrating on providing service to patients in long-term care settings can be conducted as a solo practitioner, a member of a larger group practice, or an employee of a large retirement complex. Besides providing direct patient care, geropsychologists can use their expertise as consultants in a variety of ways, settings, and purposes, with creativity and energy being the only sources of limitation.

APPENDIX A: SAMPLE FORM FOR CASE PROGRESS NOTES FOR PSYCHOTHERAPY AND HEALTH AND BEHAVIOR INTERVENTIONS

Name of client: _____

Date of Service: _____ CPT code, procedure: _____

Start time _____ ending _____ minutes; Tx session: _____

GAF score: _____ Other measures: _____

Diagnoses: _____

Change in target symptoms: _____
_____

Observations: _____
_____
_____

Treatment provided: _____
_____
_____

Current medications or changes: _____

Date of planned follow-up: _____

Prognosis: _____

Homework: _____

Notes: _____

Signature: _____ Title: _____ Date: ____

REFERENCES

Abeles, N., Cooley, S., Deitch, I. M., Harper, M. S., Hinrichsen, G., Lopez, M. A., et al. (1998). What practitioners should know about working with older adults. *Professional Psychology: Research and Practice, 29,* 413–427.

American Bar Association Commission on Law and Aging & American Psychological Association. (2005). *Assessment of older adults with diminished capacity: A handbook for lawyers.* Washington, DC: ABA and APA.

American Psychiatric Association. (1994). *Diagnostic and statistical manual of mental disorders* (4th ed.). Washington, DC: Author.

American Psychological Association. (2004). Guidelines for psychological practice with older adults. *American Psychologist, 59,* 236–260.

Areán, P., & Ayalon, L. (2005, Fall). Assessment and treatment of depressed older adults in primary care. *Clinical Psychologist: Science and Practice, 12,* 321–335.

Gray, G. V., Brody, D. S., & Johnson, D. (2005). The evolution of behavioral primary care. *Professional Psychology: Research and Practice, 36,* 123–129.

Haley, W. E. (2005, Fall). Clinical geropsychology and primary care: Progress and prospects. *Clinical Psychologist: Science and Practice, 12,* 336–338.

Hartman-Stein, P. E. (1998a). HCFA crackdown on fraud, abuse, suspect billing procedures heats up. *National Psychologist, 7,* 12–13.

Hartman-Stein, P. E. (1998b). *Innovative behavioral healthcare for older adults: A guidebook for changing times.* San Francisco: Jossey-Bass.

Hartman-Stein, P. E. (1999). Expect harsh, intensive scrutiny if your Medicare claims are audited. *National Psychologist, 8,* 6–8.

Hartman-Stein, P. E. (2000). Inspector general urges psychologists to set up voluntary compliance procedures. *National Psychologist, 9,* 1–2.

Hartman-Stein, P. E. (2001). Team-based approach to managing client's problem is psychologist's path for future. *National Psychologist, 10,* 16.

Hartman-Stein, P. E. (2002). Medicare records review: Problems will continue for those who document poorly. *National Psychologist, 11,* 8.

Hartman-Stein, P. E. (2004a). Feds help transform psychology researchers and clinicians into entrepreneurs. *National Psychologist, 13,* 8.

Hartman-Stein, P. E. (2004b). Proper documentation helps withstand Medicare audits. *National Psychologist, 13,* 11.

Hartman-Stein, P. E. (2005a). AMA restructures CPT testing codes. *National Psychologist, 14,* 20.

Hartman-Stein, P. E. (2005b). Geropsychology provides a new frontier of consulting opportunities. *Psychologists in Long Term Care Newsletter, 19,* 2.

Hartman-Stein, P. E. (2005c). Persistent psychologist wins change in Medicare regulation. *National Psychologist, 14,* 17.

Hartman-Stein, P. E., & Ergun, M. (1998). Marketing strategies for geriatric behavioral healthcare. In P. E. Hartman-Stein (Ed.), *Innovative behavioral healthcare for older adults: A guidebook for changing times* (pp. 179–199). San Francisco: Jossey-Bass.

Hartman-Stein, P., & McClure, L. (2006). A model of service delivery: Meeting the behavioral healthcare needs of community residing older adults. *Register Report, 32*, 36–43.

Heavey, S. (2004). *Reuters health information: Medicare aims to cut errors in half by 2008.* Retrieved December 28, 2004, from http://www.reutershealth.com /archive/2004/12/13/eline/links/20041213elin008.html.

Hellman, I. (2005). Consulting in geropsychology. *Psychologists in Long Term Care Newsletter, 19*, 1.

Klein, J. (Ed.). (2003). Practice Issues: What can you expect in a Medicare audit? *Psychotherapy Finances, 29*, 1–3.

Lichtenberg, P., Smith, M., Frazer, D., Molinari, V., Rosowsky, E., Crose, R., et al. (1998). Standards for psychological services in long-term care facilities. *Gerontologist, 38*, 122–127.

Moye, J. (2005). Determining capacity of older adults in guardianship proceedings: Overview of a benchbook for judges. *Psychologists in Long Term Care Newsletter, 19*, 4.

O'Donohue, W. O., Naylor, E. V., & Cummings, N. A. (2005). Disease management: Current issues. In N. A. Cummings, W. T. O'Donohue, & E. V. Naylor (Eds.), *Psychological approaches to chronic disease management.* Reno, NV: Context Press.

Office of Inspector General's Compliance Program Guidance for Individual and Small Group Physician Practices. 65 Fed. Reg. 59, 435–59, 452 (October 5, 2000).

Pope, K. S., & Vasquez, M. J. (2005). *How to survive and thrive as a therapist: Information, ideas, and resources for psychologists in practice.* Washington, DC: American Psychological Association.

Stewart, M. (2005). *The Martha rules.* New York: Martha Stewart Living Omnimedia.

World Health Organization. (2005). *International classification of diseases* (9th ed.). Los Angeles: Practice Management Information Corporation.

Author Index

Abeles, N., 191, 230
Abrams, R., 53, 57, 168
Acredolo, C., 190
Adams, K. B., 55
Adelstein, L., 116
Adey, M., 53, 55
Adorno, E., 32
Akiskal, H. G., 112
Alessi, C. A., 56
Alexopoulos, A., 168
Alexopoulos, G., 30, 31, 33, 38,
        46, 48, 49, 53, 57, 133, 135,
        149, 167
Alford, B. A., 83
Allen, K. R., 19
Allen, N. B., 48, 53
Allender, J. R., 88
Amsterdam, J. D., 83, 106
Anderson, S. W., 48
Anstey, K. J., 84
Anthony, J. C., 38, 39
Antonuccio, D. C., 166
Aranda, M. P., 12
Areán, P., 53, 133, 135, 136, 138,
        139, 167, 168, 242
Arensman, E., 34
Arlt, S., 47, 57, 69
Arnold, B., 187
Auerbach, S. M., 168
Austin, M.-P., 31, 39

Ayalon, L., 242
Azar, A. R., 33

Bachar, J. R., 38
Baillargeon, L., 85
Baker, F., 133
Baker-Thomas, T., 194
Baldwin, R. C., 33
Baltes, P. B., 6, 7
Bandinelli, S., 66
Bandura, A., 14
Barber, M., 66
Barbour, F., 134
Barker, W. W., 57
Bartels, S. J., 30
Bass, J., 112
Bebbington, P. E., 33
Beck, A. T., 53, 83, 99, 166
Becker, G., 68
Belin, T. R., 84
Belle, S., 192
Bengtson, V. L., 19, 95, 115
Bennett Johnson, S., 161
Benton, A., 48
Benvenuti, E., 66
Berezin, M., 3
Berkman, L. F., 111
Bernstein, L., 38
Berry, C., 116, 117
Betancourt, H., 181

Beutler, L., 54, 88, 165, 167
Biblarz, T., 95
Birren, J. E., 168
Bissonnette, L., 167
Blazer, D., 38, 46, 56, 57, 58, 61, 88
Boada, F., III, 48
Bogner, H. R., 38
Bogumill, S., 193
Bolstrom, A., 139
Bolton, P., 112
Bonanno, G. A., 35, 36
Bookwala, J., 11, 12
Boss, P., 95
Bosworth, H. B., 116
Bothwell, S., 124
Boyce, P., 39
Brandt, J., 66
Brater, D. C., 50
Breckenridge, J., 54
Breckenridge, J. N., 47, 48
Breckenridge, J. S., 166, 167, 168
Brilman, E. I., 34
Brink, T. L., 53, 55
Brodaty, H., 31, 39, 84
Brody, D. S., 242
Brody, E., 62
Brown, G. K., 53
Bruce, M. L., 30, 38, 115
Brugha, T., 33
Buckner, R. L., 136, 137
Buckwalter, J. G., 57, 58, 61
Buckwalter, K. C., 192
Burke, W. J., 63
Burnam, A., 119
Burnight, K. P., 5
Burns, A., 33, 46
Burns, D., 167

Burt, T., 32
Bush, D. E., 46
Butzlaff, R. L., 111

Caine, E. D., 53
Callahan, C., 50, 53, 170
Campbell, J. M., 167
Campbell, S., 31, 33, 46, 48
Caplan, A. L., 222
Cappeliez, P., 168
Carstensen, L. L., 6, 7
Casey, D. A., 92
Caspi, A., 34
Cavanaugh, J. C., 68
Cervilla, J., 33
Chambless, D. L., 83, 161
Champion, L. A., 94, 95
Chao, L. L., 137
Charles, S. T., 7, 32
Charlson, M., 31, 33, 46, 48
Cheng, J., 32
Chevron, E. S., 111, 112, 114, 116, 118
Chodosh, J., 57, 58, 61
Chopra, H. P., 38
Christensen, H., 39
Christopher, F., 133, 135, 167, 168
Chun, M., 183
Ciechanowski, P., 171
Clark, D. A., 83
Clarke, E., 95
Clarke, M., 192
Clarkin, J. F., 168
Clougherty, K. F., 112, 119, 127, 222
Coates, A., 162, 165
Collins, J. F., 112
Conwell, Y., 38

Conyers, L. M., 182
Cooley, S., 191, 230
Coolidge, F. L., 57, 59, 67, 68
Coon, D. W., 165, 170
Corbishley, A., 54, 165
Corbishley, M. A., 88
Cornes, C., 112, 114, 117, 118, 123,
    127, 165, 169
Coryell, W., 38
Cox, C., 53
Craig, I. W., 34
Craig, S., 46
Crits-Cristoph, P., 83, 161
Crose, R., 230
Crystal, S., 191
Cuellar, I., 187
Cuijpers, P., 36, 160
Cummings, J. L., 30
Cummings, N. A., 246
Cutler, N. E., 115

Dahlman, K., 39
Daniels, M., 119
Datan, N., 93, 96
D'Ath, P., 47
Davies, I., 134
Davis, S., 167
Day, A., 133
DeBerry, S., 167
Deitch, I., 191, 230
Dekel, N., 124
Del Lungo, I., 66
DelMaestro, S., 168
DeRubeis, R. J., 83, 106
Deutchman, D. E., 168
Devanand, D. P., 32
Dew, M. A., 115

Dick, L. P., 85, 166, 167
Diehr, P., 171
Dietrich, A. J., 150
DiMascio, A., 112
Dixon, R. A., 5, 6
Duara, R., 57
Duffy, M., 222
Dunn, G., 33
Dura, J. R., 11
D'Zurilla, T. J., 135, 137, 138

Elderkin-Thompson, V., 30
Elkin, I., 112
Ellis, T., 101
Emery, E. E., 37
Emery, G., 83, 99, 166
Endicott, J., 112
Engels, G. I., 160
Erbaugh, J., 53
Ergun, M., 244
Evans, L. K., 57
Evans, S., 47

Fan, M. Y., 136
Faragher, B., 46
Farrell, M., 33
Ferrell, R. E., 34
Ferrucci, L., 66
Fink, P., 46
First, M. B., 58
Fishman, B., 112
Fiske, A., 34, 38, 47, 48, 84, 161
Flacker, J. M., 56, 61, 69
Fleissner, K., 11, 12
Florio, L. P., 30
Floyd, D. L., 167
Floyd, M., 167

Folkman, S., 12
Folstein, M., 65, 66, 217
Folstein, S. E., 65, 217
Ford, A. B., 62
Foucault, M., 182
Fox, A., 192
Fox, L. S., 12, 37, 84, 161
Frances, A. J., 112
Frank, E., 112, 114, 120, 127, 165, 169
Frank, E., III, 112, 117, 118, 123, 127
Frasure-Smith, N., 35
Frazer, D., 208, 230
Fry, P. S., 167
Frydenberg, M., 46
Fukui, M. B., 48
Fung, H. H., 7

Gabrielle, M., 38, 49
Gallagher, D., 54, 158, 166, 167, 168
Gallagher-Thompson, D., ix, 1, 69, 85, 88, 90, 91, 92, 93, 98, 100, 139, 165, 166, 167, 168, 170
Gallo, J. J., 30, 38, 39
Ganguli, M., 192
Gant, L. M., 186
Ganzer, S., 47, 57, 69
Garfield, S. L., 169
Gath, D. H., 133
Gatz, M., 31, 32, 34, 38, 47, 48, 84, 161, 168
Gaugler, J. E., 36
George, L. K., 35, 116
Gerson, S., 84
Giarusso, R., 95
Gibbon, M., 58
Gilby, J., 192

Gist, Y., 189, 190
Gitelson, M., 3
Glantz, M., 84, 87, 88, 89, 99
Glass, G. V., 159
Gochneaur, K., 167
Goklaney, M., 112
Goldberg, J. H., 47, 48
Goldstein, A. P., 18
Goldwasser, A. N., 168
Gonzalez, G., 187
Goodwin, R. D., 30
Goossens, L., 6
Gorman, J. M., 39
Gottlieb, G. L., 30
Gould, S. J., 180
Grant, B. F., 30
Grant, R. W., 92
Gray, A., 134
Gray, G. V., 242
Greene, A. F., 186
Greene, R., 36
Grembowski, D., 192
Greving, A. M., 192
Grossman, H. T., 39
Guerette, A., 85
Gum, A., 139
Gunning-Dixon, F., 135
Guralnick, S., 192
Guralnik, J. M., 66

Habermas, J., 182
Haley, W. E., 242
Halpain, M. C., ix
Hamblin, D., 54, 165, 167
Hamilton, M., 53, 124
Hammen, C. L., 84, 89, 92, 158
Hansen, M. S., 46

Hansen, N. D., 186

Hanson, A., 51, 162, 165

Haring, M., 35

Harker, J. O., 56

Harkins, S. W., 168

Haroutunian, V., 39

Harper, M., 191, 230

Harpole, L., 170

Harrington, H., 34

Harris, M. J., ix

Hartman, M., 137

Hartman-Stein, P., 232, 233, 234, 235, 236, 237, 238, 239, 244, 245

Harwood, D. G., 57

Hasin, D. S., 30

Hawley, K. M., 162, 169

Hays, R. D., 119

Heavey, S., 235

Heck, E., 211

Hegel, M. T., 135, 136, 138, 150

Hellman, I., 246

Henderson, A. S., 39

Henderson, B. E., 38

Hendrie, H. C., 50

Heo, M., 135

Hernandez, N. A., 116

Herring, R. D., 182

Hersen, M., 57, 59, 67, 68

Hertzog, C., 53

Hetzel, L., 189, 190

Heun, R., 39

Hickie, I., 31, 39

Higgins, M., 118, 127

Hihus, R. S., 50

Hill, M. A., 158

Hilliard, K. M., 193

Hinrichsen, G., 37, 116, 118, 119, 127, 191, 222, 230

Hnat, S. A., 186

Hoffman, R. R., 11

Hollon, S. D., 83, 106

Holzer, C., III, 30

Hooley, J. M., 111

Horowitz, M., 168

Hoyer, W. J., 6

Hoyl, M. T., 56

Huang, K., 193

Huang, V., 53, 55

Hughes, D. C., 38

Hui, S. I., 50

Hultsch, D. F., 5, 6, 53

Hunkeler, E., 170

Hurwicz, E. A., 47

Hussain, R. A., 135, 167

Imber, S. D., 112, 117, 118, 123, 127, 165, 169

Iwamasa, G. Y., 193

Jackson, A., 33

Jackson, B. A., 62

Jacobsberg, L. B., 112

Jacomb, P. A., 39

Jaffe, M. W., 62

Jamison, C., 46, 167

Jarrett, D. B., 112, 114

Jarvik, L., 84, 158

Jefferson, A. L., 54

Jenkins, R., 33

Jeste, D. V., ix, 30, 47

Jocic, Z., 166, 167

John, R., 187

Johnson, D., 242

Johnson, S. B., 83
Joiner, T. E., 112
Jordan, C. B., 150
Jorm, A. F., 39, 46
Joseph, T., 133, 135, 167, 168
Josephson, K. R., 56
Juang, L., 181
Judd, L. L., 30, 112

Kabacoff, R. I., 68
Kahn, R. L., 94
Kakuma, T., 33, 38, 49
Kalayam, B., 38, 49
Kaltreider, N., 168
Kane, R. A., 36, 222
Kane, R. L., 36
Karel, M. J., 31
Karpe, J. M., 51
Kaskie, B., 84, 161
Kasl, S. V., 116, 125
Kasl-Godley, J. E., 31, 47, 48, 84, 161
Kastenbaum, R., 115
Kaszniak, A. W., 49, 61, 63
Katon, W., 96, 170
Katona, C., 47
Katona, P., 47
Katz, I. R., 55, 149
Katz, S., 62
Kaufman, M. S., 84
Kawachi, I., 111
Kemele, K., 192
Kendler, K. S., 32
Kiecolt-Glaser, J., 11
Kim, J. H., 183
Kimbarow, M. L., 166
King, D. A., 53
Kiosses, D. N., 49, 135
Kirkish, P., 165

Kjellander, C., 193
Klausner, E. J., 168
Klein, D. F., 54
Klein, J., 234
Klerman, G. L., 111, 112, 113, 114, 118, 121, 127
Knight, B., 3, 10, 12, 21, 36, 37, 63, 84, 87, 91, 92, 93, 107, 116, 118, 169, 183
Knight, R. T., 137
Knott, K., 38, 118, 127
Kockler, M., 39
Kocsis, J. H., 112
Koder, D. A., 84
Koelfgen, M., 56
Kohn, R., 38
Koin, D., 165, 170
Korten, A. E., 39
Kraaij, V., 34
Krause, N., 53
Kumar, A., 30
Kupfer, D. J., 112, 114
Kurlowicz, L. H., 57

Lagana, L., 190
Laidlaw, K., 84, 85, 88, 91, 92, 93, 98, 106
Landreville, P., 85, 167
Landry, J., 85
Larson, E. B., 193
La Rue, A., 49
Latham, A. E., 36
Latorre, J. M., 168
Lavretsky, H., 30
Lawrence, P. S., 135, 167
Lawton, M. P., 55, 62, 202
Lazarus, R. S., 12
Leaf, P. J., 30

Lebowitz, B. D., 85
Lehman, D. R., 35
Lenze, E. J., 34, 115
Leon, A. C., 38, 112
Lesperance, F., 35
Leventhal, N., 38
Levy, B. R., 96
Lewinsohn, P., 35, 48, 53, 97, 166
Lewis, G., 33
Liang, J., 53
Lichtenberg, P., 33, 166, 230
Light, L. L., 21
Liming Alspaugh, M. E., 36
Lipsey, M. W., 159
Liss-Bialik, A., 124
Liu, K., 198
Logsdon, R., 147, 166, 220
Longmire, C. V.F., 183
Lopez, M., 191, 230
Lopez, S. R., 181
Lorion, R. P., 18
Lovestone, S., 92
Lum, O., 53, 55
Luscombe, G., 31, 39
Lutzky, S. M., 36
Lyketsos, C. G., 136, 138
Lynch, M. S., 192
Lyness, J. M., 53

Mab, R., 47, 57, 69
Mackin, R. S., 136
MacKinnon, A. J., 39
MacNeill, S. E., 33
Maislin, G., 57
Mallinger, A. G., 112, 114
Mallinger, V. J., 112, 114
Mann, U., 47, 57, 69
Marcoen, A., 6

Marin, B. V., 183
Marin, G., 183
Markides, K. S., 53
Markowitz, J. C., 112, 113, 118, 121, 127
Martire, L. M., 115, 143
Maser, J. D., 112
Maslow, K., 211
Mast, B. T., 33
Mathews, H. F., 56
Matsumoto, D., 181
Matteau, E., 85
Matto, H. C., 55
Mazure, C. M., 111
McCallum, T. J., 12, 37, 63, 161
McCarley, T., 158
McClearn, G. E., 32
McClure, F. S., ix
McClure, L., 245
McCulloch, C., 139
McCullogh, J. B., 192
McCullum, T. J., 84
McCurry, S., 147, 166, 220
McElreath, L., 84, 160
McHugh, P. R., 65, 217
McKendree-Smith, N. L., 167
McMeniman, M., 116
McQuoid, D. R., 116
Melton, M. A., 68
Meltzer, C. C., 48
Mendelson, M., 53
Meyers, B. S., 31, 33, 38, 46, 48, 49
Miller, M. D., 112, 117, 118, 123, 127, 165, 169
Miller, T. I., 159
Mintz, J., 84, 158
Miranda, J., 53, 96
Mirowsky, J., 32

Mitchell, J., 56
Mitchell, P., 39
Mock, J., 53
Moffitt, T. E., 34
Mojtabai, R., 33, 34
Molinari, V., 230
Montanes, J., 168
Montgomery, M., 190
Morales, K. H., 38
Morales, P., 181, 182, 183, 187, 188
Moreau, D., 112
Morris, L. W., 84
Morris, P., 166
Morris, R. G., 84
Moskowitz, R. W., 62
Mossey, J. M., 118, 127
Moye, J., 222, 246
Mpofu, E., 182
Mueller, T. I., 38
Mufson, L., 112
Mukamal, K., 88
Mullan, E., 47
Muller-Thomsen, T., 47, 57, 69
Mulsant, B. H., 115
Munin, M. C., 34
Munk-Jorgensen, P., 46
Murphy, C., 49, 135
Murrell, S. A., 33, 34
Musil, C. M., 193
Muthén, B. O., 38, 39
Mynors-Wallis, L., 133, 134

Nahemow, L., 202
Nakao, K., 183
Naylor, E. V., 246
Neale, M. C., 32
Nebes, R. D., 48

Nesse, R. M., 36
Nesselroade, J. R., 32
Neu, C., 112
Neugarten, B. L., 93, 96
Neugebauer, R., 112
Newman, C., 101
Nezu, A. M., 133, 134, 135, 137, 138, 141, 167, 168
Nezu, C. M., 167
Niederehe, G., ix, 1, 85
Nielsen, C., 137
Nies, G., 54
Nitcher, R. L., 63
Norcross, J. G., 169
Nordhus, I. H., 3
Norman, S., ix, 1
Norris, F. H., 34
Norris, J. T., 54
Null, J. A., 68

O'Brien, A. T., 11, 12
O'Donohue, W. O., 246
Oldenhinkel, A. J., 34
Olfson, M., 33, 34, 191
Ollendick, T. H., 161
Onyike, C. U., 136, 138
O'Reardon, J. P., 83
Ormel, J., 34
Ory, M., 11
Otero-Sabogal, R., 183
Ownby, R. L., 57
Owsley, C., 68
Oxhoj, M., 46

Paganini-Hill, A., 38
Paniagua, F. A., 182, 186, 187
Parisi, S. A., 54

Parker, G., 31, 39
Parks, S., 190
Parmalee, P. A., 55
Parris Stephens, M. A., 36
Patrick, D. L., 192
Paulus, M., 112
Paykel, E., 111, 112
Pedersen, N. L., 32, 34, 38
Pelton, G. H., 32
Pepitone-Arreola-Rockwell, F., 186
Perel, J. M., 112, 114, 117, 118, 123,
       127, 165, 169
Perez-Stable, E. J., 183
Perri, M. G., 133, 134, 135, 167, 168
Persons, J. B., 83, 93
Peters, C. A., 68
Peters, K., 39
Pietruszka, F. M., 56
Pignone, M. P., 56
Pilisuk, M., 190
Pinquart, M., 21, 160
Plomin, R., 32
Pollack, S., 116
Pollack Dorta, K., 112
Pope, K. S., 83, 161, 229, 230
Pope, M., 54
Post, E. P., 38
Potter, J. F., 68
Power, M. J., 94, 95
Powers, D. V., 54
Prigerson, H. G., 36
Prince, M., 33
Prusoff, B., 112, 116, 117
Pupo, C., 168
Purandare, N., 46

Qualls, S., ix, 1, 12, 15, 93

Rabe-Hesketh, S., 33
Rabins, P. V., 38, 136, 138
Rabkin, J. G., 54
Radloff, L. S., 53
Rapp, M. A., 39
Rapp, S. R., 54
Raue, P., 133, 167
Reinhard, K. E., 167
Reynolds, C. A., 32
Reynolds, C., III, 149
Reynolds, C. F., 48, 112, 117, 118,
       123, 127, 165, 169
Richlin-Klonsky, J., 95
Richter, D., 46
Ridderinkhof, K. R., 137
Roberts, R., 48, 53, 95
Robinson, G. S., 183
Roccaforte, W. H., 63
Rogers, J. C., 115
Rogers, W., 119
Rohde, P., 35, 97
Rokke, P. D., 166, 167
Rollman, B. L., 115
Roodin, P. A., 6
Roose, S. P., 32
Rose, J., 168
Rose, T. L., 53, 55
Rosendahl, E., 124
Rosow, I., 115
Rosowsky, E., 230
Ross, C. E., 32
Ross, R. K., 38
Ross, R. W., 149
Rothblum, E. D., 117
Rothman, J., 186
Rotter, J. B., 14
Rounsaville, B. J., 111, 112, 114, 118

Rovner, B., 140
Rowe, J. W., 94
Rush, A. J., 83, 99
Rush, J., 166
Russell, D., 192
Rutter, C., 192
Ryan, C. F., 68
Rybash, J. M., 6

Sabogal, F., 183
Safran, J., 90
Salani, B., 66
Salomon, R. M., 83, 106
Salthouse, T. A., 5, 21, 64
Sambamoorth, U., 191
Sanders, S., 55
Sanderson, W. C., 83, 161
Sano, M., 39
Satre, D. D., 3, 107
Saxton, J., 48
Schaie, K. W., 5, 6, 23
Schein, R. L., 133, 135, 167, 168
Schieber, F., 68
Schmaling, K., 171
Schneider, L. S., 117, 127
Schneider, M. G., 69
Scholer, S. G., 68
Schretlen, D., 165
Schulz, R., 11, 12, 36, 143, 211
Schwartz, S., 171
Scogin, F., 46, 51, 54, 55, 63, 64, 84, 160, 162, 165, 167
Scott, K., 46
Seeberg, E., 192
Seeley, J. R., 48, 53, 97
Seeman, T. E., 57, 58, 61
Segal, D. L., ix, 1, 68

Segal, D. T., 57, 59, 67, 68
Segal, Z., 90
Serrano, J. P., 168
Seville, J. L., 150
Shadlen, M. F., 193
Shamoian, C. A., 53, 57
Shanas, E., 115
Shanmugham, B., 135
Shaw, B., 83, 99, 166
Shea, M. T., 112
Sheikh, J. I., 47, 48, 56
Shelton, R. C., 83
Shiang, J., 193
Shoham, V., 83, 161
Sholomskas, A. J., 116, 117
Shuchter, S. R., 35
Silberman, R. L., 117, 127
Silbersweig, D., 31, 33, 46, 48
Silverstein, M., 12, 37
Simon, G., 192
Simpson, S., 33
Sirey, J., 49
Siskin, L., 124
Siskin-Dick, L., 85, 88, 91, 92, 93, 98
Sloane, M. E., 68
Sloane, P. D., 211
Sloane, R. B., 117, 127
Small, B. J., 5
Smith, A. D., 6
Smith, M., 159, 192, 230
Smyer, M. A., 15, 93
Solomon, D., 38
Sommer, B. R., 165, 170
Sondergaard, L., 46
Sonnega, J., 35
Sörensen, S., 21, 160
Sotsky, S. M., 112

Sowell, T., 182
Span, M. M., 137
Spanier, C., 120, 127
Speer, D. C., 69
Spencer, M., 66
Spielman, L., 112, 168
Spinelli, M. G., 112
Spinhoven, P., 34
Spiro, L., 56, 61, 69
Spitzer, R. L., 58
Stamm, B. H., 192
Staples, F. R., 117, 127
Staudinger, U. M., 6, 7
Steer, R. A., 53
Steffen, A., 9, 70, 84, 89, 92, 100, 167, 168
Steffens, D. C., 116
Steinberg, M., 136, 138
Steinmetz, J., 54
Steuer, J. L., 84, 89, 92, 158
Stevens, S., 46
Stewart, A., 119
Stewart, M., 230, 231, 244
Stinson, F. S., 30
Stott, D. J., 66
Stratton, B., 137
Strumpf, N. E., 57
Stukenberg, K. W., 11
Stump, J., 162, 165
Sue, D., 182
Sugden, K., 34
Sullivan, H. S., 111
Sullivan, M., 96
Sullivan, P. F., 32

Talajic, M., 35
Talerico, K., 118, 127

Tayback, M., 46
Taylor, A., 34
Teirny, W. M., 50
Ten Have, T., 38
Tennstedt, S., 11
Teri, L., 90, 147, 166, 220
Thomas, P., 33
Thompson, L., 54, 84, 85, 88, 90, 91, 92, 93, 96, 98, 139, 147, 158, 165, 166, 167, 168, 170
Tomhave, J. A., 166, 167
Toone, L., 136, 138
Tower, R. B., 116, 125
Townsend, A. L., 36
Tran, T. V., 53
Tranel, D., 48
Trent, L., 38
Tschanz, J., 136, 138
Tuma, T. A., 38
Turk-Charles, S., 6
Turkel, E., 124
Tweed, R. G., 35

Unutzer, J., 96, 136, 170, 192
Uomoto, J., 147, 166, 220
Usala, P. D., 53

Vaillant, G. E., 88, 94
Van Alstine, J., 53
van der Molen, M. W., 137
Vangel, S. J., 166
Van Hasselt, V. B., 68
Vannoy, S., 136
Varney, M., 160
Vasquez, M. J., 229, 230
Verdeli, H., 112
Verhagen, P., 6

Wagner, E., 171
Waidmann, T. A., 198
Walker, D., 192
Walker, E., 192
Walkup, J., 191
Wallace, C. E., 54
Walsh, D. A., 54
Ward, C. H., 53
Watkins, J. T., 112
Watson, L. C., 56
Watt, L. M., 168
Weatherall, M., 47
Wei, W., 191
Weissman, M., 30, 111, 112, 113,
    114, 118, 121, 124, 127
Weisz, J. R., 162, 169
Wells, K. B., 119
Welsh, D., 51, 162, 165
Wengel, S. P., 63
Whitfield, K., 194
Wickramaratne, P. J., 112
Wilhelm, K., 31, 39
Williams, B., 171
Williams, J. B.W., 58
Williams, J. W., 170
Williamson, G. M., 36
Wilson, A., 54
Wilson, D. B., 159
Winograd, C. H., 54
Wolinsky, F. D., 53
Wong, M. G., 187

Wortman, C. B., 35, 36
Wragg, R. E., 47
Wyckle, M. L., 193

Yang, Y., 35
Yee, J. L., 11
Yesavage, J. A., 53, 55, 56
Yochim, B., 33
Yoediono, Z., 53
Yost, E. B., 88
Young, P. R., 106
Young, R. C., 31, 33, 38, 46, 48, 49,
    53, 57

Zahalsky, H., 46
Zarit, J. M., 15
Zarit, S. H., 15, 36
Zehr, M., 222
Zeiss, A. M., 9, 35, 69, 70, 84, 89,
    92, 97
Zelinski, E. M., 5
Zeller, P. J., 112
Zevenbergen, P., 192
Ziegelstein, R. C., 46
Zimmerman, S., 211
Zisook, S., 35
Zubritsky, C., 38
Zuckerman, M., 180
Zweig, R. A., 124
Zwilling, M., 112

Subject Index

Abuse prevention, elder, 246
Activities of Daily Living Scale
    (ADLS), 62, 204, 209
Adaptation level, 202
Adapting psychotherapy to older
    adults. *See* Psychotherapy with
    older clients
Adult children, referrals from, 243–244
Adult Protective Services, 208
Age:
    demographics of residents in
        nursing homes and assisted
        living facilities, 204
    onset of depression and, 31
    young-old and old-old, 8
Aging. *See also* Older adults
    depression and (*see* Depression in
        older adults)
    social model versus medical model,
        209
Alcohol consumption, 67
Alzheimer's disease. *See*
    Dementia/Alzheimer's disease
American Psychological Association, 70
Anxiety factor, 55
Apathy/withdrawal factor, 55
Apprenticeships, 231–232
Area Agency on Aging (AAA/Triple
    A), 16, 206, 208
Assessment. *See* Depression in older
    adults, assessment
Assisted living facilities (ALFs),
    208–212
    confidentiality/privacy concerns,
        224–225
    measurement of outcomes, 212
    promoting well-being, 210–211
    regulations, 209–210

staff, 210, 212
    treatment approaches, 211–212
Attorney, powers of, 223–224
Audits, Medicare, 234, 235

Beck Depression Inventory II (BDI-
    II), 53–54, 58
Behavioral therapy, evidence-based,
    166. *See also* Cognitive behavior
    therapy (CBT)
Bereavement/grief, 11, 35–36
Billing, Medicare. *See* Medicare
Brief therapy:
    brief psychodynamic therapy
        (BPT), 167
    interpersonal psychotherapy (IPT),
        119

Capacity evaluations, 245–246
Caregiving:
    case example, 100, 126, 154
    CCMSC model, 11–12
    depression and, 36–37
Case examples:
    Dorothy, Alzheimer's family
        caregiver, 64
    Helen, depression and family
        caregiver:
        case definition, 79–82, 152–155
        from perspective of cognitive
            behavioral therapy, 198–105
        from perspective of interpersonal
            psychotherapy (IPT),
            125–127
        from perspective of problem-
            solving therapy (PST),
            141–147
    Rita, depression, 49–50

Case management:
    problem-solving therapy (PST) and, 139–140
    psychotherapy versus, value conflicts, 17
Case mix index (CMI), nursing homes, 214
Case program notes, 239, 247
Casework services, 15–16, 17
Categorical reviews with older adults, 161–169
CCMSC model. See Contextual, cohort-based maturity/specific challenge (CCMSC)
Center for Epidemiologic Studies Depression Scale (CES-D), 53, 57, 58
CERTprovider.org, 234
Charting, 238–239, 247
Codes, clinical procedural, 233, 237–238
Cognitive behavior therapy (CBT), 83–106
    application/adaptation with older adults, 87–92
    appropriateness with older adults, 84–87
    case example (Helen), 79–82, 98–105, 152–155
    versus cognitive bibliotherapy, 168
    cohort beliefs, importance of the cohort, 93
    communication style of older people and, 89
    conceptualization framework for, 92–98
        cohort beliefs, 93, 104
        intergenerational linkages, 95–96, 103–104
        physical health, 97, 105
        sociocultural context, 96, 104–105
        transitions in role investments, 93–97, 104
    evidence-based treatment, 166–167

    goal-oriented approach, 85
    here-and-now focus, 84
    in meta-analysis, 160
    overview/introduction, 83–84, 105–106
    pace/length of treatment, 88, 99
    phases, distinct, 85
        final, 86–87, 102–103
        middle phase, 86, 102
        termination, 86–87
    practical problem-solving skills, 84
    primary mode of effectiveness, 83
    problem-focused strategies, 89–90
    psycho-educative approach, 84
    role-play, 87
    self-monitoring, 84
    structured approach, 84
    suitability for, 90–91
    Thompson study, 170
Cognitive bibliotherapy, 167
Cognitive impairment, 10–11
Cognitive modifications, problem-solving therapy (PST), 136–138
Cohort(s):
    adaptations based on, 13–14, 17–19, 23
    CBT, and beliefs of, 93, 104
    CCMSC model and, 4–5
Collaborative care model, 170–171, 242
Collaborative empowerment, in interpersonal psychotherapy (IPT), 114
Communication style of older people, 89
Community services networks, 16
Competence level, 202
Compliance plan, Medicare, 239–241
Complicated grief versus bereavement-related depression, 35–36
Comprehensive Error Rate Testing Program, Medicare, 234
Concentration, decreased, 55
Confidentiality/privacy concerns, residential settings, 224–225
Confirmatory factor analysis (CFA), 55

Conflict of interest, 225–226
Consulting opportunities, 245–246
Context of geropsychology practice,
    23, 177–178. *See also*
    Geropsychology practice; Long-
    term care environments;
    Sociocultural context
Contextual, cohort-based
    maturity/specific challenge
    (CCMSC) model, 1, 3–13, 80
  caregiving, 11–12
  chronic illness and disability, 9–10
  cohort differences, 4–5
  grief, 11
  maturity-related differences, 5–7
  overview, 12–13
  social context factors, 4
  specificity of challenges in late life,
    7–9, 10
Continuing care retirement
    community (CCRC), 205, 208
Continuing education programs,
    geropsychology topics, 231
Controlled Oral Word Association
    Test, 49
Coping style, escape-avoidance, 36
Cornell Scale for Depression in
    Dementia (CSDD), 47, 56, 57
Course of depression, 37–38
Crystallized versus fluid intelligence,
    6, 21
Cue and review techniques, 138
Culture. *See* Sociocultural context
Current procedural terminology
    (CPT) code, 237

Daily hassles, 142
Decision-making capacity, older
    adults, 223–224, 246
Decision-making stage, problem-solving
    therapy (PST), 134, 138, 146
Dementia/Alzheimer's disease:
  Alzheimer's Association, 16, 207,
    244

caregivers, 64, 100
  demographics of residents in
    nursing homes and assisted
    living facilities, 205
  depression and, 32, 47
  depressive symptoms and severity of,
    47
  following chronic depression, 38
  group programs, 246
  memory neighborhoods, 209
  Telephone Interview for Cognitive
    Status (TICS) and, 66
  therapy and, 10
Demographics:
  assisted living facilities, 204–205
  gender, 189–190
  Geriatric Depression Scale and, 55
  nursing homes, 204–205
  projections, number of elderly, 179
Depression in older adults, 29–40
  assessment, 45–70
    case examples, 49–50, 64,
      141–142
    client history, 61
    confounds, and difficulty of
      diagnosis, 46–48
    consulting collateral sources,
      62–63
    functional abilities and daily
      activities, 61–62
    initial interview, 60–61
    instruments, 52–58
    interdisciplinary nature of, 69–70
    medical status, medication, and
      substance use, 66–67
    mental status, 64–66
    overview/introduction, 45
    purpose, 46–49
    sensory issues, 67–69
    structured and unstructured
      interviews, 58–60
  bereavement and, 35–36
  biological changes, and depression,
    32

Depression in older adults (*Continued*)
  caregiving and, 36–37
  context of geropsychology practice,
      23, 177–178 (*see also*
      Geropsychology practice;
      Long-term care environments;
      Sociocultural context)
  course, 37–38
  definition and diagnostic categories,
      29–31
  educational levels and, 33–34
  etiology, 31–33
  exemplary studies, 169–171
    Ciechanowski et al. (2004), 171
    Thompson et al. (2001), 170
    Unutzer et al. (2002), 170–171
  gender and, 33–34, 39
  as illness, 119–120
  overview/introduction, 1–2, 29,
      39–40
  physical illness/disability and, 34–35
  presentation of, 38–39
  psychotherapy with (*see*
      Psychotherapy with older
      clients)
  risk and protective factors, 33–37
  social factors and, 37 (*see also*
      Sociocultural context)
  socioeconomic disadvantage and, 33
  stressful life events and, 34
  subtypes, 56
Development, adaptations due to,
    19–22
Developmental diathesis-stress model,
    31–32
Developmental perspectives, 23
Diabetes, demographics of residents in
    nursing homes and assisted living
    facilities, 205
Diagnosis of depression:
  categories, 2, 30–31
  difficulty of, 46–48
Directive role in therapy, 120
Disability/illness, 8, 9–10, 34–35, 97

Disease management programs, 246
Dorothy (case example, Alzheimer's
    family caregiver), 64
Dysfunctional thought record (DTR),
    86, 102
Dysphoria factor, 55
Dysthymia, 30, 48

Ecological theory of adaptation and
    aging, 202
Education levels, 18, 33–34, 191–192
Emotional changes over adult life
    span, 7, 22
Emotional versus neutral material,
    older adults' memory of, 6
Emphysema/asthma/COPD,
    demographics of residents in
    nursing homes and assisted living
    facilities, 205
Empirically supported treatments
    (ESTs), 161
Empirically validated treatments
    (EVTs), 161
Environmental modifications, 140–141
Environmental press, 202
Ethical issues in residential settings,
    222–224
  conflict of interest, 225–226
  decision-making capacity, 223–224
  privacy and confidentiality, 224–225
Ethnicity. *See* Sociocultural context
Etiology, 31–33
Evidence-based medicine (EBM), 158
Evidence-based treatments (EBTs),
    157–172
  acronyms, similar/synonymous, 157,
      161
  behavioral therapy, 166
  brief psychodynamic therapy (BPT),
      167
  categorical reviews with older adults,
      161–169
  cognitive-behavioral therapy,
      166–167

cognitive bibliotherapy, 167
criteria for, 164
evidence-based practice (EBP)
    movement, 157, 158–159
exemplary studies of geriatric
    depression, 169–171
    Ciechanowski et al. (2004),
        171
    Thompson et al. (2001), 170
    Unutzer et al. (2002), 170–171
identifying, 169
meta-analyses with older adults,
    159–160
overview/introduction/conclusions,
    157–158, 168–169, 171–172
problem-solving therapy, 167
reminiscence therapy (RT), 168
winnowing process, 163
Executive dysfunction, 38, 48–49
Expertise and cognitive complexity,
    21–22

Family:
    as collateral sources, in assessment,
        62–64
    descriptions of by minorities, in
        therapy, 184–185
    filial piety, among Asian
        Americans, 187
Fatalismo/fatalism, 186
Fees, nominal, 244–245
Filial piety, among Asian Americans,
    187
Fluid versus crystallized intelligence,
    6, 21
Form for case progress notes, 247
Functional abilities:
    daily activities and, 61–62
    demographics of residents in
        nursing homes and assisted
        living facilities, 204
Funding:
    grants, 245
    Older Americans Act and, 15

Gays/lesbians, 193
Gender:
    demographics of residents in
        nursing homes and assisted
        living facilities, 204
    differences in depressive symptoms,
        39
    life expectancy and, 190
    psychotherapy and, 189–190
    risk for depressive disorders and,
        33–34
    sex-roles, culture and, 186
Genetic risk for depression, 31–32
Georgoulakis, James, 233, 234, 238,
    239
Geriatric depression. *See* Depression
    in older adults
Geriatric Depression Scale (GDS):
    Collateral Source (GDS-CS), 63
    defined/described, 51–52, 55–57,
        58
    factor analyses, 55
    Short Form (GDS-SF), 47, 52,
        56–57, 208
    visually impaired respondents, 69
Gerold, Kevin, 234, 235
Gerontological explosion, 179
Geropsychology practice, 229–247
    apprenticeships, 231–232
    consulting opportunities, 231–232,
        245–246
    continuing education programs,
        231
    fees, 244–245
    grants, 245
    health/behavior interventions with
        older adults, 246
    joining established group practices,
        241–242
    learning the business, 230–241
    Medicare regulations, 232–241
    overview/introduction, 229–230,
        246
    recommended reading, 230–231

Geropsychology practice (Continued)
   sample form for case progress notes, 247
   sources of referrals, 242–244
   tenets, core, 241–246
Global Assessment of Functioning (GAF), 124, 208, 239
Goal setting/orientation:
   cognitive behavioral therapy (CBT), 85
   problem-solving therapy (PST), 134, 145
Grants, 245
Grief/bereavement, 11, 35–36
Group practice, 241–242
Group programs in retirement communities, 245–246

Hamilton Rating Scale for Depression (HRSD), 53, 54–55, 118, 124
Handicap, versus impairment/disability, 97
Health, physical:
   cognitive behavior therapy (CBT) and, 97, 105
   demographics of residents in nursing homes and assisted living facilities, 204
   GDS correlations, 55
   illness and disability, 34–35
   interventions, 246
Health psychology, 246
Hearing precision, 68–69
Heart disease, 32
Helen (case example):
   background, 79–82, 152–155
   from perspective of cognitive behavioral therapy, 98–105
      cohort beliefs, 104
      intergenerational linkages, 103–104
      investment in role transitions, 104
      physical health, 105
      sociocultural context, 104–105

   from perspective of interpersonal psychotherapy (IPT), 125–127
   from perspective of problem-solving therapy (PST), 141–147
      assessment, 141–142
      decision-making stage, 146
      goal setting stage, 145
      problem definition, 144–145
      problem orientation, 144
      solution generation stage, 145–146
      solution implementation and evaluation, 146–147
      strategy, 142–144
Helplessness factor, 55
Here-and-now focus, CBT, 84
Hip fractures, demographics of residents in nursing homes and assisted living facilities, 204
Historical time, placing client's life history in, 18–19
History, client, 61
Hopelessness factor, 55
Hopkins Symptom Checklist, 57
Housing bureaucracy, 17

Illness, depression as, 119–120
Illness/disability:
   depression and, 9–10, 34–35, 97
   notions of old age and, 8
IMPACT, 136, 149, 170–171
Impairment/disability/handicap, defined, 97
Income:
   demographics of residents in nursing homes and assisted living facilities, 204
   as factor, 191–192
Independent residential settings, 205–208
   measurement of outcomes, 208
   promoting well-being, 206–207
   regulations, 206
   treatment approaches, 207–208

In-home problem-solving therapy (PST), 140
Initial assessment interview, 60–61
Initial sessions, interpersonal psychotherapy (IPT), 112–113, 121–122
Instrumental Activities of Daily Living Scale (IADLS), 62, 209
Instruments/scales, 52–58
  Beck Depression Inventory II (BDI-II), 53–54, 58
  Center for Epidemiologic Studies Depression Scale (CES-D), 53, 57, 58
  Cornell Scale for Depression in Dementia (CSDD), 47, 56, 57
  Geriatric Depression Scale (GDS):
    Collateral Source (GDS-CS), 63
    defined/described, 51–52, 55–57, 58
    factor analyses, 55
    Short Form (GDS-SF), 47, 52, 56–57, 208
    visually impaired respondents, 69
  Hamilton Rating Scale for Depression (HRSD), 53, 54–55, 118, 124
  Montgomery and Aspert Depression Scale, 47
  Nurse's Observation Scale for Geriatric Patients, 47
  Social Adjustment Scale (SAS), 124
Intellectual skills, cohort differences in, 5
Intelligence, crystallized versus fluid, 6, 21
Interactive Model of Negative Live Events, Problem Solving, and Depression, 134
Interdisciplinary nature of depression assessment in older adults, 69–70
Intergenerational linkages, framework for CBT, 95–96, 103–104

Interpersonal psychotherapy (IPT), 111–127, 152, 168
  candidates for, 120
  case example (Helen), 79–82, 125–127, 152–155
  client pessimism, 120–121
  clinical experience/research, treatment of late life depression, 115–118
  conceptualization of depression as illness, 119–120
  directive role of therapist, 120
  evidence-based treatment, 168
  general issues, 119–121
  initial sessions, 112–113, 121–122
  intermediate sessions, 113–114, 122
  Late Life Maintenance (IPT-LLM), 117
  outcomes assessment, 124–125
  overview/introduction, 111–112, 127
  selecting life problems as focus of, 121–122
  structure, 112–114
  techniques and therapeutic ethos of, 114–115
  termination, 114, 123–124
  therapist role, 122
  time constraints, 119, 121, 123–124
Interviews, structured/unstructured, 58–60
Investment in role transitions, 93–97, 104

Learning-based therapies, and memory impairment, 138
Legal consultation, 245–246
Life events, negative, 34
Life expectancy, 190
Life patterns, cohort differences, 18
Long-term care environments, 178, 201–227
  assisted living settings, 208–212
  conflict of interest and, 225–226

Long-term care environments
(Continued)
continuum of social press, 203
decision-making capacity, 223–224
demographics of residents in
nursing homes and assisted
living facilities, 203–205
discharge criteria, 202
distressed mood program performed
by certified nursing assistants,
221
distressed mood program performed
by nurse supervisor, 219–220
ethical issues, 222–224
general principles of psychotherapy
across all settings, 201–203
independent residential settings,
205–208
measurement of outcomes:
assisted living facilities, 212
independent residential settings,
208
nursing homes, 222
nursing homes, 213–222
options not necessarily a continuum
of care, 203
overview/introduction, 201, 226
privacy and confidentiality,
224–225
promoting well-being:
assisted living facilities, 210–211
independent residential settings,
206–207
nursing homes, 216
regulations:
assisted living facilities, 209–210
independent residential settings,
206
nursing homes, 214–216
staff:
assisted living facilities, 210, 212
nursing homes, 218–222
therapeutic context, overview
diagram, 215

treatment approaches:
assisted living facilities, 211–212
independent residential settings,
207–208
nursing homes, 216–218
virtual team, 203
Loss-deficit model, 8, 10

Major Depressive Disorder, defined,
29–30
Marianismo/marianism, 186
Marital status, demographics of
residents in nursing homes and
assisted living facilities, 204
Maturity-related differences, CCMSC
model, 5–7
Medicaid, 213
Medical status, assessment of, 66–67
Medicare, 232–241
applying to become provider,
232–233
audit triggers, 235
CMS directives, 234, 235–236
coding, 233, 237–238
compliance plan, 239–241
documentation imperative,
238–239
inappropriate/unnecessary services
and errors in billing, 234
medical-necessity imperative,
236–237
mental health screening services
disallowed, 237
monitoring audits, 234
National Correct Coding Initiative
(NCCI), 237
overview/introduction, 14, 178
regional insurance carriers,
235–236
Medication, assessment of, 66–67
Memory:
impairment, and learning-based
therapies, 138
older adults, 5–6, 21

Memory neighborhoods, assisted living facilities, 209
Mental illness/disorders:
  demographics of residents in nursing homes and assisted living facilities, 205
  stigma of, 85
Mental status, assessing, 64–66. *See also* Mini Mental State Exam (MMSE)
Meta-analyses with older adults, 159–160
Mind-as-computer metaphor, 6
Mini Mental State Exam (MMSE), 47, 56, 64–66, 217
Minimum Data Set (MDS), 213, 214, 217, 218, 220
Minority status, defined, 181–182. *See also* Sociocultural context
Montgomery and Aspert Depression Scale, 47

National Correct Coding Initiative (NCCI), 237
Native Americans, interdependence and nonverbal communication, 187
Naturally occurring retirement community (NORC), 205
Neurotic personality traits, 34
Nurse's Observation Scale for Geriatric Patients, 47
Nursing homes, 13, 213–222
  case mix index (CMI), nursing homes, 214
  confidentiality/privacy concerns, 224–225
  Distressed Mood Program performed by certified nursing assistants, 221
  Distressed Mood Program performed by nurse supervisor, 219–220
  measurement of outcomes, 222

Minimum Data Set (MDS), 213, 214, 217, 218, 220
  promoting well-being, 216
  reform process, 213
  regulations, 214–216
  staff involvement, 218–222
  therapeutic approaches, 216–218
  therapeutic context, 215

OBRA '87, 213
Office of Inspector General (OIG), 234
Older adults:
  biological changes, and depression, 32
  communication style, 89
  decision-making capacity, 223–224, 246
  depression and (*see* Depression in older adults)
  emotional changes, 7, 22
  expertise and greater cognitive complexity, 21–22
  fluid versus crystallized intelligence, 21
  memory, 21
  misconceptions about, 14
  psychotherapy with (*see* Psychotherapy with older clients)
  slowing, 20–21
  wisdom and aging, 6–7
  young-old and old-old, 8
Older Americans Act, 15
Optimism, 24–25
Outcomes assessment:
  assisted living facilities, 212
  independent residential settings, 208
  interpersonal psychotherapy (IPT), 124–125
  nursing homes, 222
Overdiagnosis, 48

Parkinson's disease, 32, 67
Personalismo/personalism, 187

Pessimism about change, client,
    120–121
Physical health, CBT and, 97, 105
Physical illness and disability, 8,
    34–35, 97
Physicians, referrals from, 243–244
Pleasant activities, low-income clients,
    140
Pleasant events theory for depression,
    153
Positive aging modifications, PST, 141
Poverty, rural, 193. *See also*
    Socioeconomic status (SES)
Powers of attorney, 223–224
Practice, building/managing. *See*
    Geropsychology practice
Presentation, geriatric depression,
    38–39
Principal component analysis (PCA),
    55
Privacy and confidentiality, 224–225
Problem-solving strategies, CBT, 84,
    89–90, 101–102
Problem-solving therapy (PST),
    133–149
    case example (Helen), 79–82,
        141–147, 152–155
    case management and, 139–140
    empirical studies, 135–136
    evidence-based treatment, 167
    in-home, 140
    Interactive Model of Negative Live
        Events, Problem Solving, and
        Depression, 134
    modifications to, for older adults,
        136–141
        cognitive, 136–138
        environmental, 140–141
        positive aging, 141
        socioeconomic, 139–140
    overview/introduction, 133–134,
        147–149, 152, 153
    in primary care (PST-PC), 170

reminiscence therapy (RT) versus,
    135
steps, seven, 134
    decision making (step 5), 134,
        138, 146
    generation of alternative
        solutions (step 4), 134,
        145–146
    goal definition (step 3), 134, 145
    problem definition (step 2), 134,
        138, 144–145
    problem orientation (step 1), 134,
        137, 144
    solution implementation (step 6),
        134, 138–139, 146–147
    solution verification (step 7),
        134, 146–147
supportive therapy versus, 135
training in, 148–149
Psycho-educative approach, in CBT,
    84
Psychotherapy with older clients, 3–25
    assessment (*see* Depression in older
        adults, assessment)
    background, CCMSC
        (contextual, cohort-based
        maturity/specific challenge)
        model, 1, 3–13, 153
        caregiving, 11–12
        chronic illness and disability,
            9–10
        cohort differences, 4–5
        grief, 11
        maturity-related differences, 5–7
        overview, 12–13
        social context factors, 4
        specificity of challenges in late
            life, 7–9, 10
    cohort-based adaptations, 13–14,
        17–19, 23
    development/maturation,
        adaptations based on, 13–14,
        19–22, 23

evidence for (*see* Evidence-based treatments (EBTs))
general principles across residential settings, 201–203
optimism, reasons for, 24–25
options not necessarily a continuum of care, 203
overview/introduction/conclusions, 23–25
social context, adaptations based on, 13, 14–17, 23
  ethnic minorities, 189–193
  gender, 189–190
  income and education, 191–192
  intersection of race, culture, and socioeconomic status, 192
  rural poverty, 193
therapy systems, 79–82 (*see also* Cognitive behavior therapy (CBT); Interpersonal psychotherapy (IPT); Problem-solving therapy (PST))
Public housing, 17

Race, defined, 180. *See also* Sociocultural context
Referrals:
  to other health professionals, 17, 70
  sources of, for your practice, 242–243
Regional insurance carriers, 235–236
Regna, Mark, 233
Religion, ethnic minorities, 185
Reminiscence therapy (RT), 135, 160, 168
Residential settings. *See* Long-term care environments
Respect for elders, ethnic minorities, 184
Risk and protective factors, 33–37
Rita (case example, depression), 49–50
Role captivity, caregiving, 36–37

Role-play, 87, 114
Rural poverty, elders in, 193

Scales. *See* Instruments/scales
Screening services, mental health, 237
Self-monitoring in CBT, 84
Senior spelling bee, 245
Sensory issues, 67–69
Serotonin transporter (5-HTT) gene, 34
Sex-role expectations. *See* Gender
Slowing, 20–21
Small Business Innovation Research grants, 245
Social Adjustment Scale (SAS), 124
Social model versus medical model of aging, 209
Society of Clinical Psychology, 162
Sociocultural context, 179–194
  adaptations to psychotherapy based on, 14–17
  adapting psychotherapy, 189–193
  caregiving, 36–37
  CCMSC model, 4, 153
  cognitive behavior therapy (CBT) and, 96, 104–105
  culture:
    defined, 181
    role of, 182–189
  definitions, 177, 180–182
  educational levels, 191–192
  ethnicity:
    defined, 181
    divergent cultural values among ethnic minorities, 186–188
    shared cultural values among ethnic minorities, 183–186
  family and extended kinship networks, 188–189
  gender, 189–190
  helpful/harmful factors, 37
  income/socioeconomic status, 191–193

Sociocultural context (*Continued*)
   minority status, defined, 181–182
   overview/introduction, 177,
      179–180, 193–194
   problem-solving therapy (PST) and,
      153
   race:
      defined, 180
      demographics (White/Non-
         White) of residents in
         nursing homes and assisted
         living facilities, 204
      socioeconomic status and, 192
   rural poverty, 193
Socioeconomic status (SES):
   assessment of depression and, 58, 61
   disadvantaged, 33
   problem-solving therapy (PST),
      modifications for, 139–140
   race/culture and, 192
Socioemotional selectivity theory, 7
Solution implementation stage,
   problem-solving therapy (PST),
   134, 138–139, 146–147
Solution verification stage, problem-
   solving therapy (PST), 134,
   146–147
Specificity of challenges in late life
   (CCMSC model), 7–9, 10
Stigma attached to mental illness, 85
Stressful life events, 34
Stroke, 32, 205
Stroop Color-Word Interference Test,
   49
Strosahl, Kirk, 243–244
Structured Clinical Interview for
   DSM-III-R (SCID), 58–60
Structure in CBT, 84
Substance use, 66–67
Substitutive judgment, 224
Subsyndromal depressive symptoms, 30

Subtypes of geriatric depression, 56
Suicide risk, case example (Helen), 81,
   101, 153
Suitability for Short-Term Cognitive
   Therapy Scale, 90–91
Supportive therapy, problem-solving
   therapy (PST) versus, 135

Telephone Interview for Cognitive
   Status (TICS/TICS-m), 66
Termination:
   cognitive-behavioral therapy
      (CBT), 86–87
   interpersonal psychotherapy (IPT),
      114, 123–124
Therapeutic focus, loss of, in
   interpersonal psychotherapy
   (IPT), 122
Therapy systems, 79–82. *See also*
   Cognitive behavior therapy
   (CBT); Evidence-based
   treatments (EBTs); Interpersonal
   psychotherapy (IPT); Problem-
   solving therapy (PST)
Trails B, 49
Transitions in role investments,
   conceptual framework, CBT,
   93–97, 104

Vascular depression, 33, 38, 48, 56
Vigor deficit factor, 55
Visual acuity, loss of, 68–69

White matter hypertensities (WMH),
   48
Wisconsin Card Sorting Task, 49
Wisdom and aging, 6–7
Withdrawal-apathy factor, 55
Worry factor, 55

Young-old and old-old, 8